An Introduction to Mesoamerican Philosophy

The philosophy of Mesoamerica – the indigenous groups of precolonial North-Central America – is rich and varied but relatively little known. In this groundbreaking book, Alexus McLeod introduces the philosophical traditions of the Maya, Nahua (Aztecs), Mixtecs, Zapotecs, and others, focusing in particular on their treatment of language, truth, time, creation, personhood, knowledge, and morality. His wide-ranging discussion includes important texts of world literature such as the K'iche Maya *Popol Vuh* and the Aztec *Florentine Codex*, as well as precolonial glyphic texts and imagery. This comprehensive and accessible book will give students, specialists, and other interested readers an understanding of Mesoamerican philosophy and a sense of the current scholarship in the field.

Alexus McLeod is Professor of Religious Studies at Indiana University. He has written a number of books on Mesoamerican and Chinese philosophy, the most recent in each area being *Philosophy of the Ancient Maya* (2017) and *The Dao of Madness* (2021).

T0382481

An Introduction to Mesoamerican Philosophy

ALEXUS McLEOD

Indiana University

CAMBRIDGE
UNIVERSITY PRESS

Shaftesbury Road, Cambridge CB2 8EA, United Kingdom

One Liberty Plaza, 20th Floor, New York, NY 10006, USA

477 Williamstown Road, Port Melbourne, VIC 3207, Australia

314–321, 3rd Floor, Plot 3, Splendor Forum, Jasola District Centre,
New Delhi – 110025, India

103 Penang Road, #05–06/07, Visioncrest Commercial, Singapore 238467

Cambridge University Press is part of Cambridge University Press & Assessment,
a department of the University of Cambridge.

We share the University's mission to contribute to society through the pursuit of
education, learning and research at the highest international levels of excellence.

www.cambridge.org
Information on this title: www.cambridge.org/9781009218771

DOI: 10.1017/9781009218726

First published 2023

A catalogue record for this publication is available from the British Library.

Library of Congress Cataloging-in-Publication Data
Names: McLeod, Alexus, author.
Title: An introduction to Mesoamerican philosophy / Alexus McLeod,
Indiana University.
Description: Cambridge, United Kingdom ; New York, NY, USA :
Cambridge University Press, [2023] | Includes bibliographical references and index.
Identifiers: LCCN 2022032053 | ISBN 9781009218771 (hardback) |
ISBN 9781009218726 (ebook)
Subjects: LCSH: Philosophy, Central American – History.
Classification: LCC B1025 .M35 2023 | DDC 199/.728–dc23/eng/20221121
LC record available at https://lccn.loc.gov/2022032053

ISBN 978-1-009-21877-1 Hardback
ISBN 978-1-009-21873-3 Paperback

Contents

Figures

Introduction

The Cultural and Historical Background

In this book, we will look at the philosophical thought of the region of Mesoamerica, specifically during the period prior to the arrival of the Spanish in the sixteenth century CE. Mesoamerica is a historically inter-linked region in the southern portion of North America, running from north of the central Mexican valley (where cities like Teotihuacan played a major early role) to the southern Maya area, in modern-day Honduras and El Salvador. Some more specific definitions of the region take it to be bounded in the north by the Sinaloa River in current day northwestern Mexico and in the south by the Ulua River in current day Honduras.[1] While there is no official boundary of Mesoamerica adopted by everyone, this book will treat the central Mexican valley and the end of the Maya region in the south as the boundaries. Within this region, numerous cultures and traditions, many of which were historically linked, thrived for thousands of years prior to the arrival of the Spanish. By this time, numerous empires had arisen and fallen in the region, and broad ranging cultural traditions could be found throughout the region. Numerous political, scientific, religious, literary, and philosophical traditions thrived in the region.

Right away, then, we have to ask the question: What happened to these philosophical traditions and many of the other elements of Mesoamerican cultures? Why did these not become a part of the narrative of the West after European arrival and colonization? There are numerous answers here. One is that these traditions (as was inevitable) *did* become part of the broader cultural tradition, but were never credited with such or celebrated, and so consequently faded into the background, unrecognized. The enormous contributions of Mesoamerican society to what we know as "Western"

---

[1] Horacio Cabezas, "Unidad Geográfica-Cultural," in Cabezas, ed., *Mesoamérica*, 11.

culture were simply taken unattributed, similar to the work of slaves in the Americas, which is attributed to Europeans when it is attributed at all. Thus, we have to do more work, to go beneath the surface, in order to find the truth about the source of many aspects of current Western tradition. Despite what we think, the "Western tradition," in science, philosophy, literature, and other aspects, is not all the heritage of the Greeks, Romans, and Western Europeans.[2] Another part of the answer is that many aspects of Mesoamerican culture were suppressed and destroyed by the Spanish, even as they were namelessly integrated into aspects of Latin American and European culture. As zealous as missionaries can be (whether of the religious, political, or other varieties), ideas tend to be impossible to stop. We can only ever succeed at relabeling them. Once seen, an idea cannot be unseen. One of the things I hope the reader learns from this book is just how much of Mesoamerican philosophy is already recognizable – this is in large part because of its largely unattributed influence on the thought of the West. The differences between the culture and ideas of Euro-America (including Latin America) and those of Europe prior to the contact with the Americas are based not on innovation by crafty and brilliant Europeans, but rather on the ways in which the old ideas of Europe and the old ideas of the Americas cross-pollenated to create new ideas.

Readers who are familiar with philosophy (and even those who are not) will, and should, recognize certain ideas discussed in this book. Hopefully after reading it, however, you will recognize many of those ideas as originating in Mesoamerica.

The best known cultures and philosophical traditions in Mesoamerica are, of course, those of the Maya and Aztec (Nahua), and those two traditions are the most prominent in this book. As we will see, both of these cultures were (and are) very broad in scope, so much so that it makes most sense to refer to each of them as a *cluster* of related cultures and traditions. This is to some extent more the case for the Maya than for the Aztecs, as the Aztec Empire represented a large and vast political entity, having control over all the people who referred to themselves as Nahua, in a way no single Maya state ever had over all people associated with Maya languages. Nonetheless, even in the case of the Aztecs, the empire

---

[2] See for example Scott Pratt, *Native Pragmatism*.

contained numerous peoples with their own cultures, languages, and traditions, tied together by the thread of the empire (in much the same way as various peoples of Europe, the Middle East, and North Africa were once tied together by Rome or various peoples in East Asia were tied together by the Han, Tang, or Ming Dynasties of China). Taking the Maya region as an example, the area from southeastern Mexico through western Honduras and El Salvador is home to numerous different peoples from a number of linguistically related but distinct cultures. There is as much diversity in this region as in other areas in the world of similar size, if not more. There is no single Maya language – rather, the Maya languages are a *family* of languages, including ones such as K'iche' and Yucatec Maya, which are discussed throughout the book. In the pre-Spanish period, there was (as explained further in the following text) a glyphic written form for Maya languages that could serve as a kind of *lingua franca* for the region (much like Chinese characters for China and historically much of the rest of east Asia).

In addition to the enormously rich Maya and Aztec traditions, however, there were a number of other lesser known peoples with rich philosophical, religious, and historical traditions, such as the Zapotec, Mixtec, and even more ancient groups such as the Izapan civilizations like the Olmec. These traditions are covered in this book as well. The hope is that the reader will come away with an understanding of the enormous breadth, diversity, and power of Mesoamerican philosophical traditions, as well as a sense of their importance as part of the history of philosophy. While I do not want to treat precolonial Mesoamerican thought as monolithic, even within the different cultural groups, much of the focus in this book is on shared features found in a variety of Mesoamerican traditions, as well as on particular views developed within each tradition.

Despite the cultural diversity of the area, Mesoamerica as an idea largely came into existence due to shared cultural features throughout the region, that made it possible to refer to this area as roughly one "culturally interactive area."[3]

The philosophical traditions of Mesoamerica discussed in this book span from the beginnings of important cultural productions of the Olmec

---

[3] Adams, "Introduction to a Survey of the Native American Prehistorical Cultures of Mesoamerica," 6.

Figure 0.1 *Map of Mesoamerica*

in the "preclassic" or "formative" period of Mesoamerican history (roughly 2000 BCE to 250 CE) through the Maya and Aztec traditions as we find them during Spanish contact at the end of the Postclassic period (900–1521 CE). While the focus of this book is mainly on precolonial Mesoamerican thought (although some of the texts we will investigate were written after Spanish contact, and almost certainly influenced to some extent by Spanish ideas), it is wrong to say that the Mesoamerican philosophical traditions (or cultures) disappeared or collapsed after Spanish colonization. Native Mesoamerican ideas and traditions continued to flourish, in new forms as well in some of the same ones, through syncretic combinations of Mesoamerican and Spanish ideas, ones that created part of the world we know today as Latin America. Latin American philosophy as it exists today is not an importation or imposition of European thought on the Americas, but rather a synthesis of indigenous American, European, African, and other traditions (just as is Anglo-American thought).

A brief historical overview can be helpful here for placing the various traditions and periods discussed throughout the book in their proper historical contexts. The oldest cultural traditions in Mesoamerica that we have access to through material culture go back to about 2000 BCE, when new forms of settlement based on agriculture, particularly concerning cultivation of maize (a staple crop that plays a major role in Mesoamerican self-conception) and ceramic construction originate in the region.[4] This took place particularly along the area of land today known as the Isthmus of Tehuantepec (named after a mainly Zapotec town along the coast in the Mexican state of Oaxaca, whose own name derives from Nahuatl – we will get into the issues of empire in due course).[5]

The first major Mesoamerican culture to emerge in this formative period after 2000 BCE, in this same Isthmian region, was that of the Olmec – perhaps the best known and most studied of early Mesoamerican cultures. The Olmec culture developed along the northern isthmus, on the Gulf coast of present-day Mexico, and was the first in the region to display evidence of the kind of social stratification and specialization found in large-scale societies.[6] Our understanding of the Olmec comes from a number of archaeological sites at ancient cities in the region where Olmec society developed, particularly the sites of La Venta and Tres Zapotes, close to the Gulf shore, and San Lorenzo, further inland on the Isthmus.

Olmec innovations influenced numerous later cultures and traditions in the region. Some of the major features of Mesoamerican culture associated with people such as the Maya and Aztec can be traced back to Olmec origins, and in the region around the Isthmian Gulf Coast.

While the diversity of Mesoamerica, in terms of cultures and even philosophical traditions, is truly immense (particularly for such a relatively small region), I focus in this book on a handful of representative traditions for which we have a great deal of material, and which have been

---

[4] Horacio Cabezas, "Unidad Geográfica-Cultural," in Cabezas, ed., *Mesoamérica*.

[5] The beginnings of ceramic construction in the region are not necessarily connected to any massive technological leap at the time, as Richard Adams points out. Rather, the origins of ceramic construction give archaeologists the first glimpse of these early cultures, as ceramics are useful as "an analytical device for defining cultural regions and marking phase boundaries." (Adams, *Prehistoric Mesoamerica*, 46).

[6] Robert Rosenswig, *The Beginnings of Mesoamerican Civilization: Inter-Regional Interaction and the Olmec*, 3.

sufficiently studied by anthropologists, linguists, art historians, sociologists, and others to give us an understanding of the shape of these traditions before the period of Spanish contact. I focus mainly on the Maya and Aztec traditions, because we have the greatest amount of textual and other sources for these traditions, but I also discuss the important Mixtec and Zapotec traditions. There are certainly many other traditions, including philosophical traditions, represented in Mesoamerica. It is only due to the limitations of space that I don't cover other Mesoamerican traditions (though I do on occasion mention some of them in the chapters ahead). So readers should certainly not take their exclusion as demonstrating that the traditions not covered here are not or were not important parts of the broader Mesoamerican tradition.

This all prompts the question: Why *these* specific traditions, if they are but a few among a broader array of important philosophical traditions? There are several reasons for this. First, while "importance" is very much a subjective matter, and is based on the perceived value of a thing (and surely all of these traditions have value), a few Mesoamerican traditions were more *influential* than others in terms of their reach and extent. The latter is an objective historical fact. That Maya and Aztec cultures each had a larger reach and more regional influence than the culture of the Otomi, for example, is a matter of the military might, social influence via trade and migration, and other nonnormative features of the people in these cultures, rather than a matter of the superiority of their ideas. When it comes to world civilizations, we too often conflate the latter with the former. The influence of a philosophical system is most often due to historical, political, and economic accidents, rather than philosophical value. This is because aptness or truth of philosophical systems does not lend competitive advantage to a society that produced the system, so any success of the society in question cannot be attributed to its philosophical tradition. This is all the more reason why we should seek out the philosophical systems of lesser known and lesser studied traditions. Why, in the West, is the thought of Greece, Rome, and selected parts of Western Europe more prominent or well known? Throughout the history of philosophy in the modern Western academy, many have tried to construct after-the-fact justifications about the superiority of these systems to other global traditions (or more often still, simply ignored these traditions), but this is done without properly investigating these other traditions and systems to which the aforesaid traditions are supposedly superior.[7] While few today would likely use the reasoning of these earlier scholars, their views have become embedded in philosophy's self-conception, and thus numerous global traditions are still neglected in the study of philosophy in the West.[8] We cannot, as pointed out above, rely on the fact that the British Empire successfully colonized much of the world as any piece of evidence whatsoever for the truth or superiority of its philosophical traditions. Likewise, the fact that the Aztecs controlled an extensive empire does not make their philosophical thought any more interesting, valuable, or true than that of the Zapotec or Mixtec, whose states never achieved such a scale. We would easily recognize the poverty of such a line of reasoning in another context. Should we take the scientific thought of the class bully as superior to that of the physics nerd because the former beat up the latter and took his lunch money? Should we conclude (as people in society often do) that CEOs must be far more intelligent than philosophy professors, because the former are making money and the latter are not? This is to conflate two separate issues. Why should we suspect that the features of a culture that lead it to be successful in forming empire are features that would lead it to forming accurate or insightful philosophical thought? We all know that philosophers rarely make excellent conquerors.

The answer to the question, then, of "why *these* traditions?" is simply that the traditions covered in this book are the most well known and widespread in the region. There is much more written about and known by scholars about them. They are fascinating and important philosophical traditions, even if they are not more important than others in the region. And these traditions share many features with other traditions in the region, as well as with each other, as we will see. There is a "family resemblance" between Mesoamerican traditions. Indeed, the same reasons we can define the region as a cultural area are the reasons we can take the philosophical traditions of the region as representing one overarching philosophical tradition. Maya, Aztec, and Zapotec thought

---

[7] Peter Park's *Africa, Asia, and the History of Philosophy* offers an account of how the modern philosophical canon was constructed in the eighteenth and nineteenth centuries so as to exclude Africa and Asia.

[8] Van Norden, *Taking Back Philosophy*, ch. 1.

resemble one another as much as do the culturally related traditions of Europe and the Middle East, or China, Korea, and Japan. In this book, I look at both specific issues within the thought of each of these groups, as well as overarching shared features of all of them, so as to illuminate not only the philosophy of Maya, Aztec, and other traditions, but Mesoamerican Philosophy more broadly.

In a brief history we must also try to see the broad-brush, big picture of the region. As discussed above, the Olmec developed innovations in material and intellectual culture, particularly concerning new forms of political structure, calendrics, and language (at least, this is what we have access to through the material record – they likely contributed more than just this to later cultural traditions in the region). The traditions discussed in this book represent four of the five linguistic families of Mesoamerica: Mixe-Zoquean (Olmec[9]), Oto-Manquean (Zapotec, Mixtec), Mayan, and Uto-Aztecan (Aztec). These cultures also remain among the largest in the present-day region, and thus have the greatest extent of available sources – written, traditional, material, and oral. In the remaining part of this section, I offer a brief historical overview of each tradition, situating it with respect to its overall development in the area as well as its relationship to the other traditions discussed in this book.

Olmec

The Olmec culture developed along the Gulf Coast of the Isthmus, with the earliest development of the kind of ceremonial centers, featuring large-scale architecture, that becomes key to Mesoamerican societies, beginning around 1400 BCE. Connected to these centers, the Olmec developed new styles of art and reshaping of their world, most famously represented in the enormous head sculptures of basalt found at the site of La Venta, one of the central sites of the Olmec. La Venta, like other important Olmec sites, was a settlement with a ceremonial structure at its core (in this case the large building referred to today as "The Great Pyramid"), following a standard that would be represented by cities throughout

---

[9] It is not known which language was used by the Olmecs, but most scholars accept that they likely were a Mixe-Zoquean group.

Mesoamerica and throughout the rest of its history (and similar to what we find in numerous other cultures – think of the medieval European town with a church or cathedral at its heart, the temples at the heart of ancient Athens on the Acropolis, or the mosque and palace directly at the center of the round city of Abbasid Baghdad). Though the Olmec head sculptures are perhaps the most famous constructions associated with the Olmec, these were not carved until around the ninth century BCE, well after the earliest developments in Olmec innovation. It was in early centers such as San Lorenzo where the first Olmec developments were found. It was, however, at La Venta where Olmec development and construction seems to have reached its pinnacle. The styles of art and construction here seem to have set the stage for almost all of Mesoamerican culture to follow, which is why the Olmec are considered by many the formative precursor or originator of Mesoamerican culture.

There are still unresolved questions concerning just who the Olmecs were, what language they spoke, or their relation to later groups. Many maintain they were a Mixe-Zoquean group, speaking a language in the family of the current languages used in the Isthmus of Tehuantepec where key Olmec sites are found. While the sites associated by most scholars with the Olmec people themselves are found in the northern part of the isthmus toward the Gulf Coast, Olmec style art and artifacts are found in a far wider area dating back to the Preclassic period, stretching from central Mexico to Guatemala. The scope and early date of Olmec influence suggests that this culture had a formative influence on the wider culture of Mesoamerica, possibly responsible for a number of the similarities we see in different cultures and traditions of the region (even though these traditions continued to influence one another throughout history). While some account for the wide spread of Olmec styles by claiming that the Olmecs migrated to these areas, a more likely explanation is the influence of Olmec culture and styles throughout the region, through trade and other cultural interactions.

One of the features of Olmec cultural production that we see throughout Mesoamerican traditions is the system of calendrics devised in the isthmus. The famous "Long Count" calendar adopted and perfected by the Maya had its origins with the Olmec, as well as possibly a number of other ritual calendric systems widely used in Mesoamerica. As we will see with later cultures, many Mesoamerican groups used multiple ritual and agricultural calendars alongside one another. Part of the explanation for this may have been the coordinated influence and synthesis of a number of different cultural practices and calendars. As we will see, one of the most unique features of Mesoamerica is the immense *diversity* represented in such a relatively small area. As mentioned above, we find *five* different language families represented in the region, as well as a few isolate languages (that is, languages that cannot be linked to other language families, and thus represent their own distinct family). To give a comparative sense of diversity, in the entirety of Europe we find only three language families, Indo-European (now the most widely distributed language family in the world, to which the vast majority of European languages including English and the Romance languages belong, as well as Persian and Indian languages), Finno-Ugric, and Basque.

In addition to the calendar, styles of construction, burials, and a number of key Olmec ideas represented in early imagery and text (such as conception of gods and the notion of the animal companion or co-essence that became the basis for embedded identity)[10] had enormous and lasting influence on Mesoamerican traditions (we will see details of these views in Chapter 4). We have access to Olmec thought not through text, as we do in the case of some other Mesoamerican traditions, but through aspects of material culture and recognition of features of later systems influenced by Olmec ideas. The Olmec developed a robust material culture that we have been able to access via archaeological research, and the key to understanding Olmec thought comes through being able to interpret material culture.

It is with the Olmec that we can recognize the earliest strain of the Mesoamerican philosophical tradition more broadly. This is not necessarily (or even likely) because the Olmec were the first people in Mesoamerica to do philosophy or to think in philosophical ways. It is simply that the Olmec had the earliest material culture still accessible to us, which allows us to understand something of their philosophical thought. Another reason why we can consider the Olmec to have constructed the foundation of the Mesoamerican philosophical tradition is that their culture went on to influence those of almost every other

---

[10] David Carrasco, *Religions of Mesoamerica*, 63.

tradition discussed in the book. In this sense, perhaps the Olmec represent the root from which the Mesoamerican traditions grow.

Maya

The Maya cultures are among the best-known groups in the Mesoamerican world, and are distributed over a large swathe of the region, from southern Mexico to western El Salvador and Honduras. It is the Maya who have the best-known and most developed writing system in the Americas, and whose culture in many ways represented an intellectual peak in broader Mesoamerican cultures during the so-called "Classic" and "Postclassic" periods. While the Maya are best known in contemporary "Western" culture for their calendric system, particularly the so-called "Long Count" calendar, and their glyphic written language, understanding of which had been basically lost in the early colonial period right up until the twentieth century (and parts of it remain undeciphered still today), there are many important aspects of Maya tradition that are less studied, and that are crucial to understanding Maya philosophical traditions.

While we often treat the Maya as a single culture or people, there is not, and never was, a single linguistically or culturally unified "pan-Maya" people. Still, there are important cultural features that can be found throughout the Maya region, enough for us to be able to consider Maya philosophy and culture a coherent and distinct tradition. Indeed, the glyphic written language itself links numerous linguistic areas in the Maya region. One interesting feature of Classic Maya written language is that it is portable between languages, much like Chinese characters. That is, glyphs are not tied to phonetics, and can be read in a number of different ways, making it possible to read them in numerous languages. Thus, speakers of two different Maya languages may have had a hard time understanding one another, but might both understand the written glyphs. Despite this, Mayan glyphs did have a phonetic element in addition to logographic elements. These phonetic elements sometimes varied according to region, depending on how people in that region said a word, and sometimes did not (as is the case with many Chinese characters used throughout East Asia). Like Chinese characters, Maya glyphs were constructed of both logographic and phonetic elements. The phonetic elements were not, for the most part, determinative – that is, one cannot look at a glyph (or a Chinese character) and determine what sound the character corresponds to just on the basis of its phonetic element. One can often *guess* the sound of the world based on this element, but it is not determined in the same way that fully phonetic written languages such as Spanish are, in which letters are connected to specific sounds. (English is a special case, because even though it is phonetically rendered, letters are not consistently connected to particular sounds as they are in many other phonetically rendered languages).

The earliest developments of Maya culture building toward the flourishing intellectual culture of the Classic Period began in the southern highlands, during the "Preclassic" period, when cities such as Kaminaljuyu (modern day Guatemala City) rose in the period after 1500 BCE, roughly contemporary with some of the main Olmec cities. During the later years of the Kaminaljuyu power, toward the beginning of the Classic Period when larger power centers began to rise in the central lowlands to the north, there may have been some connection to and influence by the massive central Mexican city center of Teotihuacan, which came to occupy a central role in Mesoamerican culture. There are notable similarities between artifacts at Kaminaljuyu and that of Teotihuacan, one of the most influential cities in Mesoamerican culture. Teotihucaan lies in the central valley of Mexico (just north of modern day Mexico City, the Tenochtitlan of the Aztecs), at the very center of the region known as Mesoamerica. While relatively little is known of the people who inhabited Teotihuacan at its height in the late Maya Preclassic and early Classic Period, from around the beginning of the Common Era to 350 CE (and this rise of Teotihuacan may have been linked to developments in the Maya world that brought about the changes and innovations that mark what we refer to as the Classic Period), there are clear lines of influence between Teotihuacan and the Maya cities during this period.

The Classic Period began with the rise of regional power and cultural development of the city-states of the southern lowlands, from cities like Tikal in current day central Guatemala and Palenque in southern Mexico to Copan in current day western Honduras. The contemporary names for these cities are not those the Classic Period Maya used, but thanks to the decipherment of many of the Classic glyphs, we have some idea of what the original names of these cities were (in meaning if not perfectly in phonetics).

In these cities of the Classic Period, we find the rise of the conception of the *ajaw* (ruler)[11] as object of centralized power and religious devotion. The elevation of the role of the ruler to political and spiritual significance inaugurates a period of development of new construction, art forms, and ideas, with the ruler central to many of the state-sponsored constructions that have stood through time. Most of the textual and artistic material available to us today through monumental construction in the Classic Period refers to the rulers and their history, as well as to religion through discussion of the rulers' connection to the gods. While rulers loom large in Classic Period text and imagery, this is likely because most of what we can access today is connected to rulers, as the monuments for rulers were built to last, carved in stone, in the stelae and architecture of the cities. Other lasting material sources, such as pottery, wall paintings, and the small number of printed texts remaining from close to this period, show us the intellectual world beyond the rulers, and demonstrate that though rulers had an important cultural role to play, they did not dominate Maya intellectual life in the way it appears if we only look at the monumental texts and artwork. Nonetheless, the Classic Period is defined in terms of the histories and accounts of the kings of the lowland Maya city-states, as it in this period that we have well-defined historical accounts, and a clear difference from what we find in surrounding periods in this regard, though we see aspects of it on the edges of the Preclassic and into the Postclassic as well.

Toward the end of the Classic Period, there was a major population and power shift away from the southern lowland cities northward into the Yucatan. This period is associated with the so-called Maya "collapse," and the abandonment of the vast city centers of the southern lowlands. While scholars still vigorously debate the causes of this collapse and just what happened during this period to lead to the abandonment of these cities, we clearly see a decline in the south, and a corresponding rise to dominance of Yucatan cities like Chichen Itza. In the northern lowland cities during the Postclassic, similarities with central Mexican culture became

---

[11] One also commonly finds the spelling "ahau" for this term. I use "ajaw" throughout, which is more standardly used in current works in Maya studies.

more pronounced, suggesting connections with cities of the central Mexican valley. Though scholars do not have a good handle on the directions in which the influence mainly flowed, it is likely, as is the case in any cultural interaction, that there was influence in both directions, and that what we find in both the Yucatan and central Mexico in and after this time was the result of hybridization of ideas, rather than the imposition of one culture on the other.

Toward the end of the Postclassic Period, after the influence of the Yucatan cities had waned and the powerful empire of the Aztecs centered at Tenochtitlan in the central Mexican valley came to be the center of political and cultural gravity in much of Mesoamerica, the large ships of the Spanish first appeared off the Gulf and Atlantic coasts. The arrival of the Spanish, and the subsequent wars of conquest, plagues, and reorganization of the political and religious structure of the Mesoamerican world, radically changed the history of the region. Still, the colonial period and the importation of Spanish ideas and culture did not eliminate or subvert the culture and thought of Mesoamerica. As hard as the Spanish tried to convert the people of Mesoamerica to Spanish ways of living, thinking, and being, these ways remained. The colonial Spanish, in their zeal for their own religion and culture, failed to understand that culture and ideas can never be suppressed or eliminated, they can only be modified and augmented. One can never undo or unlearn ideas. While certain outward forms may be suppressed, how can we un-alter worldviews or conceptual schemes shaped by particular ideas? How can we negate the effect that ideas had have? I may forget or otherwise lose some of the things I've encountered and learned over the years, but how can I lose or forget the ways these ideas shaped my experience and thinking? Ideas have an indelible effect on mind and development, just as physical objects have effect on the world. And just as we can destroy an object but can never destroy the effect that the object had on the world, and thus can never erase it as such, the same is true, of ideas. Maybe if everyone who encountered a particular idea died without imparting it to another, if we had a case of spontaneous cultural extinction, an idea might go out of existence for all intents and purposes. But this was certainly not the case with the Maya or any other people of

Mesoamerica. Thus, while Mesoamerica largely took on Christianity, the Spanish language, and numerous cultural aspects of Europe, the native ideas of Mesoamerica remained, and the culture of the region became a hybridization of Mesoamerican and Spanish ideas and cultural elements. We see the early form of this hybridization in texts such as the K'iche' Maya *Popol Vuh*, a rich philosophical text to which I devote a great deal of attention in this book. While early Maya ideas are found throughout the text, in many parts of the text we see the influence of Christianity, and an interpretation of earlier Maya ideas through the intellectual framework of Spanish Christianity. But just as Maya and Mesoamerican ideas were not left unchanged in the introduction of Spanish ideas to Mesoamerica, Christian and Spanish ideas were not left unchanged either. While we recognize and study the changes that Spanish ideas made to Mesoamerica, we often neglect the ways Mesoamerican thought changed Spanish, Christian, and more broadly European culture. This is largely because European texts and self-conception prevented Europeans from attributing the changes in their own culture to Mesoamerican ideas. Historical investigation of these ideas and the changes in Spanish and Christian intellectual culture in the sixteenth century and onward can reveal to us the unattributed influence of Mesoamerican culture. The difference between Spanish and Mesoamerican culture in this period is not that one influenced the other without reciprocal influence, but that only one was willing to *attribute* the sources of influence to the other. The Spanish were convinced of the superiority of their religion and culture, and were thus unwilling to admit any influence from Mesoamerica *as* influence. Given that God had established this religion and this way of life, they believed, any changes must have come from the Spanish themselves and from Christianity itself, not from the people and ideas of Mesoamerica. Thus, Mesoamerican ideas were absorbed yet not attributed, like an act of cultural plagiarism. Just as in the case of the central Mexican cities and the Maya cities of the Yucatan in the Postclassic Period, we should always expect influence to move in both directions in any exchange between people. When we find similarities between Maya ideas in the *Popol Vuh* and other texts and the ideas of Spanish Christianity, we should ask ourselves not only whether this represents Spanish and Christian influence on the

Maya, but whether the similarity between these ideas and our association of them with Christianity represents Maya influence on Christianity.

Aztec

The people known by many today as the "Aztec" are more properly referred to as the Nahua, a large group of related people speaking versions of the Nahuatl language, of which there are numerous dialects. Unlike the Maya languages, Nahuatl does not represent a language *family*, rather Nahuatl is part of the broader Uto-Aztecan language family. The distribution and reach of Nahua culture at its peak, however, was roughly similar to that of the various Maya groups in the Classic Period. The best-known and most prominent of the various Nahua groups were the Mexica people, associated with the city-state of Tenochtitlan (current day Mexico City). This city headed the alliance of three central Mexican city-states, which in turn comprised the core of the Aztec Empire that began in the early fifteenth century and held central influence in the region for the next hundred years, until its destruction by the Spanish in 1521.

The Nahua, while associated most closely with the central Mexican valley that became their homeland and center of power, migrated from what is now northern Mexico around the time of the flourishing of the southern lowland cities of the Maya region during the Maya Classic Period, in the sixth century CE.[12] The Uto-Aztecan languages originated in roughly this region, in the desert of current day northwest Mexico and southwest United States. Uto-Aztecan speakers traveled north and south, to become people as diverse and widely distributed as the Aztec and Pipil (Nawat) in the south and the Comanche, Dine (Navajo) and Paiute in the North. Thus, Uto-Aztecan languages are spoken today in an area spanning from Idaho and Wyoming to El Salvador, down much of the length of Western North America.

Most of the Aztec thought available to us in writing comes from the period of empire, and around the colonial Spanish period. Nahua people certainly did philosophy and thought about their world in the period

---

[12] See Macri and Looper, "Nahua in Ancient Mesoamerica."

before the rise of the Aztec Empire, but it was with this political unit that the textual tradition associated with the Aztecs that we have today took form. Some have argued that Nahuatl speaking people had a significant influence on language and culture far before this time, hypothesizing that we find Nahuatl origins of terms in Classic Mayan languages, for example (see Macri and Looper). The earliest Nahuatl writing to which we have access comes from the imperial period around the time of Spanish contact, such as the texts known today as the *Codex Boturini, Codex Xolotl,* and *Codex Mendoza*, dating to 1541 (*Mendoza*) and earlier. As with Maya texts, Nahuatl codices in the original precolonial language likely existed in greater numbers, but were not kept and did not endure well in the conditions of Mesoamerica. And unlike the Classic Maya, the Aztecs did not tend to include text in their monumental stone construction, a medium that lasts much longer than paper. However, there is one feature of Aztec history that leads to our having a much more robust textual picture of Aztec culture during its height. Many Nahuatl texts and traditions were written in texts in Latin script during the period after Spanish contact. When the Spanish arrived in Mesoamerica, the Aztec culture of central Mexico was flourishing, and literate professional classes were around to record Aztec thought, which was kept in these new forms, in phonetic Latin script, and saved in forms common to the Spanish.

The written script of the Nahuatl language itself prior to Spanish contact was a very different writing system from the one we are familiar with. While it was much more like Classic Mayan, or even Classical Chinese than it was like phonetically rendered languages such as Spanish or English, it also differed from Classic Mayan. Unlike Mayan languages, which were rendered in a combination of logographic and phonetic elements (similar to Chinese characters), Nahuatl writing was more purely a form of "sign writing," in which ideographs dominated rather than phonetic symbols. There has been discussion of Nahuatl writing moving toward developing phonetics[13], but this seems to me to presume the superiority of phonetics in writing, which is far from obvious. The development of written languages like that of China and the Maya seem to tell against this. While early Chinese characters and forms of Maya glyphs

---

[13] See the discussion in Laack, *Aztec Religion and the Art of Writing*, 259–261.

were complicated, simplified versions were eventually made that allowed for faster and more condensed expression. There is no particular reason to think that Nahuatl writing would have moved in a phonetic rather than a simplified ideographic direction. In many ways, ideographs are far more useful for writing, particularly in a multilingual area. They allow, as we also see in Chinese, for the mutual written intelligibility of different languages (assuming grammatical differences can be bridged). Ideographic script is "portable" between languages in a way phonetic script is not, and thus has distinct advantages in particular situations. A written language can thus serve as a *lingua franca* uniting a region, even in the absence of shared spoken languages – something that cannot happen with phonetic script. This (I suspect) is part of the reason why we find such continued linguistic diversity across Mesoamerica even with the existence of vast networks, empires, and cultural areas – a situation we do not find with Indo-European or Afro-Asiatic languages, where written intelligibility requires spoken facility.

The fact that humans can separate visual and spoken language, using them for different purposes, shows that the possibility of developing in these independent ways is open (as we see in historical examples). The nature of Mesoamerican written languages, as discussed later in this book, is important to understand to grasp some important features of Mesoamerican Philosophy. While perhaps language does not fully determine the ways we think, the shape and format of our language almost certainly suggests certain ideas, and makes some more natural to have than others. It is one among many features that shape and contribute to the ways humans think about the world.

Aztec Philosophy has become the most natural Mesoamerican tradition (along with Maya Philosophy) for philosophers and intellectual historians to access, because of this written tradition. In the case of the Aztecs, we have a wealth of Nahuatl-language literature in Latin script as well as Nahuatl writing dating to the early colonial period and the time of the end of the Aztec Empire. This is indeed a rich source to draw from for understanding Aztec Philosophy. I argue in the next chapter, however, that we should expand our conception of where philosophy is found to nontextual sources as well, such as artwork, construction, oral tradition, and cultural practices. When we do this, a rich vista of philosophy opens up before us that we do not otherwise recognize. And there are particular reasons for some philosophy being done outside of texts, as we will see in discussions of the Maya tradition. *Performance* was a central part of philosophy throughout Mesoamerica, and performance happens in person, through speech and movement. There may be a textual *layer* to a performance, just as there is usually a script for a play or film, but just as often the performance is passed through practice and personal transmission, like religious ceremonies. Trying to make sense of a Catholic mass through a written description will be difficult and inadequate – one has to learn much of it through experiencing the ritual. Likewise, engagement with the visual, oral, and performance aspects of Mesoamerican philosophy opens up new possibilities and new information. That said, in this book, the five traditions I focus on are all connected to textual traditions, as philosophers (including myself) are most accustomed to dealing with textual traditions. I will also discuss nontextual aspects of these traditions, but we stick fairly closely here to text. This should be understood as a *first step* toward understanding Mesoamerican philosophical traditions. In order to understand these traditions fully, philosophers will need to learn new methods of engaging with material culture and cultural practices. We will need to learn skills from anthropologists, sociologists, and art historians (among others) as part of our own professional toolkit. This kind of borrowing from other fields is not something foreign to philosophers. We have seen ourselves as linked to the sciences and science-related fields for many years. In the "analytic" tradition of philosophy that predominates in the Anglo-American world, it is not at all unusual to find philosophers adopting the tools of mathematicians, linguists, or physicists. As an undergraduate I took a course in philosophy that covered quantum mechanics, using the mathematical tools of physicists, and another in philosophy of neuroscience, using the analytical tools of biologists and psychologists. These courses would not at all have been out of place in departments of physics, biology, or psychology. This is all seen as central to philosophy. I took courses in graduate school that were cross-listed with mathematics and linguistics. Yet, I never saw a course in philosophy in which the methods of archaeology, art history, sociology, or religious studies were used. Part of what is going on here has to do with the "self-image" of contemporary Western (particularly "analytic") philosophy, which tends to see itself as more akin to the empirical sciences such as physics, biology, and off-branches such as mathematics than to literature, performance, religion, or culture.

Thus, while I stay fairly close to the textual philosophical tradition in this book, I both suggest and point the way toward other ways of accessing philosophical thought in Mesoamerica. To become better historians of philosophy with respect to the Mesoamerican traditions, we need to become familiar with and gain facility in the techniques and tools of people in fields not often associated with philosophy, particularly archaeology, art history, and sociology.

Aztec intellectual culture at the beginning of the colonial period and in the closing years of the Empire was flourishing, and we have a wealth of Nahuatl texts from which to gain an understanding of this thought. As with colonial period Maya texts, there are influences from Spanish thought and European thought more broadly (as there are in the other direction), but we find here the people of a flourishing culture speaking for themselves in accessible language that for the "Western" tradition was our earliest contact with a Mesoamerican tradition. We have to remember that while the Classic Maya philosophical texts are older than the Nahuatl texts, the rendering of Nahuatl texts in Latin script since the colonial period has meant that these texts have been "accessible" to the West for far longer than the Classic Maya texts. Since people were using Nahuatl writing itself at the beginning of European contact, this script has also long been better understood. Today, much of Classic Maya written language has been deciphered, but it has only been in the last 60 years or so that this has happened. This is because by the time the Spanish arrived in Mesoamerica and texts were rendered in Maya languages in Latin script, much of the knowledge of Classic glyphic script was lost, and the rest died out with the rise of the use of Latin script.

The history of the roughly hundred years of the Aztec Empire is well known, and better attested in text than any other history of a people in the Americas with the exception of certain Maya states. This history (or rather mytho-history in the case of origins) begins with the Mexica's migration to the central Mexican valley. According to legend, the people originated in the land of "Aztlan" (the word that forms the basis of "Aztec"). This semi-mythical origin place of the Mexica was associated with a special destiny of its inhabitants in their migration to central Mexico, to a "promised land" associated with prophecies and the divine mission of the Mexica people. The Aztec histories discuss a long migration of the Mexica people, under the rulership and guidance of Huitzilopochtli, who was both god and "earthly" ruler (an association commonly made in Mesoamerican thought and crucial to understanding its philosophy).[14] After a long migration, the Mexica founded the city of Tenochitlan on an island, in the lower portion of the large Lake Texcoco. This lake no longer exists, having been drained nearly completely dry over the long period of colonial rule, through massive drainage projects that reduced and eventually eliminated it; it is the remnants of this lake on which the modern day Mexico City sits. The establishment of Tenochitlan is a story that loomed large in the imagination of the Mexica people's association with the city, and its importance can still be seen today. According to the story, the people of the region to which the Mexica had moved were hostile to the Mexica and attempted to drive them away, led by Copil, the nephew of Huitzilopochtli, the son of his sister Malinoxochitl, a vicious magician who was effectively exiled by Huitziilopochtli and then became the founder of a related people. Huitzilopochtli commanded his people to defeat Copil and in return bring him back Copil's heart, and on receiving the heart, the god ordered a priest to throw it into Lake Texcoco. After this followed more warfare between the Mexica and the people of this area, who still struggled to drive the Mexica off. The Mexica suffered a number of defeats, and were on the verge of collapse, when they discovered the signs foretold by their god that marked the place of the promised land they would call their own, capped by the discovery of the heart of Copil, sitting on a stone in the center of Lake Texoco. A prickly pear had sprouted from the stone, and an eagle sat perched on the plant. This was the prophetic sign the Mexica had sought, and here they knew they had finally found their new homeland. Tenochtitlan was founded on this spot, and the name glyph for the city incorporated this image. Today, this image can be found at the center of the flag of Mexico – the eagle holding in its beak a serpent, a colonial innovation on the original symbol, of the eagle holding

---

[14] We will see numerous other gods associated with earthly counterparts, such as Kukulkan/Quetzalocatl, an important god/ruler figure in Yucatan Maya and Aztec thought.

a symbol of power and warfare, the *atl tlachinolli*, which represents fire and water, in its beak.

The establishment of Tenochtitlan was the beginning of Aztec history proper. In its early years, through the reign of its first king Acamapichtli, who reigned between 1375 and 1395 CE, Tenochtitlan was hardly the major power it became later. It was a small city-state beset on all sides by more powerful neighbors, who levied heavy taxes on the Mexica state in lieu of driving it off. This situation led to the near impoverishment of the Mexica state by the end of Acamapichtli's reign. In the following years, the position of the Mexica improved, as alliances were secured with the dominant Azcapotzalco state, a nearby city-state and center of the Tepanec Empire, through marriage of the Tepanec ruler's daughter into the Mexica royal family. This connection led to the improvement of Mexica fortunes, but also to the resentment of numerous factions within Azcapotzalco. The ruling council of the city, going against the wishes of their king, had the Mexica ruler and his son killed, which plunged the Mexica into a new crisis.

It was the next act that formed the foundation for the empire that would rise from Tenochtitlan. The next ruler, Itzcoatl created an alliance with two other nearby cities, Tetzcoco and Tlacopan, in order to generate the economic and military power to have a chance of resistance to the Tepanecs – a chance that none of the cities had on its own. The new "triple alliance" not only successfully resisted Tepanec power, but invaded and destroyed the city of Azcapotzalco, bringing the Tepanec Empire to a close and establishing a new regional power that would expand its influence and power throughout the wider region – the Aztec Empire. In the following years and under successive rulers the Aztecs would expand their domain, colonizing a number of areas throughout central Mexico and eventually beyond. Under the rulership of Motecuhzoma I (r. 1440–1469 CE), the empire expanded its scope, and the Mexica became the dominant member of the triple alliance. Motecuhzoma's expansion of the Aztec Empire through military dominance set the stage for a prolonged period of peaceful development, during which many of the elements of Aztec culture encountered in their philosophical thought developed.

The next series of kings to lead the Empire continued its expansion, which culminated under the rule of Motecuhzoma II, who was ruler when the Spanish arrived in central Mexico in 1517, with the first expeditions to the region. Motecuhzoma knew about the movements of the Spanish visitors and had them tracked over the few years they returned to the region, until he finally came personally into contact with them on the arrival of Hernan Cortes at Tenochtitlan in 1519. In the ensuing struggle between the Aztecs and the Spanish, Motecuhzoma was captured and eventually killed in the fighting that led to the Spanish retreat from Tenochtitlan. In an eerie echo of the Aztecs' own conquest of the Tepanec Empire, the Spanish formed an alliance with the people of Tlaxcala against the Aztecs, which ultimately led to the downfall of Tenochtitlan and the Aztec Empire.

While the story of the fall of the empire and the Spanish conquest has been presented as a story of the total superiority and dominance of the Spanish over the natives of central Mexico, the true story, as we see in brief from the above, is far more complicated than that. Just like the Aztecs themselves, the Spanish needed to ally themselves with other local groups in order to take down the Aztec Empire. And like the Aztecs, they eventually came to dominate this alliance, writing history in ways that elevated them, just as the Aztecs and others had before them. Accounts such as that of the *Historia verdadera de la conquista de la Nueva España* (*The True History of the Conquest of New Spain*) of Bernal Díaz del Castillo mythologize the Spanish role in the fall of the Aztec Empire. Spanish history of the establishment of "Nueva España" turns out to be no more or less mythical than origin accounts of many other peoples, groups, and empires around the world. What we find in these accounts is a blend of history, myth, self-aggrandizement, and imperial/colonial propaganda.

Zapotec, Mixtec

The Zapotec and Mixtec were two other Mesoamerican cultures which developed systems of writing, and to which reference will occasionally be made in this book. The Zapotec society developed in the southern Oaxaca valley, in what is now southern Mexico, and the earliest known structures associated with the Zapotecs in the region are connected to the site of the highland city of Monte Albán, the most powerful city center of the Zapotec between its time of establishment around 500 BCE through the next 1000 years or so, to around 700 CE, when, similar to the Maya Classic Period city states of the time, it was abandoned. This suggests that whatever causes led to the Late Classic Maya "collapse" were not limited to the Maya, but also affected Monte Albán. While activity and inhabitation continued to some extent at the site in the years after this, up till the arrival of the Spanish, this occupation was on a far smaller scale.

Archaeologists mark five phases of development at Monte Albán, I–V, spanning the nearly 2000 years of the history of occupation of the site before the arrival of the Spanish. The Zapotec empire reached its largest extent during the Monte Albán II period, around the second century CE. Early Zapotec writing has been found dating back to the sixth century BCE, thus making Zapotec writing perhaps the earliest writing system in Mesoamerica. It is difficult to know exactly when writing originated in this region, but it was already established by the sixth century BCE, in a Zapotec form.[15] This writing style was used in the Zapotec region until around the end of the first millennium CE, when other writing systems came into use with the political decline of Monte Albán during the beginning of the Monte Albán IV period (900–1350 CE). Writing in general seems to have declined during this period as well, with few examples of these new hybrid styles in the Zapotec region. This style drawing on Mixtec forms of writing was more widespread in the region during this period. While Zapotec writing declined in this period, there were almost certainly influences from Zapotec on the hybrid Mixtec style writing that became more common in the wider region.

Zapotec texts are few, just as in the case of other early writing systems. As in the Maya case, many of those that exist are inscriptions on architecture and stelae. We also have, as in the case of other Mesoamerican traditions, colonial period texts written in Latin script, that give us some additional sense of precolonial Zapotec ideas. And of course, as in the case of the other traditions mentioned, we also have access to contemporary views and practices, and what these might tell us about the past. We have to demonstrate caution with this, as Zapotec culture and philosophical tradition, like that of any other part of the world, is not static and stuck in time. We can expect the views of today

---

[15] Scholars such as Javier Urcid have pointed out that there may have been earlier forms of writing that have not been preserved, because they were written on perishable materials. (Urcid, *Zapotec Writing*, 5)

to be as different from those of the precolonial ancestors of the Zapotec as the views of English people today are from those of their distant ancestors.

In the tenth century CE, the influence of Monte Alban waned, and other cities in the region filled the political gap left by this retreat. A number of the distinctive features of earlier Zapotec culture merged with first Mixtec and then Nahua/Aztec features, including language and writing. The Mixtecs move into the Zapotec region, including Monte Albán, in the years following the decline of the Zapotec city in the tenth century, and for the remaining history of the Zapotec before the Spanish arrival in the sixteenth century, they are engaged in conflict with both Mixtec and Aztec groups. While the Aztec Empire came to dominate the region in the early fifteenth century, the Zapotecs maintained a separate kingdom and successfully resisted Aztec domination until the opening years of the sixteenth century, when the Aztec expansion with the rulers Ahuitzotl and then Motecuhzoma II finally overcame the Zapotec resistance.

The Mixtec society developed very close to the area of the Zapotec region, in what is today Oaxaca. This relatively small region is one of the most linguistically and culturally diverse in Mesoamerica and in the world. The reasons for this are not altogether clear, though the terrain of the region, between numerous mountain ranges and the sea, and its location seemingly at a crossroad between a number of different cultural regions, may have something to do with this. Because of this, a number of different groups were able to be relatively isolated for long periods in this region despite being relatively close to one another. Numerous language families can be found in this tiny region, as well as a number of languages representing isolates, not linked to any known language family.

The Mixtec society developed centralized settlement around the beginning of the first millennium CE, with the city center today known as Yucuita becoming one of the first developed city centers in the Mixtec region. As described above, the Mixtec come to engage with the Zapotec, the Aztec, and other people in the region in the years after 1000 CE. The Mixtec developed their own writing system, which became influential through the wider region, and is similar to writing systems like that of the Aztecs, with which there were almost certainly connections. Six precolonial Mixtec codices are known today.

Mesoamerica in the History of Philosophy

The history of Mesoamerican cultures intersects with that of Europe and the "West" more generally beginning in the sixteenth century, with the Spanish arrival in the Americas. While we tend to think of the history and intellectual traditions of Europe and the colonial world in the last 500 years as a solely European construction, this is far from the truth. As is well known, many of the physical resources that made the Spanish Empire possible came from the Americas, including Mesoamerica. Spanish influence on Mesoamerica is well known and oft discussed, but Mesoamerican influence on Europe tends to be neglected or denied. No cultural exchange, even ones between conqueror and conquered, is one-way. It is no coincidence that the periods of cultural and intellectual growth and innovation in Europe (as elsewhere in the world) happened at the same time people in the region made contact with and learned from those in other areas of the world. If the Spanish encounter with Mesoamerica radically changed the latter, it also radically changed the former.

Mesoamerican traditions are not as "foreign" as we think. We tend to think of our tradition (in the Western academy) as "Euro-American" only because we have ignored the fact that much of what constitutes it does not have a European origin at all. The Western tradition is not solely (or not even mainly, if we go back far enough) a European construct, it's just that it's only the European figures we choose to give credit for it. In the case of almost everyone else, ideas were taken but the originators were neglected and forgotten. This, I think, is the true harm of "cultural appropriation" (even though I think much of our current discourse about that idea is badly flawed). There's nothing wrong with taking ideas – ideas can't be stopped, and can't be owned. Rather, the problem is misattribution of the sources of our ideas, and the way that serves (often intentionally) to belittle certain cultures and lionize others. Thus, the history of ideas in the West has been one focused on the West, and with the contributions of the rest of the world to the ideas "of" the West edited out. If philosophers have a responsibility to seek truth, then we also have a responsibility to correct this long lived but inaccurate view of the history of "Western thought."

Part of what is necessary here is to engage with ideas in their historical contexts, and with an eye toward understanding where these ideas originated, how, and what their purposes were. Having this historical context is independently important to help us understand what a given historical tradition, thinker, or text aimed to do, but it is also important in helping us to see what the true origins of ideas are, what the influences between cultures was, and the ways in which numerous traditions we often take as distinct are linked, and often intimately linked. To do this, we must look beyond the ahistorical approach to texts. We have to do more than simply pull arguments and positions that seem appealing to us out of texts, with no context and no evidence for reading the texts the ways we do. This is not to say that the purely ahistorical approach is illegitimate, but it holds dangers, particularly as a way of engaging in the history of philosophy. The historical background sketched in this chapter, although too brief to give more than a rudimentary understanding of the history and culture of these Mesoamerican traditions, is a necessary starting point for understanding the Mesoamerican philosophical traditions themselves.

Further Reading

There are a number of excellent works dealing with the historical, cultural, and philosophical background sketched briefly above. For fuller and in-depth accounts of what is briefly sketched here, see Adams and MacLeod, eds., *Cambridge History of the Native People of the Americas, Volume II: Mesoamerica*, Part 1; Sharer, *The Ancient Maya, 6th edition*; Nichols and Alegría, *The Oxford Handbook of the Aztecs*; Joyce, *Mixtecs, Zapotecs, and Chatinos: Ancient Peoples of Southern Mexico*. For excellent shorter overviews aimed at a more general audience, see Soustelle, *The Olmecs: The Oldest Civilization in Mexico*, Coe and Houston, *The Maya, 9th edition*; Foster, *Handbook to Life in the Ancient Maya World*; Coe and Koontz, *Mexico: From the Olmecs to the Aztecs, 8th edition*; Carrasco, *The Aztecs: A Very Short Introduction*; Townsend, *Fifth Sun: A New History of the Aztecs*; McKillop, *The Ancient Maya: New Perspectives*. Full publication details for all of these works can be found in the bibliography.

1   The Nature of Philosophy
in Mesoamerica

In this chapter, I consider the issues of the role of philosophy in Mesoamerica and its sources. Offering an expansive account of philosophy, I argue that the sources of philosophy in ancient Mesoamerica include, but are not limited to, textual material. While there is a long textual tradition in Mesoamerica, particularly in Maya and Aztec cultures, we find philosophy in other sources as well, including architecture, art, oral tradition, and performance. I describe the ways philosophy can be found in these numerous sources and argue for the importance of philosophical interaction with anthropology, art history, and other relevant fields.

What Is Philosophy?

Mesoamerican philosophy, as a particular representative tradition or cluster of traditions, has long been neglected as such. While the philosophical traditions of various Mesoamerican cultures have been studied and explored by a number of excellent scholars across numerous disciplines (most often archaeology, sociology, linguistics, and art history), few philosophers have brought the insights and tools of philosophy to this project. There are likely a number of reasons for this, some of which are interrelated.

First, within the discipline of philosophy, the history of philosophy has been largely seen as a European phenomenon. Many texts still today chart this history as beginning with the ancient Greeks, running through Rome and then Medieval Europe into the modern period and finally to the contemporary philosophy of Europe and the extended European colonized world

(Anglo America, Australia, etc.).[1] Today, there are some signs of this slowly beginning to change, as more histories add at least nods to the so-called "Non-Western" traditions (i.e., the philosophy of everyone in the world outside of Europe and the European colonized world). There are still large parts of the globe left out of the story of philosophy told in academia, however. Mesoamerica is one glaring omission. The decolonization of philosophy is revealing the existence of these traditions to philosophers, as we reenvision what the discipline is and can be.

Second, philosophy's self-conception in the West has long been as a text-based tradition. While there are numerous texts in Mesoamerican traditions, from both before and after the arrival of the Spanish in the Americas, these texts give us only a partial picture of the philosophical systems of Mesoamerica. One of the unique features of Mesoamerican philosophy is its lack of complete reliance on text. It is not that people in Mesoamerican traditions did not see text as important and playing a role in preserving ideas, but rather that the role of text was not as central as it was in a number of other global philosophical traditions. We will see, in precontact texts in Mesoamerica, that the kinds of things selected for inclusion in text tended to be commemorative or instructional. In the precontact texts, we find almanacs, ritual manuals, divination guides, and histories. After the colonization of the Spanish, we find a host of other texts, often written in Mesoamerican languages using Latin script, giving us a deeper glimpse into Mesoamerican philosophy. Texts such as the *Popol Vuh* of the K'iche' Maya and the Aztec text known today as the *Codex Magliabechiano*, as well as Bernardo de Sahagun's late sixteenth-century study of the Nahua, known today as the *Florentine Codex*, show us a more detailed picture of Mesoamerican philosophy in

---

[1] Here, my use of "European colonized world" refers not to all of the areas in the world that were colonized by Europeans but specifically to ones in which Europeans became a majority and affiliated with the "dominant" culture of this new place. Thus, nations such as the USA, Canada, and Australia count, while nations such as India, Nigeria, and Malaysia do not. In the case of the latter countries, while they were colonized, Europeans never became a majority of the people of these nations and did not transplant their people or culture as fully as in the previously mentioned places. Another group of nations not on the list is somewhere between these – such as the nations of Latin America that came under the rule of the Spanish and Portuguese in the sixteenth and seventeenth centuries.

text. Why, we might ask, were these ideas not included in earlier texts before the arrival of the Spanish? One part of the answer to this question, I contend, is that a great deal of philosophy was not done in text prior to the Spanish colonization. We find explicit claims to as much in texts such as the *Popol Vuh*, which explain that the contents of the text are being written down because they can "no longer be seen." Among the last lines of the *Popol Vuh* are contained:

> Xere k'ut u k'oje'ik K'iche', ri'rumal maja b'i chi ilb'al re, k'o nab'e ojer kumal ajawab', sachinaq chik.

> Here then is [written] the essence of K'iche', because there is no longer the means to see it [the *ilb'al*]. That which was enacted by the ancient kings (*ajawab'*) is now lost.[2]

The *Popol Vuh* was originally meant to be performed with ritual performance, enacting the story of creation and the emergence of humanity. Philosophy done in this way, in the Maya tradition and other Mesoamerican traditions, was *performative* in nature. Not simply oral, in the sense of information passed through discussion, but performative in the sense of movement, speech, song, and enacting of character and events meant to uncover particular aspects of the world.[3]

In philosophy today, we tend to deal with *texts* when thinking about and uncovering the past. Philosophical traditions, we assume, were always textual traditions. Accordingly, when we work on the history of philosophy, we translate, interpret, and discuss texts and textual traditions. While our focus on text is clear, we also recognize that philosophy can be done without text. Indeed, the philosopher often pointed to as the archetype of philosophy itself, Socrates, has no writings attributed to his name, and we only know of him at all through his students and others who knew him. While we access Socrates through Plato (and to a lesser extent Xenophon and others), we are willing to recognize what he did, in oral and not textual transmission, as not only philosophy but the very definition of

---

[2] *Popol Vuh*, 8710, author's translation. From K'iche' text, in Christenson, *Popol Vuh: Literal Translation*, p. 304.

[3] Mesoamerican philosophy shares this feature with other traditions of the Americas, in particular North American indigenous thought, which placed emphasis on performance in similar ways. See Welch, *The Phenomenology of a Performative Knowledge System*.

philosophy.[4] This recognition that philosophy is not necessarily (or perhaps even originally, or mainly) something done in text should open for us new possibilities of understanding. If philosophy might be done independently of text, in what other ways might it be done? How much philosophy might we be missing in the world and its history due to our overreliance on text? It turns out, quite a bit. Not only is there philosophy in oral tradition and transmission as in Socrates' case, which we find in numerous traditions throughout the world (including in Mesoamerica), but philosophy can also be done through other nontextual media. We find philosophy in art, architecture, monumental construction, and other aspects of material culture. This, of course, would not be news to art historians, archaeologists, and other scholars who attempt to draw meaning from nontextual material artifacts. Yet it can be a stumbling block for philosophers.

The act of translation needed for interpreting nontextual material is different from that required for translating one language to another. Here, images must be translated into words, cultural practices interpreted for philosophical meaning. This is not to say that there are no texts to work from as well. Indeed, there are – the Mesoamerican philosophical tradition is the sole tradition of the pre-Columbian Americas that we know of with a precolonial textual tradition. As we will see, the Maya, Aztecs, Mixtec, and Zapotec (the other four traditions covered in this book) all had systems of writing, and numerous texts containing religious, political, philosophical, and historical ideas, long before Europeans arrived in the Americas. Even given this, however, there is much to be found in Mesoamerica, including these traditions, in aspects of material culture. Even in cultures that had textual traditions, we find philosophy outside of texts. After all, ancient Greek society was literate and had texts as well; yet Socratic philosophy was not textual in nature at its inception. According to Plato, Socrates' practice of philosophy was an oral activity, within a world with a robust textual tradition. Socrates lived in a world with numerous texts, including the massive historical

---

[4] Numerous scholars have written about the issue of oral philosophy in various cultural contexts, for example "sage philosophy" in African traditions. Lucius Outlaw discusses the issue of Socrates and the textual/oral in "African Philosophy; Deconstructive and Reconstructive Challenges," 230. There are additional sources of philosophy beyond the oral or textual, discussed in the following text.

works of Herodotus, the Homeric epics (which were transmitted orally for many years before they were put into print in the eighth century BCE), vast numbers of poems and plays, and many other texts. So it can hardly be said that text was rare or difficult to produce when Socrates lived. Yet philosophy for him proceeded differently, not through text but through conversation. And even when we see the move of this style of philosophy to text, with Socrates' students such as Plato, it still mainly takes place through conversation, but conversation now translated into print, as with the Socratic dialogues of Plato. Though there were other forms of philosophy during the time that were text based, this Socratic form of philosophy (which Plato identified exclusively with philosophy) was first done primarily orally.

This all raises the question of just what the nature of philosophy is, so as to determine in what sense Mesoamerican philosophy should be considered a part of this wider phenomenon. It turns out that we do not need to significantly expand or relax the conception of philosophy used by those in academia in order to see that Mesoamerican philosophy, like a number of other philosophical traditions that have been neglected in the West, falls perfectly within the category. That is, even *by our own lights*, Mesoamerican philosophy is clearly philosophy, and so barring it from that designation cannot but be for reasons falling outside of our determination of the definition of philosophy.

Thought about the nature of philosophy in the West (focusing here on contemporary philosophy in the Western academy), despite debates and disagreements, has been somewhat surprisingly consistent over the past half century or so. It has been a common move in defining philosophy to point back to the views of the originators of the term, in ancient Greece. Here, we see that *philosophia* (from *philosophos*) is understood differently from the way many of today's professional philosophers understand their work. The term seems to have originated initially as an insult to flag people who arrogantly strove and failed to become *sophoi*, political advisors. The association of philosophy with "love of wisdom" was a later reenvisioning of the name by those who had by then adopted it as their own.[5] On this later conception, immortalized by Plato, a philosopher was understood as

[5] Christopher Moore, *Calling Philosophers Names*, 1.

a person who strives for truth, through attempting to uncover definitions. This is a very broad description, of course, and if applied to our own time, could capture every single academic field. Plato's conception of philosophy is much closer to *academic research in general* than it is to any particular field.

Even by the definition of the activity of philosophy found in the works of the ancient Greeks, however, a far wider range of global cultures engaged in philosophy than those most often picked out by the Western philosophical tradition, and our departments of philosophy today. Current day descriptions of the activity of philosophy likewise pick out a wide range of activities throughout the world and history that we seem nonetheless unprepared to accept as philosophy. The twentieth-century American analytic philosopher Wilfrid Sellars famously wrote: "[T]he aim of philosophy, abstractly formulated, is to understand how things in the broadest possible sense of the term hang together in the broadest possible sense of the term." While many philosophers today accept this, and refer to Sellars' famous quote, they often fail to extend this to people who engaged and still engage in this activity in areas we associate with the "developing world" (a somewhat insulting phrase that has come to replace the also problematic but less insulting "Third World" of the Cold War era).[6]

The self-conception of philosophy in the Western academy has changed over time, and continues to change. While decades ago, the religious philosophy of the medieval period of Europe (and sometimes the Middle East) was seen as a key part of the history of philosophy, today it is less so, except at religious institutions. Today, philosophers in the academy affiliate themselves for the most part with the sciences (with some exceptions), and the naturalistic methods of the sciences, as well as the assumptions and intuitions of a world fully explained by the sciences, are often assumed.

---

[6] I take it that "Third World" is less problematic because it at least has no normative connotations. The phrase referred originally to unaligned nations in the Cold War struggle between the West ("First World") and the Soviet sphere ("Second World"). The phrase came to take on implications of poverty and global insignificance, presumably because many of the unaligned nations were poorer and/or less connected to these larger conflicts. But the phrase "Third World" itself has no such meaning, in the way "developing world" contains in its meaning the assumption that a region or nation is lesser than some compared nation or region. We could just as easily find things that the wealthiest or Western nations struggle with compared with the nations classed as "developing" and describe them as "developing" on the basis of that.

While philosophers often accept concepts, ideas, and positions that cannot be fully captured in scientific explanation, they attempt to make these views as consistent as possible with the dominant scientific positions of the day. Often, views such as those of the ancient Mesoamericans are dismissed because of the sense that they are inconsistent with contemporary scientific views (a sense that is not always accurate). We should be careful to notice, however, that for the most part, our contemporary Western philosophical views *also* fail to maintain consistency with scientific naturalism as such, as does most premodern Western philosophy. The only fully consistent view would be a kind of scientific reductionism that rendered almost every metaphysical concept eliminable. While some philosophers, particularly in the previous century, did take such a line, such views are far less prevalent in philosophy today and even more rare in the history of philosophy anywhere in the world.

Many scholars have challenged the idea that philosophy is something limited to the European "West" and to the methods and styles of thinkers of this tradition. Philosophy, like religion and culture more broadly, is as old as humanity itself. It is almost inconceivable that any human ever existed anywhere without thinking about the nature of his or her life and world, and using the tools enabled by his or her brain to think through these issues in an extra-empirical way. We would be much better served following the general rule that *anything that is found in one place, or among one people or person, is almost certain to exist elsewhere too.* That is, we are much more likely to be correct if we operate from the assumption of our ordinariness (or that of anyone else we find) than of our uniqueness. When we allow our cognitive biases that give us a sense of personal value into our attempts to understand the world, we cannot be surprised when we get things wildly wrong. And perhaps the mistakes of this bias can teach us something important about how we construct value, and suggest different possibilities for doing it. Why do we have to be *different* to have value? Why not think that there is value in the common?

When we talk about philosophers, *whom* are we talking about? Seemingly, it cannot be only people working at academic institutions and publishing in journals of philosophy, because we refer to many historical figures who did nothing anywhere close to this as philosophers. And for most of the population, the term "philosopher" refers to these bygone historical figures rather than modern-day academics. "Philosophy" is tantamount to "history" or "history of philosophy" for most people outside of the walls of academia. But even if we stick to the views of professional philosophers, the category of "philosopher" must be broad enough to include at least diverse figures such as Plato, Aquinas, Kant, Descartes, Nietzsche, and Frege, people whom all professional philosophers will accept as philosophers. How can a category broad enough to capture all of them fail to capture figures such as Dharmakirti, Ibn Arabi, Xunzi, or the Aztec *tlamatinime*?

Sources of Philosophy in Mesoamerica

We will not spend much time here considering the questions, then, of whether there is Mesoamerican philosophy and whether the content of this book counts as philosophy, rather than culture, religion, or something else. All philosophy usually counts as something else besides. The more important question for our purposes here is *how* philosophy was done in precolonial Mesoamerica, and *where* it could be found – that is, what were the sources of philosophy in early Mesoamerica?

Precolonial Mesoamerica did have textual traditions. Texts were written throughout the region, on stelae and architecture, as well as in bark paper books, some of which are still extant today. Most of the paper books from the precolonial period have been lost due to a combination of reasons. Such books generally do not keep well in the conditions of most of Mesoamerica; even when texts have been found by archaeologists in burial sites, they are generally so badly decayed that they are unreadable. Another reason is the Spanish suppression of native textual traditions in the colonial period. Texts were not copied in their original forms, instead shifting to Latinized versions of native languages, such as we see with the K'iche' Maya *Popol Vuh*. Nonetheless, today we have access to a handful of precolonial Mesoamerican books, including Maya texts such as the eleventh century CE *Dresden Codex* and *Maya Codex of Mexico* (formerly known as the *Grolier Codex*),[7] as well as the fourteenth-century Mixtec *Codex Tonindeye*

---

[7] Precolonial texts are given such names as there are no titles affixed to the texts; thus, we do not know what they were called when they were written and read.

(also known as *Codex Zouche Nuttall*)[8], and the fifteenth-century Aztec *Codex Borgia*. In addition to these texts, there are a host of colonial period texts likely based on earlier lost native texts, such as the *Popol Vuh* of the K'iche', the *Chilam Balam* books and the *Songs of Dzitbalche* of the Maya in the Yucatán, and Aztec texts such as *Cantares Mexicanos* and *Florentine Codex*.

In addition to text, however, there are a number of other important sources of philosophy in precolonial Mesoamerica. Indeed, text may not have even been the most important or primary source of philosophical thought, even though it is one that philosophers and other scholars working on Mesoamerica today need, because of our lack of access to the performances, artwork, and discussions that the people of early Mesoamerica had (and which some still have today in these regions). We are then working at something of a disadvantage – we have a window into early Mesoamerican philosophy, but it is one that is muddied and unclear. Like the authors of the *Popol Vuh*, we have to rely on the texts, remnants of artifacts, and words of people today in Mesoamerica to glimpse early Mesoamerican philosophy, because to a large extent, it can "no longer be seen" in its original character. Of course, this is also true for the philosophy of the style of Socrates and his followers in ancient Greece or Confucius and his students in ancient China. Texts, artifacts, and oral histories, for example, allow us to get a handle on what philosophy would have been like in the times and places we are considering. From this, we can try to *reconstruct* a philosophical tradition, always keeping in mind a fact that Mesoamerican philosophers knew (and know) well – that any reconstruction is always a partnership between the source and the observer. Just as nature itself is constructed via the cooperation of the gods and human beings, reconstructions of philosophical systems can never be pure transmission from earlier times and places. They are products of cooperation between the material and the interpreter. This is why translation and interpretation remain valuable, even when texts or traditions have been translated and interpreted many times before.

---

[8] Many precolonial Mesoamerican texts were given modern names after Western collectors or places associated with the text – some have attempted to give these texts names more appropriate to their cultural and linguistic context – such as in this case the Dzaha Dzaui (Mixtec) term *tonindeye* ("lineage history"). See Jansen and Perez-Jimenez, "Renaming the Mexican Codices," 269.

When we look at textual sources of philosophy in Mesoamerica, we have to consider the question of genre, style, and the relevance of each for philosophy. *Poetry*, or rather ritual verse, intended for performance, was a key textual style of philosophy in Mesoamerica. The best-known texts of the region, such as the *Popol Vuh* and the philosophical songs of the Aztec ruler Nezahualcoyotl (recounted in the sixteenth century *Romances de los señores de Nueva España*) are in poetic form, as are many of the greatest philosophical texts in human history. There is something particularly powerful about the poetic form for invoking the suggestive, incomplete, interpretive, and cooperative nature of human understanding of the world. A poetic rendering of philosophy makes clear the role of our own creativity in making the world as it is – a key feature of Mesoamerican philosophical thought. As we will see, this human creative role does not, however, entail that truth is simply invented by us. While we *assist* in making the world as it is, we cannot make the world any old way we like, we cannot change the features of the world that bind our creative operation. Just as with the molding of clay into a statue – we cannot make the underlying characteristics of the clay other than how they are, and we are limited in what we can mold by the medium. What we create will always still have the features of clay, but using this medium, we can create a host of things. It is the human mind that makes the clay shaped a particular way into an image of a person, or a tree, or a bird, etc. Considered outside of the perspective of the human, such a shaped clay is still just clay. It is the human mind that makes this shaped clay more than just clay. Notice that the clay does not take on the features of a person when we shape it in a certain way so as to resemble a person in our eyes. The clay formed into a statue has the exact same physical features as the clay that has been naturally shaped into the form of a rock. The statue will appear to a bird the same as will an unshaped piece of clay. It will show up on an infrared sensor the same way as a piece of clay will. What makes one the statue of a person and one a rock is our own recognition and accordance of meaning. We can see that this is not something that happens just as a result of the world itself, as if through natural processes, a piece of clay formed into something that perfectly resembled Abraham Lincoln, we would consider it an image of Abraham Lincoln. But the difference between the construction of this clay and the rock is our recognition, our conceptualization. We can see this in the way we recognize or conceptualize certain natural features of the world as objects such as faces, or familiar human items. We see the image of a face in a rock, for example(a commonly recognized feature in human society, given the human brain's tendency to interpret visual features faces[9]), or the image of a man in the moon. These are all human conceptualizations and constructions we impose on our natural environment – no less so than the ways we create or recognize the image of a person in a molded piece of clay that we shape specifically to resemble a certain person, or the mixture of pigments and paint to resemble a certain landscape, or the ways we manipulate pixels on a television screen to present to us an image that seems to perfectly resemble a scene of our choice. Human creation of the world from the natural stuff of the cosmos happens on numerous levels – not only the construction of artifacts and tools, as in the case of the television, but also in the ways we conceptualize and perceive the untouched parts of "nature." Poetry can help capture either of these senses of human creation – making more explicit the ways in which the human mind works in shaping our world. This can all-too-easily be hidden behind the language of technical analysis. When we describe a rock face using the terminology of the sciences, we often miss the ways our own conceptualization contributes to the formation of what we are discussing. It makes it seem as if we are observing something completely independent from us.[10] Poetry, on the other hand, in its creative play with language, brings right to the fore the sense in which human creativity is involved in the way we grasp and understand things in the world, and necessarily so because human creativity is central in the construction of the things in the world as we understand them.

---

[9] This phenomenon, known as face pareidolia, likely evolved in humans due to our reliance on social cues to navigate interpersonal activity. See Palmer and Clifford, "Face Pareidolia Recruits Mechanisms for Detecting Human Social Attention."

[10] Although today plausible interpretations of quantum mechanics show us that we can never get away from the fact that observation makes a difference in the states of things in the world.

This is why we see that philosophical systems, schools, and traditions that stress the human role in the construction of nature, such as many systems in early Mesoamerica, as well as the Daoists in China, certain schools of Buddhism in south and east Asia, and Western figures such as Nietzsche or Wittgenstein (who wrote "one should only really do philosophy as poetry"[11]), often express their positions in poetic form.

The *Cantares Mexicanos*, a sixteenth century collection of Aztec poems, and the K'iche' Maya *Popol Vuh*, a ritual text on the origin of the cosmos and humanity,[12] show us two examples of philosophical texts in poetry and verse. The Aztec "flower and song," according to the *Cantares Mexicanos*, expresses truths about the world that can be expressed in no other way, and gives us insight into the human condition as well. While the *Cantares* is clearly heavily influenced by Spanish ideas, particularly Christianity, the poetic form of the text is likely an older structure in the Aztec tradition. Poetry, according to a number of the verses in the text, is both a balm to human suffering and a way to access other worlds, including that of those who have died. One poem in the collection reads (in Bierhorst's translation):

> Flowers are our only adornment. Only through songs does our pain on earth subside. [...]
>
> I suffer and grieve, I, Prince Nezahualcoyotl. With flowers, with songs, I recall the departed princes Tezozomoc and Cuacuauhtzin.
>
> Do we truly live in the Place Unknown? Let me follow these princes. Let me bring them our flowers. With good songs let me touch this Tezozomoc, this Cuacuauhtzin.[13]

Just as the poetry of "flower and song" accompanies one into other generally unseen parts of the world, such as the places where the dead still live on, we can gain access to these other realms through ritual performance of the kind of poetry written in the *Popol Vuh*. A passage near the beginning of the *Popol Vuh* explains why it was written down in this textual form, when the *Popol Vuh* had previously been primarily performed (although there is also suggestion here of earlier glyphic text):

---

[11] *Culture and Value*, 24, Z#160.
[12] Though both of these texts were written during the colonial period, their contents are almost certainly older.
[13] *Cantares Mexicanos*, song 40, Bierhorst trans., 213–215.

This account we shall now write under the law of God and Christianity. We shall bring it forth because there is not longer the means whereby the Popol Vuh may be seen, the means of seeing clearly that had come from across the sea – the account of our obscurity, and the means of seeing life clearly, as it is said. The original book exists that was written anciently, but its witnesses and those who ponder it hide their faces.[14]

In addition to poetry and more straightforward verse, we find a number of different sources for philosophy in early Mesoamerica. These sources will perhaps be most unfamiliar to readers steeped in the traditions of the Eurasian continent, as in those traditions, philosophy is most closely associated with text and textual tradition. In the Mesoamerican context, text certainly plays a role, but we also find philosophy in monumental imagery, art, architecture, performance, ritual, language, and construction of tools. In this and later chapters, I look to all of these sources to clarify Mesoamerican philosophy. In the West, we are unaccustomed to looking at these sources for philosophy, so this will require a certain extent of *retraining* one's philosophical sense. Fortunately, this is something that can be done, and indeed something we *already* do in numerous ways, and simply fail to understand this activity as philosophical. My hope is that once we see these ways of understanding philosophy via other nontextual sources, we will recognize the enormous number of philosophical tools in both the Mesoamerican tradition and outside of it, that we often leave unutilized, and the rich areas we leave unexamined. The philosophical terrain of human culture is a vast continent with sweeping mountain ranges, deserts, swamps, lush forests, rolling rivers, seemingly eternal plains – but we often limit ourselves to a small clearing, a grove within a single woodland, rendering the rest of the world on our map with dragons.

While I do not have the space here to discuss *all* of the ways we can encounter philosophy in the world, I can discuss some of the central ways beyond textual culture that we find practiced in Mesoamerica. We often find poetry in oral tradition, particularly in premodern history.

---

[14] *Popol Vuh*, Christenson trans., 55–56. One interesting issue here is the question of whether this passage refers to earlier textual versions of the *Popol Vuh* in native Maya scripts. It is likely that such texts existed, as we find references to events from the *Popol Vuh* in the Classic Period imagery. The glyphic text itself, however, as we will

The epics of ancient India, the Homeric epics of Greece, and even the *suttas* of early Buddhism were passed down through memorization and recitation long before they were rendered into textual form. Another source of Western knowledge of oral tradition is, of course, the robust oral tradition of the indigenous Americas. Most readers of this book (i.e., English-speaking audience) will be familiar with the emphasis of indigenous groups throughout the Americas on knowledge contained in and passed through oral tradition. Much (but not all) of this oral tradition has been put into text over the years, by native people themselves, and students of their traditions. There are still things that have *not* been put into text, however, and on purpose, following the view that there are certain ideas that can only be understood and appreciated in non-textual forms.

Likewise, some ideas can only be properly understood against some background context, as developing other ideas. Just as we would not expect someone with no background in analytic philosophy to get much from a specialized journal article on metaphysics, philosophy of mind, or any of the other areas in which we work, we could not expect someone without the requisite ritual, performance, or aesthetic formation to understand the nuance, complexity, and significance of certain ritual performances, constructions, artworks, etc. And since this context, for many

---

see in the chapter on identity, would have been understood as itself a performance, with the words containing the essence of the entities referred to. This suggests a different understanding of the relationship between language and reality than obtains with a text written in Latin script. The Maya authors of early Latin script forms of the *Popol Vuh* were likely familiar with the very different conception of the relationship between language and reality of the Spanish, and their understanding of text, which differed from native Maya understanding of text. It is possible that these different theories of language were associated with the use of particular languages or scripts – that is, writing in Latin script entailed Western conceptions of the connection between language and reality, whereas writing in Maya script entitled native conceptions. Native conceptions of language held glyphs to have identity with the represented things – the glyph for a god contained the essence of that god, for example. Spanish conceptions of language relied on reference rather than identity or manifestation of essence. Thus, writing about the world in Latin script was perhaps seen as referencing the world, while writing about it in Maya script would be understood as presenting or manifesting the world, such that it could be *seen*. This is likely what the author has in mind when claiming that the Popol Vuh can no longer be seen.

non-native readers, will be very unfamiliar, we must learn some of this background – this is something I will attempt to translate for readers throughout this book.

Performance, particularly ritual demonstrations in presentations of important "plays" or ceremonial events (the two categories were not completely separated, though there could be longer and shorter such everts), was one source of philosophy in early Mesoamerica. While some important performances, such as those recounted in the *Florentine Codex*, the *Chilam Balam* books, or the *Popol Vuh*, were ultimately written down after Spanish contact, while others were not. Fortunately, some of these performances, or at least descendants of them, are still made by people in Mesoamerica. It is thus important, in understanding the philosophical traditions of Mesoamerica, to look to anthropology, sociology, and the practices of the current day indigenous communities of Mesoamerica. While their practices cannot tell us *exactly* what their ancestors practiced, they can give us important insights and hints that we can combine with other sources (in addition to being valuable in their own right). We are fortunate to be able to draw from the extensive work of generations of anthropologists and sociologists who have studied the practices of current day Mesoamerican indigenous groups, as well as people from these communities who have explained their practices to outside communities, scholars, and audience.

Often such ritual performances relied on nonlinguistic features of movement to express meaning. This is an issue that has been discussed to some extent by philosophers in aesthetics. It has not been fully appreciated by philosophers across the field, however, that physical movement, nonlinguistic sound, color, and motion can convey philosophical meaning or content. This is a very important feature of Mesoamerican performance. In performances of the K'iche' Maya *Rabinal Achi*, and presumably also the *Popol Vuh* before it, particular motions, colors, and sounds have important meaning and significance, and understanding the import of the performance requires attending to those features. Reading a text of the *Rabinal Achi*, for example, will leave one who does not understand this perplexed, as the textual content itself seems sparse and repetitive. But focus on the text obscures the fact that the most important aspects of the performance are given in *movement*, in a way that cannot be captured in text without elaborate description and translation, and even then text misses something crucial inherent in movement.

We find other examples of such things in traditions across the world. Even if Mesoamerican ritual performance is unique in just how much of the work of communicating meaning is done through the nontextual aspects of performance, and the sense in which philosophical content particularly is expressed this way, we do find the idea of movement as expressing meaning in cultures and traditions throughout the world. In the West, we are familiar with the notion of dance as expressive in communicative ways. In everything from Broadway musicals to ballet, we find meaning expressed through physical movement – whether emotion, statement, or other communication. We also recognize the ways movement can (perhaps to a lesser extent) express meaning in the context of sports, or even gestures between people. A shrug of the shoulders, for example, can express that one is uninterested, or a particular kind of glance can demonstrate surprise, interest, boredom, or many other things. The movements of boxer or MMA fighter in the ring or octagon can communicate confidence, arrogance, respect, timidity, or a host of other meanings. We all know of the idea of "jumping for joy," which can happen at a sudden victory in sport, or a sudden unexpected windfall for an individual – an acceptance letter or call from a school or a job, a notification of winning the lottery, and other such things. And while emotion is commonly expressed through movement, we can express other meanings as well. Wide motions can express directness, wooden and still stances can express guardedness, careful and ritualized motions can express a sense of importance or significance.

We see that movement can express basic ideas. At a more abstract and complex level (which we are less familiar with concerning movement, but that is common in Mesoamerican performance), movement can express more technical, complex, and philosophical ideas. Some forms of dance in the West have attempted to move in this direction, and it is in the area of the movement arts that we find most discussion and understanding of this. In the historical Indian philosophical tradition, there was also focus on performance both in terms of the significance of sound and recitation (retained today in the importance of the chanting of mantras or texts in ritual and religious contexts), as well as on the spiritual and philosophical significance of certain forms of movement.[15] Recently, some philosophers in Western academia have also developed views of movement as expressive of meaning.[16] Some readers may find this aspect of Mesoamerican Philosophy particularly new, unusual, or confusing, and I will try my best to unpack the issues associated with this source of philosophical thought and the cultural background necessary to understand it in the following chapters of this book.

Physical art and architecture are perhaps the most unique ways Mesoamerican philosophy was presented. As with performance, many of us will recognize the ways art and architecture can bear meaning – any course in art history or even a stroll through your local art museum will reveal this. The creative physical arts – painting, sculpting, printing, construction, and more – have always held and been intended to impart meaning. This is perhaps most obvious in the case of artworks depicting people, scenes, events, or places. We shape things into a likeness, a representation of some original, including the artist's interpretation of, commentary on, or way of thinking about this original. Representational art shows us that there is no "view from nowhere," no perspective-independent view on a scene or thing. Even a photograph is taken from a particular location, under particular lighting, at a time and angle, through human eyes, etc. And the subjective mode is more pronounced in other art forms. When we look at Picasso's "Guernica," we see not just a historical scene, but a particular take on the emotions, the terror, the chaos, the dissonance of that scene. Volumes have been written on particular paintings, sculptures, and other artworks to explain their meaning in text form. We recognize such artwork as a potentially extraordinarily rich source of meaning and information (think of the common phrase "a picture is worth a thousand words"), but we are for some reason less inclined to take such artwork as the source of *philosophy*. In the Mesoamerican traditions, philosophy emerges through such artwork.

---

[15] The concept of *natya*, or stylized movements meant to express certain emotions and ideas through dance, was extensively discussed in the *Natyasastra*, a text on drama dating to somewhere between the second century BCE and the second century CE.

[16] See for example recent literature in philosophy of dance, such as Katan-Schmid, *Embodied Philosophy in Dance*; Welch, *Choreography as Embodied Critical Inquiry*; among numerous others. Also see Nail, *Being and Motion*.

A natural question one might ask here is whether Mesoamerican traditions *intentionally* presented philosophical ideas through artwork, performance, and the other sources we are discussing, or instead whether
scholars of Mesoamerican philosophy are *finding* philosophical meaning
in these sources, in the same way we might find philosophical meaning
in artworks and performances in other cultures, even when such meanings were not intended or explicitly given to the artwork? There are a few
additional questions raised by this: 1) does doing philosophy require a
conception by the people engaged in it of themselves doing philosophy as
such, or at least a single coherent activity, whatever they might call it? 2)
Is explicit philosophical intention in creation of a thing necessary for that
thing to convey philosophical ideas?

Let's take the second question first. While we know that there are certainly *some* ideas and content that do not require creative intent to be
carried by an object (artwork, text, etc.), we generally take philosophical
meaning to require particular kinds of intent. This may be the result of
our tendency to think of philosophy as involving something like conceptual analysis and related projects, or along the lines of the physical sciences, which shows why many reject the idea that poetry can be a source
of philosophy. If philosophical meaning can be held by poetry, though,
there must be some hermeneutic freedom, some sense in which autho-
rial intention does not constrain philosophical meaning. If this is so, the
question becomes just what the role of such intention is, and whether *any*
such intention is necessary for something to carry philosophical meaning. If not, then it seems that natural objects, or anything else in the
universe, could carry philosophical meaning. But is this what we want
to say? It turns out that this is very much what Mesoamerican traditions
will say, and for a number of reasons. First, the structure of the world *is*
at least in part created by the human mind, according to a dominant view
in these traditions. The ways we conceptualize and conceive of the world,
which completes it and makes it what it is, can be found within the natural world itself, and investigating these things can reveal much about
these ways we conceptualize the world – the patterns in which we do so.
Though perhaps we don't *intentionally* create things in this way, we do
create them through conceptualization, and insofar as philosophy can be
understood as engaging with concepts (including conceptual analysis!),

these objects in the world can be understood as providing philosophical meaning. But is there any sense in which *philosophical positions* are to be found in these objects (or artworks, etc.?) Even if the stuff of nature gives us something we can philosophize *with*, this is different than the claim that philosophy is going on and is presented by the objects in question. Concepts themselves are not philosophy, even though we can do philosophy with them. In Mesoamerican philosophical views, however, objects do not just contain the static concepts we have constructed, but also convey the activity of continually constructing these objects. That is, investigation of objects reveals the ways humans think about and construct our world through conceptualization, not only the concepts themselves. And this activity, conscious or not, is the activity of philosophy. Much of Mesoamerican philosophy is concerned with explaining and uncovering the ways human conceptualization works, revealing the structures of the world that turn out to be identical to the structures of our own thinking and activity. So this is one way that objects, including human-made objects, can present philosophical content. When we think about created objects such as artwork or architectural construction, there is another level of presentation involved. What we will find here in Mesoamerican philosophy is works constructed so as to *draw our attention to* particular ways we engage in conceptualization and thinking about the world, and creation of the world. The inherent meaning in objects, even natural objects, is vast, and certain operation on objects by humans can reveal or be suggestive of certain aspects of those objects. For example, one well-known way of thinking about sculpture reveals this thinking. A block of stone has many potential shapes contained in it, and a particular statue is created by cutting away the parts of that stone that do not immediately reveal this shape. When we see Michelangelo's David, we are seeing a block of stone, and the initial block of stone contained that which we see before Michelangelo ever carved his statue. That same block potentially also contained an image of Abraham Lincoln, or the Great Wall of China, or many other things (and still does, as the stone can be cut down further to reveal those things). The view here is that all of those images are inherent in the stone itself, that the stone can be conceptualized so as to represent (and thus contain the essence of) a particular thing, and that a particular carving brings out this inherent feature of the thing. We will find different views on this in Mesoamerica, including the view that such a carving establishes or actualizes the essence of an object, where multiple essences are *possible* because of the containment of all possibilities of conceptualization within the object.

Ways of Accessing the Philosophy of the Past

As shown above, there are numerous sources of philosophy in precolonial Mesoamerican thought. But we also have to be thoughtful about the ways we *access* this philosophy. Understanding the philosophical views of people using such a variety of sources also requires the ability to access and understand those sources. Thus, we have to look beyond texts and to rituals, practices, oral traditions, architecture, and more. The history of philosophy must become more methodologically diverse in order to allow for our access to such information.

We find patterns when we see them emerge across a range of different ways of thinking. We have to go out and do the work of investigating people and places and different worldviews, and also to look for different sources of thought and use different methodologies to access it. Looking for particular kinds of argument structure and drawing those out of texts (generally removed from historical context) may give us *something*, but it will obscure much of philosophical value when we investigate a tradition or text. To use an analogy – when we're asking what a house is made of, it's not going to suffice to stay in one room and look at the wall. We have to have a broader understanding of the different rooms, parts of the house, and how they fit together. Is it possible to do this "from the armchair," as the philosopher generally (but not always) works? Does the philosopher have to become a field archaeologist or materials expert? At least in part – yes! But fortunately, twenty-first century technology has given us massive assistance in making this a less daunting task than it would have been not long ago. We have an enormous amount of information at our fingertips, and can learn a great deal about other times, places, worldviews, etc. from our own homes. We have this incredible resource that we often fail to use, for a number of different reasons. First, we still have not learned great strategies to navigate this high-information environment, and this is apparent in the growth of online echo chambers, disinformation, etc.

One of the seeming drawbacks is that because all of this information is so easy to access, it can be overwhelming, and we can become unable to evaluate what we encounter. Information overload can lead to a simple breakdown in our ability to process things. We have to develop a strategy to move through such environments that allows us to skillfully navigate them without being overwhelmed – we need to form guiding principles, otherwise it becomes all too easy to get lost in the woods.

One potential response to the information overload is to retreat back into narrower ways of thinking, as a protective response. I suspect this is at least partly the explanation for the rise of nationalism, conservatism, and a certain antiquarian kind of traditionalism around the world. This new world can be baffling and overwhelming, especially when we have not developed strategies to deal with it, and a natural response to what is overwhelming can be to retreat to a place of safety, a place in which all features of the environment are defined, well-known, familiar. But this response is in essence a failure – a failure to make use of and learn from an incredible opportunity. Instead of retrenching in narrower forms of thought, we should invest our energy in discovering and learning strategies for navigating this new situation, so as to take advantage of it, to make use of what it promises. The enormous wealth of information online makes it possible for the philosopher to widen the scope of their investigations beyond text and pulling arguments from text, without having to take on the completely new tasks of learning field archaeological techniques or having practical experience with the physical properties of clay. Such experience, of course, will still be immensely valuable for the philosopher who aims to understand a particular tradition, and absent constraints of time, energy, etc., we should all aim to gain such intellectual breadth, as it will aid our understanding of philosophy. But it is not strictly necessary to do all of this today, with the invaluable treasure of what the Internet makes possible, thus making it possible for a wider range of philosophers to access and understand the variety of ways philosophy is approached across global traditions.

Even when we cannot fully access or understand a particular philosophical tradition (and this is inevitable, as we cannot hope to learn *everything* relevant to understanding a tradition), we can do enough to have a sufficient handle on it, particularly in the ways it differs from traditions we are more familiar with. A guiding principle of the project of learning from the history of philosophy should be that our own worldviews are incomplete, necessarily narrow, and always in need of development. Learning stops where certainty begins, so the more confident we are that our own ways of thinking are the correct or only ways, the less inclined we will be to learn from others, whether of other times or other places. And at that point we become trapped in our cage, unable to recognize the value of anything else, unable to change, to grow. We can only learn from others when we think that there is something we have to learn, can only appreciate different insights and ways of conceiving of the world when we recognize that our own ways are not the only or necessarily the best ways. Faced with information overload, we can entrench in our own worldviews and thus become impervious to learning – that certainly is one way to handle it. But a better way is to make use of the abundance of information to learn and reshape our worldviews into something better, more flexible, more inclusive, more informed.[17]

Philosophical traditions like those of Mesoamerica, which are (sometimes radically) different from those most of us in the contemporary West

---

[17] I use the language of "we" and "our" here with some hesitation. The reason for this is that in this discussion I do not want to exclude those from *outside* Western ways of thinking about these ideas, such as those familiar with or within Mesoamerican traditions, from being assumed part of the readership of this book. I stick with this terminology mainly because the point here is to suggest to philosophical audiences in the West, most of whom are unfamiliar with Mesoamerican philosophy (as most readers of this book will probably be reading it to gain some knowledge about this area – it is after all an *introduction*) that *they* stand to gain in these ways from understanding Mesoamerican philosophy. For those readers familiar with Mesoamerican traditions or who have connections with these traditions – it is not my intention to leave you out here. Indeed, the ways we think about what reflexive group terminology refers to is an essential point, but one we often do not think about. What does it mean when an author uses terms like "we" or "our"? Who are they referring to? I want to be explicit here that I am referring to something like "academic philosophers in the West without familiarity with Mesoamerican traditions." This "we" is of course rhetorical, as it is one that does not even include the author of this book who employs the terminology. I am an academic philosopher in the West, but I also am familiar with Mesoamerican philosophy, take its worldviews seriously, and am committed to the development of broader worldviews (as I hope should be clear from the discussion above).

are familiar with, have much to teach us about what is possible, about the limitations and boundaries of our own philosophical presuppositions, and about how we might modify our own narrow conceptions of the world. These systems can not only help us to see new (to us, perhaps) ideas, ways of thinking about the world, and ways of understanding what we are doing when we do philosophy.

One thing I try to minimize throughout this book, and for reasons connected to the above discussion, is the use of familiar Western philosophical categories or Western thinkers to frame Mesoamerican philosophical ideas. One might argue that I have already violated this principle by using "philosophy" as a way of understanding a particular kind of intellectual activity in precolonial Mesoamerica. While this is true to some extent, I use this term in a flexible way, not assuming a particular kind of activity as connected with it. Thus, rather than using the idea of philosophy as a tool to narrow the investigation of Mesoamerican thought to particular kinds of ideas, I use it as a starting point from which to enter Mesoamerican thought, trying to allow the major concerns of Mesoamerican philosophers to determine our categories of investigation.

Finally, it is also important to point out that our understanding of precolonial Mesoamerican philosophy, like our understanding of other aspects of Mesoamerica before European contact, is very much dependent on interpretations of the existing material. The issues I discuss in this book are very much still live, and there are robust scholarly debates surrounding interpretations of Mesoamerican sources. While I present a number of these interpretations here, including my own, in order to offer a coherent big-picture view of Mesoamerican thought, the reader should not take from this that what I offer here is settled academic consensus on the issues. In some discussions later in the book, I explicitly reference interpretive debates, while in others, I bypass these. This is all done for the sake of presenting as clear of an overview of the main themes and views of Mesoamerican traditions as possible. For almost every position about Mesoamerican traditions found here, alternatives or disagreements can be found somewhere in the scholarly literature. This is generally the case for any philosophical tradition, but even more so for Mesoamerican traditions, because of the relative paucity of extant textual sources (compared to traditions like those of China, India, or Greece), our relatively new and still changing understanding of precolonial glyphic written language in Mesoamerica, and the fact that academic scholarship on Mesoamerican philosophy is still very much in its infancy by comparison with scholarship on many other philosophical traditions. I aim to help the reader gain a big picture understanding of the Mesoamerican philosophical traditions, but I also invite the reader to learn more, to see and verify for him or herself, to grapple with the material, learn the languages, become familiar with the areas, and then challenge our interpretations and offer new ones.

Important Philosophical Themes in Mesoamerica

The philosophical concerns of Mesoamerican traditions, while to some extent overlapping with those of philosophers today in the English-speaking West, do not perfectly align with those concerns and interests. There are conceptual differences, as well as differences of focus even where the same concepts or issues are dealt with. It is important to keep these differences in mind even as we find parallels between precolonial Mesoamerican thought and that of the modern West, because this will ultimately help us to better understand and to learn from Mesoamerican philosophy. At the same time, we should be careful not to overemphasize such differences, as it becomes easy to find them where they do not exist and force our interpretations so as to create desired alternatives to certain aspects of contemporary Western thought. But we should try as much as possible to attend to native Mesoamerican ways of accessing concepts and thinking about the world, in order to achieve insight into those traditions. In the following text, I outline a few themes central to Mesoamerican Philosophy, around which the remaining chapters of this book are organized.

Creation – A common theme in Mesoamerican philosophical traditions is the robust human role in the creation of the cosmos, as well as the continually unfolding and ongoing nature of creation. Mesoamerican philosophers recognized that the world we inhabit, and our access to that world, is dependent at least partly on us. The world as we perceive it, as we understand it, is dependent on our communal activity in creating aspects of culture, and cooperating with the gods in the construction and maintenance of the cosmos. This happens continually, rather than at a single time at the beginning of the cosmos. Creation is connected to the issue of the nature of reality, as it is an ongoing process, and being is thus linked with continual creation. The cosmos must be continually ordered in order to stay in existence. It is understood more properly as a process or event than a static and self-enduring object. This is the reason for the necessity of continual renewal as well. As we will see, the focus on sacrifice (a sadly misunderstood concept in Mesoamerican thought) and rebirth in Mesoamerican traditions is connected to the continual creation and thriving of the cosmos.

We find numerous accounts of the continuous and cooperative nature of creation in Mesoamerican accounts. Creation accounts are found in textual sources, performance and oral tradition, and imagery from early sources such as pottery, architecture, stelae, and wall paintings. We will look at a number of these creation accounts, most prominently the K'iche' Maya *Popol Vuh*, the Yucatec Maya *Chilam Balam* books, the Aztec *Florentine Codex*, but also a number of other texts, including Mixtec and Zapotec accounts, as well as discussions of early Mesoamerican imagery and oral tradition. Creation is a central issue in almost all of the precolonial and colonial period texts available to us, and is linked to ritual. Ritual itself plays an important role in discussion of creation because it is largely through ritual that humans contribute to creation of the cosmos. As we will see, humanity contributes to the formation and maintenance of the world through upkeep of rituals connected to calendrics, sacrifice to the gods (in the variety of different senses), and (re)enactment of formative events.

Personhood and Essence – Conceptions of the person in Mesoamerica for the most part surround conceptions of essence or vital energy – concepts captured by a number of different terms representing a cluster of related concepts. There are a number of distinct concepts referring to essential aspects of the person, associated with spirit, soul, co-essence, and other individuating features. There are numerous conceptions in Mesoamerica of what makes a person, how a person is identified, and the relationship between the person and the essential parts, personal identity, and the connection between the person and nonpersonal aspects of the world.

Time – The topic of time has been of great interest to scholars and the general public, in part because of the unique and interesting calendric systems of Mesoamerica that have been passed down through text and ritual practices. The role of time and its maintenance is clearly central to numerous Mesoamerican traditions, which can be seen in the memorialization of calendric ideas, dates, and events in ancient texts, as well as the centrality of ritual practices associated with time even into the colonial period and persisting today. While time *may* be overestimated as a foundational concept in Mesoamerican thought due to the nature of the physical record (monuments involving and referring to time, in rock, survived the ravages of time that more ephemeral sources did not), it is still clearly an important topic in Mesoamerican Philosophy. Particularly central to the Mesoamerican concern with time is the idea of correlation between time and other aspects of the cosmos, such as humanity, the gods, and different unseen realms. Each thing that exists can be expressed in terms of time, and has a fundamental relationship with time that makes this concept central to Mesoamerican metaphysics.

Ethics and action – The questions of proper action in Mesoamerican Philosophy focus on role performance, the responsibilities of individuals and the community in the maintenance of the world, and the individual relationship with the community and the cosmos. There is a focus on what we might call individual and collective character traits or virtues. Central ethical concepts include sacrifice, humility, and balance – all of which have important political implications as well. The organization of society is based on these virtues, which are supposed to be represented by the ruler, thus the elaborate rituals tying the ruler to the community through sacrifice, commitment, and public display of role activity.

Vision and Knowledge – The concerns with knowledge in much of Mesoamerican philosophy are with the means of generating knowledge, rather than with the issue of what knowledge is. Knowledge is associated with *vision*, the ability to understand the world, what things are in it, and how these things operate. This is thought of in terms of sense, as the ability to see connects to the ability to use, predict, and navigate. We generate this ability in a number of ways, with certain kinds of ritual central to the process. There is a great deal of focus in Mesoamerican traditions on particular classes of people with the role of bearing knowledge for the community, in terms of calendrics, medicine, and general learning. These classes were in the precolonial period connected to forms of government, and persist in new forms still today in the region.

Further Reading

For excellent overviews of some Mesoamerican philosophical traditions, including discussions of the nature of philosophy in Mesoamerica, see Maffie, *Aztec Philosophy*; Leon-Portilla, *La filosofía náhuatl* (translated as *Aztec Thought and Culture*); Schele, Friedel, and Parker, *Maya Cosmos*; Knowlton, *Maya Creation Myth*; Carrasco, *Religions of Mesoamerica*. For some of the primary sources from the colonial period that offer the fullest accounts of Mesoamerican philosophical traditions, see *Popol Vuh* (Christenson trans. or Tedlock trans.), *Florentine Codex* (12 volumes, especially Volume 6. "Rhetoric and Moral Philosophy," Dibble trans.). The *Chilam Balam* books, such as the *Chilam Balam of Chumayel* (see Roys trans.) and the *Chilam Balam of Tizimin* (see Edmonson, *The Ancient Future of the Itza*) contain much on this as well. For more on performance, see Tedlock, *Rabinal Achi*. Full publication details for all of these works can be found in the bibliography.

2 The Nature of Language

Truth and Meaning

This might seem like a somewhat odd heading for a chapter to those familiar with Mesoamerican philosophy. The link between language and truth, and the centrality of language in the philosophical project of uncovering the nature of reality, seems like a very Indo-European idea, one we often think is not shared by traditions such as those of Asia, Africa, or the Americas. I believe this is mistaken. As I have argued at length elsewhere[1], we tend to see the same themes emerge in philosophical traditions across the globe, even though we find sometimes very different conceptions of these themes. There is, of course, an inherent interpretive danger here – if we go to other traditions seeking out something to fit a preconceived category, we will generally find it, correctly or not. We will ultimately force a worldview into our sought-after categories, whether they are relevant in this tradition or not. We see an example of this very thing from the history of European interaction with Mesoamerica.

The Franciscan priest and later bishop Diego de Landa (1524–1579) created a syllabary for Yucatec Maya using glyphs, which led to confusion in attempts to decipher the glyphic script of Classic Mayan inscriptions and texts in the coming centuries. It turned out that de Landa assumed the glyphs must have represented sounds, just as did letters in European languages, and forced the language into this categorization in which it did not fit. He asked his Maya informants for corresponding signs to Spanish syllabics, rather than investigating the language to determine whether it was primarily syllabic in nature. Because of this mistake, he missed the fact that the Maya glyphs were partially logographic in construction

---

[1] See, for example, *Theories of Truth in Chinese Philosophy*, ch. 1, and *Transcendence and Non-Naturalism in Early Chinese Thought*, chs. 1–3.

rather than phonetic. The syllabary de Landa created was not *wholly* wrong, as glyphs could be and were provided that were pronounced in ways similar to the syllabic de Landa sought. However, Maya glyphs were not constructed on the basis of syllabic construction, and for a number of the corresponding glyphs in the syllabary, de Landa's informants had provided him with *words* the sounds of which approximated the sounds of the Spanish syllables de Landa sought.

This shows us the danger of approaching a tradition with a preconceived notion of its nature. We can simply force the tradition into the framework we assume. We can take aspects of this tradition to do work they are not in fact doing because of surface resemblances to elements we are seeking in these traditions. So we have to be careful. The fact that the concept of truth and its link to language is not prominently discussed in almost any of the secondary literature on Mesoamerican thought and not obviously in any of the primary texts of Mesoamerica should give us pause. We don't want to make a modern philosophical version of Diego de Landa's mistake.

Our investigations of other philosophical traditions, like our investigations of other cultures, languages, etc. do however have to be guided by certain assumptions about human thinking and categorization. The crucial point is that we *get these assumptions right* – and this requires thinking about them in terms of general human activity, ways of human concept formation, and the like. And how do we learn about this? Through examination of traditions, learning languages, behavior, societies. There is some difficulty here – the assumptions we make about human thought are necessarily going to be based on our investigation of human thinking, and if we already enter into the second project with uninformed assumptions, we will simply project these all the way through. Luckily, however, this is not how things seem to work. What more often happens is that the initial assumptions which we have begin to give way as we encounter more cultures, more traditions, that either do not fit or can fit only awkwardly with our initial assumptions. When we bring problematic assumptions to our investigation of a new tradition, we ultimately notice something is wrong – just as scholars did with the syllabary of Diego de Landa. The more traditions we investigate, the more we will recognize that our initial assumptions were inadequate and have to be changed. Thus, application of the informed assumptions that come from investigation of a variety of traditions and cultures will be far more reliable guides than those that come from a single tradition or cultural context. Of course, even these well-informed assumptions will have to be open to revision, if we find that they do not fit comfortably with the new tradition we are investigating.

Concern with language, in a broad sense (not quite the same as the concern that philosophers in the West will be most familiar with), and its connection to truth does seem to be a general feature of all philosophical traditions, and one we can find in Mesoamerican traditions as well. This philosophical concern fits comfortably in the interpretation of Mesoamerican philosophy, and does not create downstream problems or awkward roadblocks in the way de Landa's forced syllabary did. In fact, we find that understanding the link between language and truth in Mesoamerican philosophy illuminates and makes sense of many other features of the tradition – a fact that demonstrates that our attribution of a concern with truth and language to the Mesoamerican traditions is well-founded.

Language and Sign

There are two central aspects of language or forms of language in the Mesoamerican traditions, as in those of other literate societies – written language and spoken language. The former category, in the Mesoamerican traditions, is understood much more broadly than in almost any other tradition philosophers are familiar with (with the closest being those of East Asia). The first hint we have as to the difference in the Mesoamerican traditions on this point are the unique features of Mesoamerican written languages. We find in Mesoamerica, prior to Spanish contact, one dominant type of written language: Logosyllabic – that is, writing systems that combined logographs (nonphonetic images representing particular words), and symbols representing phonetics (symbols representing particular sounds, such as the letters in Indo-European languages). Logosyllabic and logographic writing systems are most prominently used throughout East Asia, with Chinese characters, but were also found in ancient Egypt and the cuneiform of the ancient Middle East. The Chinese-derived writing system is the only logosyllabic writing system still in wide use today.

One interesting feature of Mesoamerican written language after the arrival of the Spanish was the development, in written Nahuatl in particular, of rebus writing. A rebus is the use of a logographic element and its associated sound reading to represent a phonetically associated word or phonetic part of another constructed word – for example, in English when we use an image of an eye as a stand-in for the indexical word "I." While at one time, scholars thought rebus writing was core to Nahuatl written language, further investigation revealed that such writing was uncommon in the precolonial period, and that rebus writing may have been used primarily to render foreign, non-Nahuatl names and words (in somewhat the same way that Japanese uses a distinct syllabary, *katakana*, to render words originally from non-Japanese or Chinese languages).[2]

Many of the known texts from the Maya and Aztec traditions originally recount performances, rituals, or other visually and orally presented accounts. Interestingly, given the unique form of written language in Mesoamerica, groups in this region seem to have been less reliant on the written form than those in other areas, in Europe and Asia. The written form was linked with the oral and performative in the conception of ritual. The distinctions concerning language we tend to make, between the written and the spoken, were not the same as the ones that Mesoamerican groups made. Language as communication in performance, understood as the most basic kind of linguistic expression, combines numerous elements that we generally distinguish. In Maya performances, speaking, movements, costumes and other visual signs, and placement can all do the linguistic work of expressing meanings. Music/singing, masks, and dance were all understood as part of expression in performance.[3] We see this in post-contact texts such as *Popol Vuh*, and plays such as *Rabinal Achi* (both of the K'iche' Maya). These sources are sometimes misunderstood because scenes in which not much appears to be going on as regards textual content are offered from contexts which are opaque to those without knowledge of Mesoamerican ways of communication. Music and song play an important role in performances, as seen in the modern *Rabinal Achi*, as does movement, in particular directions and in the relation between

[2] Laack, *Aztec Religion and Art of Writing*, 259.
[3] Looper, *To Be Like Gods: Dance in Ancient Maya Civilization*, 3.

the performers on stage.[4] Movement and song are so central to these performances that the performance would be unrecognizable or lose crucial components of meaning without them – thus in written translations of the *Rabinal Achi*, stage instructions about the movements and song are included.[5] Unlike a play by Shakespeare, which we can pick up and read, appreciate, and fully understand from only the texts, the words, which are the main focus, Maya performances such as *Rabinal Achi* cannot be captured only by written description of what is *said* in the performance. The expression of language happens through multiple sources.

The communication of meaning in song is a common feature across Mesoamerican groups as well – recounted in texts such as the *Chilam Balam* books of the Maya of the Yucatan, or the Nahuatl codices, which speak of the *cuicatl* (songs).[6] According to Isabel Laack, "the Nahuas [Aztec] did not separate 'speech' from 'song'."[7] This is relevant also in considering the terse and streamlined nature of glyphic text in Mesoamerica. We do not find sources, either in book form or monumental text, that present prose in the long, conversational, way we find it throughout other parts of the world. Dennis Tedlock writes of the Maya texts: "[H]ieroglyphic texts tend to be extremely terse, so their relationship to vocal performances was probably more like that of a set of program notes than a libretto."[8] Much of the reason why the philosophical traditions of Mesoamerica cannot be pieced together from precolonial texts alone is not just the relative scarcity of these texts, but also the fact that Mesoamerican texts were not intended to be used disconnected from such things as performance, speech, and other aspects of ritual presentation. Literary culture in Mesoamerica was not the kind of private and personal access to text found in some other cultures like our own, in which reading is mainly a solitary and silent act, but was tied closely to ritual and communal performance.

---

[4] Tedlock, *Rabinal Achi*, 164–165.
[5] Tedlock, *Rabinal Achi*, 23–25.
[6] Laack, *Aztec Religion and the Art of Writing*, 204.
[7] Laack, 205.
[8] Tedlock, *Rabinal Achi*, 158. See also Tedlock, "Toward a Poetics of Polyphony and Translatability," 190–191.

This, of course, also has implications for the views of language, meaning, and truth found in Mesoamerica. Language, as understood in Mesoamerica, has numerous dimensions that are not generally treated as linguistic in the Western context, although we can certainly recognize these as linguistic. When we understand dominant Mesoamerican conceptions of language, we see the way a concept of truth as connected to language, representation, and activity also emerges from this consideration. The importance of performative aspects of language can be seen in different ways throughout Mesoamerican traditions, from the ritual performance of the Maya to the focus on speaking through the idea of the *tlatoani* (speaker) of the Aztecs.

Nahuatl Language and Truth

I begin here with a consideration of the Aztec written language, despite its being a later development than the Maya written language discussed in the next section, because the Aztec case gives us a chance to understand some of the most unique features of a shared Mesoamerican conception of the connection between language and reality, due to the very different nature of Aztec writing. Classic Maya writing, as discussed in the next section, is much closer to what we generally associate with written language.

We see in Aztec literature a number of different categories of linguistic expression, presented in numerous genres. As in the Maya case, language for the Aztecs had the capacity to reveal unseen aspects of the world – linking it with ritual performance. The Aztecs had a distinct category for such revelatory ritual language, *nahuallatolli*, dealing with capturing the essence of things, beyond the usual abilities for humans.[9] This category of language is linked with ritual, and its revelatory quality offers a particular insight into the conception of truth in Aztec thought. (A similar category existed in Mixtec systems[10]) To capture features of the world through song, gesture, sign, etc., shows us a representational system of language, in which some semantic unit, understood in any of these ways, expresses

---

[9] Laack, 204,

[10] Mikulska, "'Secret Language' in Oral and Graphic Form: Religious-Magic Discourse in Aztec Speeches and Manuscripts."

particular meaning. But representation can also happen through substitution or invocation, with the sign coming to gain *identity* with, through possession of the essence of, the represented entity. This, we will see, is a common theme of Mesoamerican philosophical traditions – the sense in which things are represented by the transformation of other things into those very things, via transshipment of essence.

This need not be understood as a magical, nonnaturalist, or far-fetched claim. This develops from a basic ontology in which distinct things in the world are related in terms of their fundamental underlying makeup, whether in terms of *teotl* in the Aztec tradition, or the unnamed "ground of being" associated with essence (*'itz, k'oje'ik*) in the Maya traditions.

In the *Romances de los señores de la Nueva España* (1582), a major source for understanding Aztec thought around the time of Spanish contact, three distinct kinds of "romances," or literary categories, are distinguished: *conjuros, huehuetlatolli*, and *netotiliztli*.[11]

Some have argued that certain aspects of Nahuatl language demonstrate or necessitate features of the philosophical system of the Nahua and concepts such as truth, connected to this. Miguel Leon-Portilla famously argued for a view of particular poetic sounds and forms of expression as having meaning in the language. While some scholars have rejected Leon-Portilla's view of the philosophical nature of Nahuatl poetry in terms of systems of knowledge or philosophical schools akin to what we find in Western traditions, others have pointed out ways in which Nahuatl language seems connected to philosophical positions.[12]

For years, there have been rich debates concerning the extent to which (if at all) language plays a role in determining certain outlooks on the world. While our best evidence seems to show that the strong linguistic determinist view is false, a weaker view that aspects of language *suggest* or make more obvious certain philosophical moves and worldviews is more plausible. The structure of our languages may make certain positions more obvious, but they generally do not serve as a barrier to philosophical thinking. And as anyone who has raised a teenager will know, the human ability continually to innovate in the realm of language is unlimited. If

---

[11] Bierhorst, *Ballads of the Lords of New Spain*, p. 25.
[12] See Laack, *Aztec Religion and Art of Writing.*

inherited language stopped us from thinking in certain ways, no invention of new words would be necessary or even possible.

The expressiveness and meaning of language in Nahuatl, similar to what we see in Maya languages, comes through the association of linguistic entities with the expressed entities. Linguistic entities, whether in writing, speech, or movement, express meaning not through *representation* of a particular thing or event, but through enactment of a thing or event, understood in terms of containing or manifestation of its essence. This seems to be common in Mesoamerican languages. Precolonial Nahuatl writing differs from those of the Maya in that it is almost solely pictorial in nature. The rebus writing used for phonetic rendering, some scholars argue, was used mainly to render foreign place names and other non-native words, and came into broader use only late in the Aztec empire, and expanded with the arrival of the Spanish[13]. While on the face of it there is no necessary difference in a society's conception of the connection between language and reality on the basis of whether the written language is primarily or wholly phonetic, logographic, or pictographic, certain connections might be more suggestive in languages using visual imagery as representation. This may be due to the fact that in such written languages, the written word will often resemble the object or activity depicted. This is most clearly the case in a highly pictographic written language such as Nahuatl before Spanish contact. There have been debates surrounding the extent to which the precolonial written language had phonetics, represented particular words as separate, or even had fixed readings.[14]

The imagery used to represent words and ideas in Nahuatl and other central Mexican forms of writing, along with certain concepts of transformation and substitution found in the cultures in question suggest, as numerous other scholars have pointed out, that linguistic imagery in Nahuatl and other Mesoamerican languages did not represent or stand for (as signs) things and events, but shared essence with those things and events and thus *included* them.[15] Meaning, in these traditions, was not a

---

[13] Boone, *Stories in Red and Black: Pictorial Histories of the Aztec and Mixtec*, 35–37. Laack, 259.

[14] Mignolo, *The Darker Side of the Renaissance* (1995), 96–109.

[15] Hajovsky, *On the Lips of Others: Moteuczoma's Fame in Aztec Monuments and Rituals*, 49.

matter of an intermediary connected to things in the world via representation, but rather a kind of direct linguistic access. Isabel Laack writes:

> Nahua language theory, at least in reference to some genres, did not merely assume that linguistic signs *mirror* reality, since this assumption rests on the idea that language represents a symbol system essentially separate from reality. Rather, Nahuatl, or some genres of Nahuatl, was most probably considered a natural language that assumed a direct relationship between the linguistic signs and reality.[16]

One type of structure common in Nahuatl texts that suggests relationship between words and essences in this way is the phenomenon known as *difrasismo*, a combination of two words in order to establish a particular kind of relation or focus a particular feature. The connection between metaphors suggests the meaning of the subject in question. Leon-Portilla points out the common use of this technique in Nahuatl, and attributes to Ángel María Garabay the earliest discussion of this in Western scholarship. Leon-Portilla focuses on "flower and song" (*in xóchitl in cuícatl*) as an important example of *difrasismo* linked to poetry. According to Leon-Portilla's interpretation, the concept of truth is linked to this form of expression. Discussing a poem from the *Cantares Mexicanos* attributed to a discussion in the residence of Tecayehuatzin, Leon-Portilla writes that the "flower and song" of poetry is the only source of truth.[17] While Leon-Portilla translates the term *nel* of the original Nahuatl here as *verdadero* (reality, truth), John Bierhorst translates it differently, as "good." Thus, we see two very different understandings of the poem – in Bierhorst's version, "how else could there be anything good on earth?"[18] and in Leon-Portilla's rendering, this becomes "es esto quizás lo unico verdadero en la tierra?" (*Is this perhaps the only true/real thing on earth?*). Both Bierhorst and Leon-Portilla touch on something important here, which also shows us the limitations of translation from original texts. The *nel* of the original text seems to have the sense of *both* truth and goodness. These two concepts are implicitly linked in discussions in other traditions as well. Consider the notion of truth

---

[16] Laack, *Aztec Religion and Art of Writing*, 240.
[17] Leon-Portilla, *La filosofia Náhuatl*, 312.
[18] Bierhorst, *Cantares Mexicanos*, 161.

as ideal – the true friend, or the true king. This use of the term is clearly normative in nature – the friend or king who is an example of the kind who lives up to a particular standard. The notion of the "good" is likewise normative, and often in the same way. A good friend is one who lives up to the ideal of what a friend should be. A good king is one who performs the duties of the king as they are supposed to be performed. In this sense, "true" and "good" become almost interchangeable. Thus we see this is not something limited to Nahuatl. The English term "true" has always had a normative component. The etymology of the term, tracing back through Old English to Proto-Germanic, has the sense of "faithfulness" or "agreeing with a certain standard." There is some suggestion of connection to even earlier Proto-Indo-European root *deru-, meaning "firm, solid, steadfast."[19] The claim of the poem from the *Cantares Mexicanos* then suggests that it may only be through flower and song that we can fully (or as fully as possible for humans) access the nature of things as they are, that what we find in flower and song comes closest to the ideal, gives us the most faithful depiction of the world.

If poetry, in terms of invoked imagery based on metaphorical descriptions, has the function of expressing truth in Nahuatl, this expressiveness seems to come through the providing of images related to the meaning in question. The term Leon-Portilla translates here in the poem as "*verdadero*" (truth) is *nelli*, which is understood as "root/foundation," and connected by numerous scholars more broadly with a conception of truth.[20] The connection between language and this concept of truth is not one of the representation of facts about the world through language, as *neltiliztli* has to do a rootedness that is not semantic in nature, or at least not primarily so.[21]

When we understand the idea of rootedness, we see that the well-rootedness of language consists in language serving as a sign or representation of some underlying reality, but rather in the fact that language as a part of this reality connects with other parts of reality in ways that reveal features of both. But, one might object, if language contains the essence of and somehow shares identity with what it is *about*, how

---

[19] www.etymonline.com/word/true.
[20] Maffie, IEP; Karttunen, *Analytical Dictionary*; Gingerich, "Heidegger and the Aztecs."
[21] Maffie, IEP.

does this differ from a kind of representational conception of language, other than that the Nahua view is simply stronger – that rather than an image of the world, language is the world itself? This question seems to me exactly the right one, and we should be careful of the tendency to draw Mesoamerican thought as being so distinct from Western or other forms of thought that we lose sight of what ultimately grounds a particular system of thought. Language fundamentally involves expression of meaning concerning the world using things in some way independent of, but representing, those aspects of the world. We can only talk or write *about* something insofar as we can use linguistic elements capable of representing those things. Just how they represent these things in the world is understood differently by different theories of language and truth. But no system can be a system of language if it is not ultimately this that is going on. The world is as it is – we would not call the structure of the world as such, or our interaction with it, a language. Language happens when we communicate information about the world using some representational structure – possibly even the things themselves.

The concept of *neltiliztli* in Aztec philosophy is regularly associated with the concept of truth, but numerous scholars point out the independence of this concept from language. James Maffie discusses the concept as "well-rootedness," explaining that to be well-rooted is to properly disclose *teotl*, the underlying essence of the world, or the sacred. *Teotl* signifies *reality* itself, in which well-rooted things gain their authenticity or truth. Maffie writes:

> That which is well-rooted ... in teotl is true in the sense of being genuine, authentic, and well-balanced as well as true in the sense of being non-referentially disclosing and unconcealing of teotl.[22]

The Aztec concept of truth, according to Maffie, is that of disclosing the nature of *teotl*, and this is associated primarily with the nature of an object (or more properly the process of the cosmos itself) rather than with language. Maffie argues that we find an *ontological* rather than *semantic* conception of truth in Aztec philosophy. But what is it to disclose the nature of *teotl*, and why can't language do this? The nature of the entire cosmos

---

[22] Maffie, *Aztec Philosophy*, 101.

is ultimately *teotl*, and so all things are of the nature of *teotl*, even those which are not well rooted in *teotl* in terms of failure to disclose *teotl*. Maffie understands this failure in terms of things revealing only one or limited features of *teotl*, and failing to reveal how these features connect to others. Yet it seems that we have a similar problem here to one that plagues other monistic systems, such as that of the Tiantai Buddhists who hold that all things are ultimately Buddha Nature. Namely, if everything is ultimately *teotl*, then all things should equally well disclose or reveal *teotl* if we properly understand them (or perhaps even if we don't). Because all things in fact contain all aspects of *teotl*. One way around this that Aztec thought seems to take is that certain things make manifest *teotl* in terms of aiding in our ability to understand its features. For this to be the case, however, there must be some sense in which certain aspects of *teotl* can *represent*, stand for, suggest, or otherwise intermediate *teotl* better than others, even though all aspects of *teotl* are equally of the nature of *teotl*. That is, if we have an ontological conception of truth in which to be true is to be *more x* than something lacking truth, then *x* cannot be the fundamental reality of a monistic system, as everything has that equally, and thus everything is true, in which case the concept loses its meaning. Thus the *disclosive* aspect of *neltiliztli* must be in some sense representational, symbolic, semantic, just as is language. The key insight of the Mesoamerican traditions is that the disclosive is not *limited* to language – or perhaps that language is not limited to certain kinds of speech and writing.

The concept of *teotl* is a difficult one, which can show us some of the inherent difficulty as well as the highly interpretive nature of Mesoamerican philosophy (as pointed out above). As Molly Bassett points out, there are a range of different understandings of what *teotl* means, tracing back to a few influential interpretive choices. Maffie's understanding of *teotl* here is influenced by that of Alfredo Lopez Austin, who understands *teotl* as a force or power, focusing on this understanding of the term rather than in the related sense of "god."[23] Bassett traces the most prevalent interpretations to Lopez Austin, Klor de Alva, and

---

[23] Bassett, *The Fate of Earthly Things*, 62. Lopez Austin, *Myths of the Opossum*, 139. Lopez Austin also renders the term as "god," even though he mainly understands it in the sense of a force in discussion of the idea.

Hvidtfeldt. Lopez Austin seems to suggest that there is no clear distinction made between *teteo* (plural of *teotl*) as forces and as gods. This position seems consistent with a number of other metaphysical views in Mesoamerican thought (discussed here and in chapters ahead), as well as with Mesoamerican understandings of language. While Western scholars often look for a single determining feature or definition of some concept, in Mesoamerican traditions concepts are generally marked by their variability, the ways in which they connect numerous aspects of the world. As we will see below in discussion of duality in creation, in Mesoamerican traditions, what is *this* is always at the same time *that*. No thing is characterized in a single distinct, discrete, and individual way, but rather each thing is understood in terms of its relations. The gods are also forces, just as they can be understood in terms of number, time periods, and a host of other identities discussed in later chapters. All of this is also suggested by features of Aztec written language.

The nature of Aztec writing reveals to us ways in which language can be far broader than we generally think. What we generally take as art, including depiction, imagery, and dance, can be used as language. The key differences between these forms concerns our methods of communication, what we intend to communicate, and a systematized form of expression. Communication of meanings can happen in numerous ways, including through gestures or rituals. What makes the difference between nonlinguistic and linguistic meaning is the standardization or systematization of certain meaning-bearing elements. Take sign language as an example here. It involves neither speech nor writing, and is constructed of gestures, yet we recognize it as a language in a way we do not recognize, say, tap dance. This is because in the case of sign languages, the physical gestures used are systematized and associated with more specific meanings than what we find in tap dance. One can certainly communicate using tap dance as well, but one does not communicate in the same way as one does with sign language. The more suggestive and less systematized a mode of communication is, the less likely we are to grant it the status of language. There is, of course, no clear line distinguishing between when a system of communication is a language and when it is not, just like there is no single clear point at which a hill becomes a mountain, or at which a certain number of hairs lost becomes baldness.

Aztec writing was systematized to a certain extent, though scholars point out that there were numerous ways of reading the images. Of
course, this is also possible with every language, as we know from the history of philosophy, where scholars spend entire careers coming up with
different ways of reading texts in a variety of languages. Reading an "is"
as predication instead of as identity can change the entire meaning of a
sentence. The extent of systematization of meanings will vary with language, and the Nahuatl written language before Spanish contact falls on
the side of less systematic written languages. Because there is no phonetic
component (unlike Classic Maya written languages), there is no particular spoken word associated with a glyph in many cases. Walter Mignolo
describes the difference between Aztec writing and phonetic writing systems thus: "[A]lphabetic writing allows for the inscription of what is said
but not for a description of the scene of speaking. Mexica [Aztec] writing allowed for the inscription of the scene but not for what was said."[24]
While Mignolo here overestimates the association of "alphabetic writing"
with spoken language (as logographic or gestural signs can also determine
specific spoken words, as with Chinese, Classic Mayan, or sign language,
and phonetic signs can fail to capture anything of meaning), he is right in
that Aztec writing was less determinative than other written language systems. If this is so, though, then why should we think of the Aztec written
system as a written language at all? Perhaps Aztec writing was something
closer to visual art. Indeed, Isabel Laack concludes that "in general, central
Mexican writing records neither speech nor language."[25]

The reason why I think this is wrong is that the primary aim of Aztec
writing seems to have been to convey particular meanings through signs,
even if these meanings were not associated in a specific way with particular words. The ideas would have occurred to readers of precolonial codices
in the same ways. That is, these texts would have been understood, in the
ways we understand another when they speak or write in our language,
even though their meanings cannot be understood in a completely determinative sense. Aztec "picture writing" would have had far less interpretive variability than a Hokusai woodblock print in Japan or a Beethoven

[24] Mignolo, *The Darker Side of the Renaissance*, 97.
[25] Laack, 259.

symphony in Europe, even if more than a text in classical Chinese or modern Spanish. Visual signs are on a spectrum of specificity, and there is no clear point on this spectrum at which a sign becomes a linguistic sign as opposed to some other kind. One lesson we can learn from Mesoamerican writing is the variability of this process – because much of Mesoamerican writing, particularly systems such as those of the Aztec and Mixtec, straddle this mid-point between semantic and non-semantic sign, this can show us how things can take the place of *both*. A semantic sign can at the same time be another kind of sign. The same thing can communicate meaning in different ways. Good poets know this well. Something like alliteration or onomatopoeia becomes possible only through a combination of semantic meaning and the significance associated with the particular sounds of words. This is one of the reasons why poetry is notoriously difficult to translate: A translator must try to capture the semantic meaning while at the same time retaining other signatory elements that may be impossible to duplicate in a different language. How does one translate English alliterative sentences into K'iche' or Zapotec and still retain the alliteration?

The imagery of Aztec writing, like ritual, movement, and other visual aspects of Nahuatl language, was able to express *truth* in terms of the well-rootedness of *neltiliztli*. This rootedness, though associated with disclosing of *teotl* and the expression of the nature of *teotl*, had to have been ultimately understood as representational and semantic. We are left then with a concept of truth connected to language that does give us something like the "correspondence" conception of truth we find in other cultural contexts, in which what makes something true (whether language or anything else that can express meaning) is that it corresponds with "reality," which in the case of Aztec philosophy is understood in terms of *teotl*. Often a notion of truth as correspondence is associated with a particular type of so-called "correspondence theory" in contemporary analytic philosophy, of the kind devised by Bertrand Russell and others. But this is a mistake – this correspondence theory was always one particular attempt to make sense of a far larger and more intuitive view that truth consists in correspondence with reality – what many philosophers refer to today as the "correspondence intuition."[26] And as philosophers who use this phrase point out,

---

[26] See Kolár, "Truth, Correspondence, Satisfaction."

numerous theories of truth beside the Russellian correspondence theory accept and can make sense of the correspondence intuition.

The key here is to determine how language, on the Aztec view, discloses *teotl* through being well-grounded, *nelli*. How does language exemplify *neltilizti*? Maffie argues that anything in the world can be thus well grounded, insofar as it discloses or represents *teotl*. This has to be understood in an epistemic sense – a thing is well rooted in that it makes clear *to us* the nature of *teotl*, it expresses this nature as meaning. As we have seen earlier, *teotl* as the nature of the cosmos itself is the nature of *everything*, so it is impossible for anything to be more *teotl* or more of the nature of *teotl* than anything else. Just in the same way, however, that it is possible for some things to tell us more about the nature of reality even though all things are part of reality, certain things can tell us more about the nature of *teotl* than others. Maffie understands this in terms of the organization or ordering of things, and in connection with activity. Truth is "a way of being and doing, a way of living, conducting one's life, and so on."[27] This active disclosing of *teotl* through the rootedness of activity must be a feature of language insofar as language is performing some activity. Language is not, on the Aztec view (shared with other Mesoamerican traditions) inert and static. Rather, language is associated with instances and activity. This can help to explain a very important feature of Aztec and other Mesoamerican traditions – the role and understanding of *performance* and of "substitution."

In contemporary Western philosophy, a distinction is made between word types and tokens, as well as between an object or event and the depiction of an object or event. In Mesoamerican views of language, these distinctions are collapsed. The concept of "substitution" (*k'ex* in Maya[28], *ixiptla* in Nahuatl), which we will look at in more depth in Chapter 4 on personhood and identity, is relevant to language and meaning as well. A representation or sign standing for some thing in the world, as semantic elements of language are meant to, are understood as *identical* with those things in the world in Mesoamerican traditions. Rather than the word

---

[27] Maffie, *Aztec Philosophy*, 102.
[28] The term *k'ex* is found in (Yucatec) Maya as well as K'iche', with a similar meaning, connected to replacement, change, or renewal.

"tree" being a sign referring to or otherwise designating a tree, the word in its image and utterance shares the essence of a tree, is identical to a tree. As Maffie says of *ixiptla*:

> Ixiptla and teotl are numerically one and the same. Teotl's medium of presentation is itself. There is neither ontological nor constitutional distinction between representation (signifier) and represented (signified). There is only teotl presenting itself.[29]

If language works in this way, as does substitution in the case of performance of roles, how do we make sense of the seeming differences in features of sign and signified, given their identity? If, that is, a glyph representing a tree is *identical* with a tree, then how come we cannot make bark paper out of the glyph, tap it for syrup, sit beneath it for shade on a hot sunny day, or build furniture with it? After all, if two things are identical, they should share all the same properties. But not so fast! On most views of personal identity, one will conclude that the one-year-old Cuauhtemoc and the 25-year-old Cuauhtemoc were the same person[30], that is, were *identical* persons. If this is so, it shows that sameness of properties is not necessary for identity, as nearly all of Cuauhtemoc's properties as a 25-year-old were different from the properties he had as a one-year-old. What makes the two identical is sameness of person. This suggests that it might also be the case that what makes the glyph for tree identical with a tree is sameness of what is essential to the tree. This is exactly what Mesoamerican traditions will say – it is sameness of essence, of *teotl* for the Nahua, of *itz* for the Maya, that grounds this identity.

But there is a new problem. Given that this essence, *teotl*, is the same everywhere and for everything, then it should turn out that *everything* is ultimately identical with everything else. There is no special thing it means for a glyph to be identical to an object that it represents or substitutes, because it shares its essence with everything else that exists, so it should be equally identical to a table, or the Taj Mahal, or Jupiter. The answer here is this: On some level the glyph *is* identical to all of those things. This

---

[29] Maffie, 114.

[30] Cuauhtemoc (1497–1525) was the last emperor of the Aztec Empire, executed at the age of 28 years by the Spanish *conquistador* Hernán Cortés.

identity is what allows a sign or a thing in the world to represent or substitute some other thing in the world. Substitution would be impossible
if there were no such identity. Signification would be impossible if there
were no such identity. But representation or substitution also requires
representation or manifestation, that is, the epistemic function of disclosing particular aspects of *teotl* discussed above. The glyph's identity with
teotl is not in itself enough for the glyph to express or disclose *teotl*.

Part of the issue here is that the manifestation of each thing of *teotl* is not
understood in terms of identity. *Teotl* (or the unnamed "ground-of-being")
doesn't preclude the existence of nonidentical things created of and
ultimately manifesting *teotl*. And these things can have their own identity
conditions – they will be identical to one another as *teotl*, but nonidentical
in other ways. The relationship between a glyph and what it represents,
like the relationship between substitute and substituted, is such that the
identity is between one another, rather than simply with each and *teotl*. A
glyph or other created thing can become identical to what it represents
because it, like what it represents, is ultimately *teotl*, which has the potential
to become anything that exists. But the identity of all things with *teotl* does
not entail the identity of all things with one another.[31]

Isabel Laack discusses this association between the written word and
what is represented through sharing of essence. She discusses an interesting difference between depiction of inanimate objects and animals in
Aztec texts, in which the essence of inanimate things can be more fully
contained in a painted glyph, while animate things are substituted most
fully by performance (an idea discussed in Chapter 4). Laack writes:

> The Nahuatl term *tlacuilolmachiotl*, used for paintings, contained the
> verb *machiotia*, which means 'making things visible and knowable.'
> Consequently, pieces of art and writing made the fundamental *teotl* quality
> of the depicted entity clearly visible. Many Nahua statues and material
> objects show a strong attention to botanical details. Most probably, the
> essence of non-animated things like plants or shells was believed to be
> visible to the human eye in their outer appearance. Nahua animal statues,

---

[31] Those concerned about the failure of transitivity of identity to which this commits
one should consider similar commitments required for proponents of theories of personal identity in Western philosophy.

in comparison, appear rather clumsy to the modern Western eye, and surface details are much coarser. The difference may be due to the idea that animal essences were not only visible in their skin and outer appearance but also in their movement and behavior patterns. Movement and behavior, however, is expressed more precisely in moving presentations than in statues, for example, by human deity impersonators.[32]

Maya Language and Truth

The Classic Maya written language is an interesting case among precontact Mesoamerican languages, as it is the only one we can say with confidence was logosyllabic and whose glyphs represented fixed words, in the sense of most modern languages. Perhaps the closest equivalents to the Classic Maya written language in use today are Chinese characters. Like Chinese characters, Maya glyphs could be read in different ways, using different sounds depending on a language or dialect, but the meanings of a term were also fixed. The Chinese character 人 can be read in Mandarin (*ren*), Cantonese (*jan*) or even Japanese (*hito* or *jin*) and Korean (*in*); it has the same meaning, "person," in all of these contexts. Likewise, the glyph for "snake" can be read as *chan* or *kan* (Yucatec Maya pronunciation), but retained its meaning, "snake," across spoken contexts. Logosyllabic scripts have this linguistic portability because they are not tied tightly to phonetics as purely syllabic scripts are. The upside of such systems is the ability to have a mutually intelligible written system across a variety of languages – thus, people who do not speak the same language can still understand one another to some extent in writing (the extent to which there is understanding will depend on the grammatical similarity). The downside is that it is impossible to learn on the basis of reading how something is said. One could learn to read a text yet never know how the text was spoken in its original language. The situation is similar with respect to spoken languages like those of the Classic Period Maya groups and the early Chinese. In the case of both of these, scholars have heroically tried to reconstruct what these sounds may have been on the basis of clues in modern languages and ancient texts, but much of this reconstruction is still guesswork, and we do not know for sure

---

[32] Laack, *Aztec Religion and Art of Writing*, 165.

how these languages sounded (of course, we have this problem to a lesser extent with syllabic scripts as well, because the way letters are pronounced in modern languages do not always correspond to the ways those letters were pronounced in the past).

The more "familiar" nature of the Maya glyphic script has led some scholars to claim that it represents the only written language system in the pre-Columbian Americas. If we require that a written language must be closely tied to the spoken language in the sense of determinate terms picked out by individual symbols, then the Maya written system indeed counts as the only known written language in the pre-Columbian Americas.[33] On a broader conception of written language, however, the Aztec, Mixtec, and Zapotec scripts count as well, although symbols did not specifically determine spoken terms.[34]

Despite the closer tie between Maya glyphs and spoken language than what we see in other Mesoamerican writing systems, we find a very similar view of the connection between language and reality in Maya thought to those in other Mesoamerican traditions. In particular, we find the notion of substitution (k'ex in a number of Mayan languages) operative in language, of written glyphs as representing aspects of the world via *identity*. The Maya case, I think, more clearly shows us that written language in Mesoamerica can be understood as both semantic and as expressive in non-semantic ways. There has been debate on whether writing systems such as the Aztec and Mixtec systems should be understood as "picture writing" without semantic determinants or writing expressive of words, but the Maya case suggests that writing can have *both* features.

The Maya writing system has often been treated differently than that of the Aztec, Mixtec, or Zapotec, because there are clearly defined phonetic elements in the script, and particular words appear to be connected to specific glyphs. While glyphs are determinate, *words* do not determine glyphs. That is, a particular word can be rendered in a number of different glyphic ways. This is a situation perhaps similar to what we find in modern

---

[33] Some proponents of this view are Alexandre Tokovinine (see Laack, *Aztec Religion*, 291) and Anthony Aveni (*Foundations of New World Cultural Astronomy*, 5); see Boone, *Stories in Red and Black*, 4.

[34] Sharer, *The Ancient Maya*, 6th ed., 125.

languages such as Japanese. In Maya writing, as in Japanese, a word can be rendered either phonetically or through nonphonetic characters. The explanation for this in Japanese is the integration of Chinese characters (*kanji*) into the language alongside of locally constructed phonetic written systems (*hiragana* and *katakana*). A particular word – for example the word for "person" – can be written using *kanji* as 人 or using hiragana as ひと. An additional complication for Japanese is that there are also multiple ways to *say* any given word. 人 can be read as *hito* (as above) or as *jin*. These two words are equivalent, but the latter is a more Sinicized way of saying the word, clearly phonetically related to the Mandarin *ren*. Chinese characters in general, because they are not phonetically linked, are portable across languages in ways phonetic scripts are not. While a letter system can be used to render words in numerous languages – just as we see with the Latinization of K'iche' in the *Popol Vuh*, Yucatec in the *Chilam Balam* books, or Nahuatl in the *Florentine Codex, Cantares Mexicanos,* and *Romances* – it cannot be used to render the same word across languages. Nonphonetic characters can do this – thus, a character representing a word in one language can also represent a completely different word in another language, generally sharing the same meaning. The character 人 can be read in any Chinese language, Japanese, or Korean. A monolingual speaker of Mandarin and a monolingual speaker of Japanese could both understand that written term, even though they may be unable to communicate the meaning of that term to one another in speech. We could, were we so inclined, even render Chinese characters using English phonetics. We could adopt Chinese characters to render English and use 人 for "person." It would be possible for us to create a written form of English fully in Chinese characters, or a hybrid version using Chinese characters and Latin script. Some English written sentences would then become nearly intelligible to speakers of languages such as Chinese or Japanese.

Like Chinese characters, the Classic Mayan writing system is a combination of logographic and phonetic elements, and was thus portable across different languages. We know that certain words were said differently in different Maya regions, because there were sometimes phonetic elements affixed to glyphs demonstrating how the word was to be said in a particular language or dialect. Words could be visually rendered in a number of ways. Purely phonetic versions of a word can sometimes be found. There

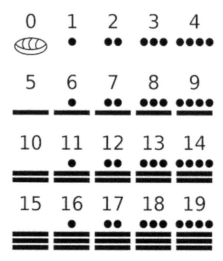

Figure 2.1 *Maya numerals*

were often also numerous glyphic ways of rendering a given word, from
the fairly simple to the artistically ornate. Maya number signs show us a
good example of this. In the most simple written form, numerals can be
rendered using a dot and dash system: one dot representing one numeral
up to four and a dash for five. Higher numbers can be rendered through a
combination of these. For example, the number 15 would be represented
by three dashes: 5+5+5, as shown in Figure 2.1. The Maya number system
was vigesimal, or Base-20, so numeral places ascend once you reach 20
(rendered by four dashes). Numerals from 1 to 20 were also represented
in some texts in a slightly more intricate glyphic form that we might call
"head variant" characters (Figure 2.2). Finally, these same numerals could
be rendered in another even more elaborate "full body" version, in which
each numeral was depicted as a god. In each of these glyphic renderings of
the numerals, the glyphs uniquely picked out a particular numeral. There
was no semantic variation in even the most elaborate glyphs.

Maya glyphs served both semantic and non-semantic or aesthetic
roles – a feature of written language that is often overlooked in Western
scholarship. This feature of language is far more obvious in cultures
with a history of artistic rendering of written language, such as East Asia
and the Arabic-speaking world, where calligraphic rendering of words
is a form of high art. And here just as in the Classic Maya case, we find

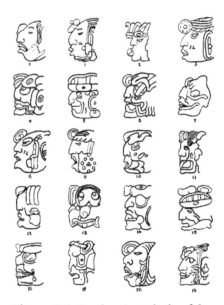

Figure 2.2 *Head variant glyphs of the numerals*

meaningful variations of words without difference in what they signify. We can change the intended message of written words through non-semantic features in English in the very same way. Think of *fonts*. One of my favorite internet memes declares that "fonts matter," rendering the same English sentence in two very different fonts, to startlingly (and humorously) different effects. In one example, the sentence "I'll be waiting for you" is rendered in a bubbly cursive script on a note, which expresses the loving anticipation of a spouse or child for you to return home. The same sentence is rendered in a harsh angular font resembling writing in blood, and the message completely changes, instead appearing as a threat, telling you that the writer of the note is preparing to harm you.

The variable rendering of Maya glyphs, which can have different forms across media (bark paper books, pottery, or stone stelae) or even within the same medium, are reminiscent of traditions like Chinese or Arabic calligraphy, or contemporary American graffiti script. Stylization is so much a part of these forms that one who knows "standard" or "universal" script often cannot read these forms without training. For the untrained English speaker, a stylized graffiti name on the side of a train or a building may be unintelligible, while one familiar with the style can read it. Maya glyphs followed a similar pattern. There were relatively simple versions that would have been intelligible to many or most people, and elaborate stylized versions that would have been the purview of only a trained group familiar with the sometimes elaborate conventions of a particular style. This becomes another way of establishing privileged groups, along with other features of language that generally do this, such as jargon or idiom.

Meaning can be expressed in Maya glyphs in numerous ways, just as in cultures with more elaborate artistic conceptions of writing. The word expressed by a particular glyph is not the only element of the signification of a glyph or sentence, but the stylistic elements also often play a major role. This is perhaps one of the biggest differences between the precolonial Mesoamerican texts available to us and modern texts. We even find this difference between the precolonial texts and their colonial counterparts rendered in Latin script. The colorful and elaborate images in accounts of creation we find in precolonial Aztec and Maya codices, for example, are silenced and dulled in the Latin script renderings of these same stories we find in texts such as the *Florentine Codex* or *Popol Vuh*. Each word can be stylized in its own way in some Maya texts (and this is even more prominent in Aztec texts). The style of many Mesoamerican texts is perhaps closer to what we know today as graphic novels or comic books. Not that the content of these texts is the same, but the integration of word and image in Mesoamerican texts is more similar to what we find in graphic novels. In Maya and Aztec texts, however, the image can often *be* the word. In graphic novels, we find drawings of people and places representing images, with words represented in speech bubbles of some kind. In Mesoamerican texts, the depiction of a person or thing can itself be a word, as well as an image. This is possible only because of the logographic nature of Mesoamerican writing.

Some texts contain more florid imagery than others. Among Maya books, the Dresden Codex is relatively subdued in its imagery as compared to the other extant codices, although it too contains full figure imagery. Regional influences as well as the purposes of particular texts likely explain these differences.

The issue of truth in representation is similar in Maya and Aztec texts. Ultimately the words/images of a text represent the essence (*itz*) of a particular thing or event. We might think of this as a version of reference, but it cannot be the standard kind. It is not that the word in a book or on a stela is a token or independent object related to some thing to which it refers through description or agreement, but that the word contains the *essence* of a thing, which we recognize in part through resemblance. Reference as resemblance and sharing of essence has largely been overlooked in contemporary Western philosophy of language, largely because the nature of written languages like English is very different from that of written languages like Mesoamerican languages. It may never occur to an English speaker that a word can *resemble* the thing to which it refers (although onomatopoeia can suggest this auditorily).[35] Such resemblance is a major aspect of reference in Maya written language. The essence of a thing is manifested by particular kinds of activity characteristic to the thing in question. As we will see, Mesoamerican metaphysical systems understand the cosmos and things within the cosmos as fundamentally and necessarily active, more akin to events or processes than inert substances. What makes a particular thing what it is, then, is its performance of certain kinds of characteristic activity.

Maya glyphic representation as well as other human-constructed imagery was taken as including or manifesting the essence of the "represented" thing to which a word referred.[36] The resemblance of certain glyphs to the object or event to which the word refers is obvious.

---

[35] Relatedly, this is why a responsible philosophy of language cannot be done monolingually. What is true for English is quite often not true for other languages, and vice versa. Philosophy of language in some of the contemporary Western academy should more properly be called "Philosophy of English" (or perhaps more properly "Philosophy of Anglo-American English." And even then, understanding how the English language works is going to be severely hampered without understanding the ways it differs from other human languages, the ways it follows or diverges from the general structures from which we construct language, and so on.).

[36] The work of Stephen Houston, David Stuart, and Karl Taube discusses one avenue of evidence for this, focusing on the concept of *baah* (self), and its glyphic representation. See Houston and Stuart, "The Ancient Maya Self," and Houston, Stuart, and Taube, *The Memory of Bones*, ch. 2. Megan O'Neil summarizes this work well, writing:

> [U]sing evidence such as the appearance of the glyph *baaj* (self or head) in the captioning of Maya images, as well as making comparisons with understandings of Mexica practices, [Houston, Stuart, and Taube] have proposed that part of the essence or soul of the person was transferred into the image. Furthermore, Houston and Stuart explain the process of this transference of essence through

Figure 2.3 *Classic Maya glyph for* balam, *"jaguar"*

The glyph for *balam* (jaguar), for example, is a glyphic image of a jaguar. This visual resemblance may present itself more naturally to the human mind as representing a closer connection between the written word and represented object than is generally taken to be the case between a phonetically written word and the represented object. The English word "jaguar" neither looks nor sounds like the animal referred to, and thus would strike a speaker of English reflecting on this topic as simply a representative token, referring in some way other than resemblance and sharing of essence. We generally take a photograph, on the other hand, to refer through resemblance, and to more properly *be* the individual or thing represented. A photographic image of me *is* me, in a way we do not generally take a written name or description as being me. If we present a photograph of a person to them and ask them what it is in the photograph, they are likely to respond "this is me," while if we present a piece of paper with their name written on it and ask them what it is, they are likely to respond something like "this is my name." Think about how awkward it would sound to hear a person say of their name "this is me" or of their image "this is an image of me."

The presence of phonetic elements in Classic Maya glyphs, then, does not suggest a radically different way of understanding the meaning and reference to what we find in other Mesoamerican contexts (Figure 2.3). Rather,

a conceptualization of "personhood" that is not limited to the physical human body but can be transferred to objects and representations. These substitutes allowed rulers – both alive and dead – to be eternally and multiply available for supplication and veneration. In other words, they suggest that stelae were not inanimate objects, but embodiments of divine rulers that contained and were enlivened by parts of those rulers' souls.

it demonstrates that this conception of meaning and truth can extend to languages rendered phonetically as well. While images associated with objects may more directly suggest an "essence" theory of reference, there is no reason why such a theory cannot also be used to understand reference in other kinds of language. Indeed, in some philosophical traditions in Indo-European languages, such as particular views of Sanskrit in India, syllabic sounds themselves are understood to hold particular essence and significance, in addition to the reference of words.

Further Reading

Issues of language and truth can be found in a number of sources on Mesoamerica, including Laack, *Aztec Religion and the Art of Writing*; Houston, Chinchilla, and Stuart, eds., *The Decipherment of Ancient Maya Writing*; Worley and Palacios, *Unwriting Maya Literature: Ts'iib as Recorded Knowledge*; Boone and Mignolo, eds., *Writing Without Words: Alternative Literacies in Mesoamerica and the Andes*. For overviews of Mesoamerican languages, see Coe and Van Stone, *Reading the Maya Glyphs*; and Whittaker, *Deciphering Aztec Hieroglyphs*. Full publication details for all of these works can be found in the bibliography.)

3 Time

One of the unique features of pre-Columbian Mesoamerican thought, in comparison to that of other parts of the world, is its development of and the centrality of particular conceptions of time, the creation of time, and the role of time. In Mesoamerican thought, time plays a crucial role in the continual creation or maintenance of the cosmos. It is an organizational principle and structure, interconnected with other aspects of the world and contains features of nontemporal aspects of the world. We can determine that time has a key significance in much of Mesoamerican thought not just because many of the textual sources document time and its features, but because time is continually linked with correlated features of reality, and described as a fundamental feature of objects and events in the world, as we will see in this chapter. Time clearly has a central role to play in the philosophical thought of Mesoamerica, though just *how* it plays this role is a matter of debate among scholars, and as we will also see, differs between and within traditions.

The idea of continual creation that we have discussed to some extent already is a large part of the story of the centrality of time. Many people, even those unfamiliar with Mesoamerican traditions, have some familiarity with the idea of the centrality of time in these traditions, particularly for the Maya and Aztecs. One of the most common associations many people have with pre-Columbian Mesoamericans (particularly the Maya) is the host of invented claims that the Maya predicted the end of time in 2012. Some also know that this so-called "prediction" was linked to Maya calendrics and one of the unique systems for keeping time used in the Maya region and Mesoamerica more widely. Despite the fact that the claims about the Maya predicting the end of time in 2012 have always been absurd, it is true that the Maya and other Mesoamerican traditions did accord calendric events with deep significance, beyond what we find in the West and other traditions. Much of the reason for this is the fact that periods of time, for most Mesoamerican traditions, had important associations with other aspects of the cosmos. Time was not *just* time, but was also all the interconnected features of the cosmos to which it was linked. There was also a connection between time and the organization and structuring of the cosmos by the human mind. Time was a crucial feature of the world in part because time was understood as the nexus between the world and humanity.

Calendric Systems and Ordering of the Cosmos: The Human Role

The calendrics of pre-Columbian Mesoamerica are among the best-known and most distinctive features of the region. Mesoamerican cultures developed numerous calendars, most of which were used throughout the wider region in largely the same form. Indeed, one of the things that marks Mesoamerica as a wider cultural area is the widespread use of the calendric systems, particularly those developed in the Isthmian region associated with the Olmecs, the oldest of the Mesoamerican groups for which we have evidence of calendric development.[1]

In the earliest Preclassic Period, the Olmecs developed a number of the best-known calendars in Mesoamerica, including the first version of what became to be known as the "Long Count" calendar (most famous in its Maya context), as well as the 260-day ritual calendar used throughout Mesoamerica (referred to by scholars as the *tzolk'in* in the Maya context, a Yucatec Maya term for "ordering of days"). In addition to these, a 360-day year calendar was used throughout Mesoamerica. All of these calendars had different purposes, with the 260-day and Long Count calendars having primarily ritual and divinatory purposes. It is with these two calendric systems that we will be mainly concerned in this chapter, as the philosophical significance of time in Mesoamerican traditions is closely connected with these purposes. We should not, however, understand the primary purposes of these calendars as unconnected to those

---

[1] Rice, *Maya Calendar Origins*, 103.

of the 360-day calendar. More "mundane" purposes such as agricultural growth cycles also held much of philosophical import, and Mesoamerican traditions generally recognized the extent to which understanding these key patterns in the world could inform our understanding of other aspects of the world, including the specifically human. As we will see, the idea of patterning and discernment of pattern is central to views of time and other concepts in Mesoamerican traditions.

The 260-day calendar is based on a cycling series of 20-day signs and 13 numbers. The set of 20 for the day sign is likely linked to the more general counting system of Mesoamerican cultures, which followed a vigesimal (base-20) system rather than the decimal (base-10) system in widest use in the modern world. The idea is that there are individual numerals within a place until reaching the end of that base, at which point further counting moves up a place, repeating those numerals at a higher place. So in base-10, for example, we have 9 numerals before moving up a place to the next 10, 1–9, 10–19, etc. Each of the 20-day signs is associated with some aspect of the natural world and/or deity, with strong similarity across cultural contexts within Mesoamerica. While the day signs do not perfectly align in every version of the calendar, they clearly share a lineage, with many of the day signs aligning. The first day sign, for example (given as the first in the *Chilam Balam* texts), is associated with a crocodile in Yucatec and Classic Maya (*imix*), Nahuatl (*cipactli*), and Mixtec (*quevui*). Most of the other day signs also show such overlap. The calendar begins with the first number attached to this beginning "crocodile" day, and successive numbers up to 13 connected with the following day signs, until the 14th day sign ("jaguar" in the three versions of the calendar mentioned above), which then again takes the number 1. The day-number combinations continue to cycle until there is a repeat, in this case of the initial 1 Crocodile, if this is what we begin with, at which point the cycle begins again. To progress through the calendar, with each day sign taking 13 unique number day values, takes 260 days (Figure 3.1).[2]

[2] Notice that neither the 260-day calendar nor the 360-day calendar will remain fixed in the same way to the true solar (tropical) year, which is roughly 365.24 days. There are a number of possible explanations as to why the Maya allowed the calendar to process like this. A more cynical take would be that the maintenance of a class of ritual and calendric experts was facilitated by having an overly complicated calendric system

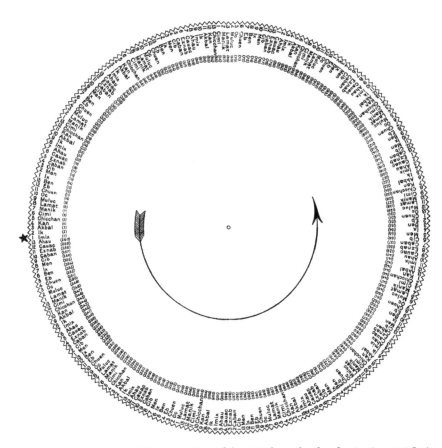

Figure 3.1 *Depiction of the operation of the 260-day calendar, beginning at 1 Imix*

One interesting feature of this calendar, as distinct from those such as the Gregorian year calendar with which most of us are familiar, is that each day in the cycle has a noncontinuous association (the importance of this will become clearer when we discuss embedded identity in Chapter 4). That is, there are 13 numbered days of each day sign, but each of these 13 instances is separated from the previous and the next instance by 19 days. This organization is different

that required specialists to make sense of it for the rest of society. A more charitable explanation would be that calendrics were more important for ritual purposes and for the marking of events than for keying annual events happening in a particular regular sequence. Planting of crops, harvest, etc, were probably keyed to astronomical observation and other indications of a coming rainy season, rather than calendric dates.

from that of the month and day organization of the Gregorian calendar, for example, with 30 or 31 day numbers, but the same month successively for that 30 or 31 days. It would be more akin to taking our weekdays, Sunday through Saturday, attached to numbers but without the month, restarting the count once we reach 30, cycling until each number, 1–30, had taken a day value of Sunday through Saturday once. It would take 210 days to cycle through all of the possible combinations. The month and day are cleverly combined in the Mesoamerican 260 day calendar, with the twenty day signs approximating the length of a month, and recurring 13 times through the ritual "year." Although there are months in the 360 solar calendar also used throughout Mesoamerica, there are none in the 260-day calendar. The months worked in much the way those in the Gregorian calendar do, and there were holidays, festivals, and other events associated with particular periods. These associations with the calendar were largely similar to ones we are familiar with. It is the 260-day ritual calendar that is further from the experience of many of us – perhaps something closer to a liturgical calendar, with its feast days for saints, ordering in terms of sacred history, and ritual significance. For most of us in the modern world, even most of those who belong to religions using such calendars, the significance of these calendars has declined massively from that in the Middle Ages.

The 260-day calendar had key ritual significance in all of the Mesoamerican traditions covered in this book. The day sign of one's birth, for example, was understood as setting particular traits and associating an individual with a *nahual* in the Aztec tradition (a co-essence or companion in nature linked with the human, taking the form of an animal or active component of nature such as storms). The concept of the *way* in the Maya tradition is similar. The link here between a particular day sign and this co-essence of a person expressed a connection between the associated character of a day, that of a person, and of different aspects of nature, expressing the idea of embedded identity (discussed further in Chapter 4). Other features of the 260-day calendar, such as the linking of days in 20-day units, seems also to demonstrate a feature of identity across time inherent in Mesoamerican traditions. Identity, as we will see, need not be *continuous*. In the cycles of time and creation, a day, god, person, or other aspect of the world can exist, go out of existence, and come back into being. That is, there can be *gaps* in identity across time.

While there is disagreement among scholars about the significance of 260 days and the reasoning behind this number of days in the ritual calendar (far less than the 365 of the solar calendar), one potential answer for this is that it roughly corresponds to the period of human gestation.[3] This could connect the 260-day calendar to generation, and the idea of continual creation that is stressed in a number of different areas of Mesoamerican thought, throughout traditions. Other scholars argue that the significance of the numbers 13 and 20 plays a central role.[4] Contemporary Maya calendric experts, or "daykeepers" in Guatemala offer the explanation of gestation for the 260-day calendar.[5] Scholars also suggest a connection between the agricultural cycle in the region.[6] Following themes throughout Mesoamerican traditions would suggest a connection between the human gestation period and the agricultural cycle, as well as potentially a number of other observed cycles in the world. As we have seen already, Mesoamerican traditions stress the interconnectivity of things and correlative identity of objects and events, processes and features of the world. To seek *one* fundamental explanation or corresponding feature grounding the 260-day calendar is very much against the spirit of Mesoamerican philosophy. While in the West there tends to be appeal to the single foundational explanation, in Mesoamerican thought there is a constant stress on the idea that no one thing, whether object, process, or explanation, is ever truly independent or foundational. Each thing mirrors, contains, and is fundamentally interconnected with other things in the world. The human gestation period corresponds to other cycles in the world as well, and thus if the gestation cycle has explanatory significance for the 260-day calendar, these corresponding cycles also do. None of them can be taken as the "real" explanation – none of them is reducible to the others.

---

[3] Earle and Snow, "The Origin of the 260-Day Calendar: The Gestational Hypothesis Reconsidered in Light of Its Use Among the Quiche-Maya"; Aveni, *Conversing With the Planets*, 79; Milbrath, *Star Gods of the Maya*, 2.

[4] Rice, *Maya Calendar Origins*, 176.

[5] Earle and Snow, "The Origin of the 260-Day Calendar."

[6] Aveni, *Foundations of New World Cultural Astronomy*, 365.

The 260-day calendar was organized into 52 year segments in all of the Mesoamerican traditions we look at here. A key difference between the Maya and Aztec calendars, however, is that the Maya used the Long Count calendar in addition to the 260-day calendar. The Long Count, as its later moniker suggests, enabled association of events in a much longer scale of time than the 52-year cycles of the 260-day calendar. Maya forms of the Long Count included everything from the smallest unit of a single day to the largest commonly used unit of the *b'ak'tun* (394.26 years, or 144,000 days). Following the vigesimal numeral system, each place count is ascended with 20 of the previous place, except for the unit that makes up the year, which, corresponding roughly to the solar year rather than to a perfect numeral count, breaks from the pattern. Thus, 20 days (*k'in*) is one *winal*, 18 *winal* is one *tun* (year), or 360 days. 20 *winal* would have given 400 days, overshooting the solar year by quite a bit, 20 *tun* is one *k'atun*, and 20 *k'atun* is one *b'ak'tun*. If the *b'ak'tun* is the largest possible unit, this gives us 7885.2 years possible to record without repetition on the Long Count calendar. Indeed, this is part of what was behind the popular view that the Maya claimed that the world would come to an end in 2012 – a claim nowhere found in Maya texts, nor suggested in any way by their calendrics. The view was based on a misinterpretation by amateurs of both the calendar and the significance of ends of *b'ak'tun* cycles, as well as lack of knowledge about higher units of time in the Long Count.

First – it turns out that the *b'ak'tun* is *not* the highest possible unit in the Long Count. Archaeologists have found reference to larger units of the count, although less commonly used than the ones mentioned, all the way up to a unit of *63 million years* (named the *alautun* by scholars). Just one single round of this unit would be many times longer than the entirety of human existence. One *alautun* before today would put us around the time of the asteroid impact (just off of what is today the Yucatan peninsula) that led to the extinction of the dinosaurs and marks the end of the Cretacious period. The *alautun* and other less common large units of the Long Count seem not to be understood in terms of discrete extension of the calendar, but as ways of expressing that the calendar is potentially *infinitely* extendable. There is no end point of the Long Count, just continually new cycles and periods, which we can capture by ever larger units should the need arise to refer to these units. Just as is the case with the numeral system we use – we can talk of billions and trillions and quadrillions and septillions and can create more and more terms for as many places as we care to ascend – we can continually talk of ever larger units of time to capture longer and longer periods.

Second – even if the *b'ak'tun* were the highest unit of the Long Count, or the calendar restarted in 2012 (which is not true), holding that to be indicative of an ending of time or the world demonstrates a fundamental misunderstanding of Mesoamerican philosophy. As we have seen earlier, the 260-day calendar's sectioning into 52 year round began anew once 52 years had passed. While the Maya had a Long Count calendar that contextualized these rounds within the longer scope of the Long Count, other Mesoamerican groups such as the Aztec did not use the Long Count calendar. For them, the 52-year cycle simply began anew after each cycle. The Aztecs certainly had a conception of periods longer than 52 years (as certainly there were even people alive at any given time who had lived longer than that number of years). The Aztecs, like many other Mesoamerican groups, had a conception of ages of creation stretching across times much longer than 52 years. The end of a cycle in one of the Mesoamerican calendars never indicated the completion of the world or the full run of creation, any more than the ending of a calendar year in the Gregorian calendar has such an implication. Cycles always begin anew – ending and beginning are necessarily linked, with one required for the other. The two are linked in a process of continual creation, in which the cosmos is continually ending and born anew. This does not happen only at certain key dates, although there are important points in given cycles, including beginning and ending dates, and these are generally celebrated. There is no single creation point and ending point of time or the cosmos in Mesoamerican thought. In the Abrahamic traditions familiar to the West, God is said to create time, which has a culmination at some future point, an "end of time" at which the world separate from God's transcendence will come to an end and all things will exist in this divine transcendence. Even in these traditions, there is continuation after the so-called end of time, otherwise God would as well have to end – but what continues after this end can no longer be understood as time in the sense of the created world. James Maffie writes of the Aztec conception of creation:

> [T]he very idea of an absolute beginning or ex nihilo creation makes no sense. It is ill-conceived. All creations are destructions (and conversely), and all acts of creation depend on previous acts of destruction (and conversely). Creation-destruction and being-nonbeing are agonistic inamic aspects of one and the same process...[7]

In Mesoamerican traditions, no such distinction is drawn between things within and outside of time, a transcendent ground on which the cosmos depends but that is not itself part of the cosmos, and the separate cosmos. There is an interconnectivity of the gods and the cosmos, with any transformation (entailed by an ending) requiring the development of something new, just as the development of something new requires an ending or change. This continual process of birth and death, of sacrifice and rebirth (prominent themes in numerous Mesoamerican traditions as we will see) is not a single timeline with discrete beginning and end, but a sequence of successive cycles. To hold that one point could be considered *the* end or *the* beginning rather than *an* end or beginning would not make sense in Mesoamerican conceptions of the cosmos and time. And with good reason! A perpetual problem Abrahamic traditions face is to explain how we can possibly understand either God outside of time, or divine time as fundamentally different than secular time. If God acts, creates, thinks, etc., how can we say that any space in which God operates in this way is outside of time? If there is activity going on, if there is movement and change, there is time in some sense (even if not "kept" or completed in the way that requires human conceptual and ritual activity according to Mesoamerican traditions). Thus, there could never be any ending of time. The successive repetition of the 260-day calendar in 52-year cycles for the Aztecs demonstrates this as well. There is no limit to the number of 52-year cycles, there is only continuation of them.

There are some interesting parallels in terms of philosophical implication of continual repetitions of the 52-year cycle of the 260-day calendar and potentially infinite continuation of the Long Count. Both the 52-year cycle and the Maya/Olmec Long Count entail the continual unfolding of time, of unending renewal of cycles. An older debate broke out over the question of whether we should consider Mesoamerican conceptions of

---

[7] Maffie, *Aztec Philosophy,* 447–448.

time *cyclical* as opposed to the supposedly *linear* conception of time found in the Abrahamic tradition.[8] This question is based on a problematic formulation of differences between traditions on the nature of time. While Mesoamerican systems do focus on cycles and the repetition of cycles, there is also a conception of the distinctness of cycles. The renewal of a cycle is not literally a starting over, a repetition of a cycle identical to the last, with the same events, objects, etc., in a kind of Nietzschean "eternal recurrence." Rather, cycles are understood as distinct but recurring periods in which particular events are enacted anew. In some sense, cycles can be understood as identical to one another, in the sense in which things can share identity over time (through things such as *substitution*, which we will discuss in greater detail in Chapter 4). But distinct things can also become identical in the sense of their sharing of essence, of the substitution of one for another. An example often discussed is that of biological descent. A plant grows, deposits its seeds into the earth, and a new plant grows from that one. The new plant can be understood as *both* distinct as well as a continuation of the old. It shares its essence, and thus resembles in every way the old plant, while at the same time it is constructed of what is new, it is numerically distinct and built of different stuff than the original. The same happens in the case of things like human procreation. This is why texts such as the K'iche' Maya *Popol Vuh* call a child the "continuation" of the parent, and claims that the former continues to exist as long as the latter does (and so on for successive generations). We also commonly see the image of maize and generation from maize used to express this idea.

There has been controversy among scholars on the question of the cyclical nature of Mesoamerican thought. While a number of scholars contrast a so-called Mesoamerican cyclical conception of time with a "linear" conception emerging from the Abrahamic traditions (a distinction made popular by Mircea Eliade), others resist this idea. The fundamental repetition of the calendar in terms of the 260-day ritual calendar and the solar calendar do demonstrate cyclicality, but such cyclicality is present in *every* human understanding of time, and every human calendric system.

---

[8] For more on this see McLeod, *Philosophy of the Ancient Maya*, ch.1; Leon-Portilla, *Time and Reality in the Thought of the Maya*, 163–164.

The key difference between cyclical and linear systems would have to be a progressive view of time in the latter – later cycles are new, further, and more importantly closer to the point of the culmination of time. While we find no such idea as the culmination of time in pre-Columbian Mesoamerica (thus the lack of sense of the 2012 end of time claim), we do find the idea of successive cycles, and the accrual of meaning and identity through these cycles. This idea shows us an important insight concerning how humans tend to think about cycles and recurrences, even though we often do it unconsciously.

Cycles, that is, gain new features, associations, *character*, each time they recur. Some recurrences add more to the character of a cycle than others. This is true of any cycle, whether it is a particular day, part of the calendar, age, or whatever else. A recurring cyclical event has certain associations necessarily, otherwise we wouldn't be able to track its recurrence. A daykeeper, a calendar, or observation of the sun's motions can tell us when the solstice is approaching. Thinking about this in terms of seasons, holidays, or even days of the week makes the point clearer. What things do you associate with the autumn? If you live in a temperate region, as I do, you probably associate this with the changing color of the leaves, maybe trips to the countryside to see the leaves. But our associations with this season developed over time as activities connected to it changed. Though autumn has recurred throughout human history, new events became associated with it over time. In the US, the game of (American) football developed in the early twentieth century, became a popular part of college sports, and its seasons were placed in the fall, at the opening of each academic year. With the growth and popularity of the sport, professional leagues developed, with seasons mirroring those of colleges. Football became part of American life, and associated with the fall. Today, most Americans have that sport, and the beginning of the school year, as part of the furniture of their minds associated with the autumn. And a newer autumnal association, one that wouldn't have existed even 20 years ago, is the now ubiquitous "pumpkin spice latte." All of the associations we have with autumn today were not fixed at the beginning of the annual cycles and recurring throughout time – rather, these associations are accrued as the cycles recur. New associations are gained, old ones are lost. I remember as a child "bobbing for apples," but who does that anymore? It was a holdover from a bygone agricultural era, and slowly fell out of practice as society changed, became more technical, then digital, moved away from the natural environment.

Mesoamerican traditions recognized the accrual of associations and character of successive cycles. Cyclical recurrence was not just renewal, but also growth and development, addition and augmentation. We see many examples of this from numerous Mesoamerican contexts. The cycles of the "five suns" in the Aztec story of creation and the world build on one another. The current age, that of the fifth sun, followed a previous cycle of destruction in which a flood devastated the world. Each of the suns was also identical with a particular god. The well-known practice of human sacrifice (and the lesser known practice of auto-sacrificial bloodletting) was associated with this modern cycle. Such sacrifice, according to the story, was meant to propitiate the gods, in order to ensure the continued survival of the sun. If such rituals were to cease, the sun would extinguish, leading to the destruction of humanity. According to Sahagún's *Florentine Codex*, the Aztec concern with the potential extinction of the sun rose to the level of near paranoia. Discussing solar eclipses, Sahagún's document claims that extra sacrificial ceremonies were carried out at these times from concern that the sun would be fully extinguished. A passage from Book 7 of the *Florentine Codex* reads:

> When this [an eclipse] came to pass, he [the sun] turned red; he became restless and troubled. He faltered and became very yellow. Then there were a tumult and disorder. All were disquieted, unnerved, frightened. There was weeping. The common folk raised a cry, lifting their voices, making a great din, calling out, shrieking. There was shouting everywhere. People of light complexion were slain [as sacrifices]; captives were killed. All offered their blood; they drew straws through the lobes of their ears, which had been pierced. And in all the temples there was the singing of fitting chants; there was an uproar; there were war cries. It was thus said 'if the eclipse of the sun is complete, it will be dark forever! The demons of darkness will come down; they will eat men!'[9]

In Maya sources we also see the idea of accrual of associations with successive cycles. An interesting feature here is that the associations with

---

[9] *Florentine Codex* Book 7, Anderson and Dibble trans., 2.

cycles can be forward looking and anticipative. Prudence Rice has argued that in the Maya region, calendric cycles were connected to a rotating political and religious center. The calendric cycles, then, accrued new associations as the political and religious center of the region would change with each renewed cycle.[10]

The purposes of the interconnecting calendars in Mesoamerica are numerous, just as are those of the interconnecting calendars in use in our modern world. We use the Gregorian calendar along with and simultaneously with others such as the academic calendars of our institutions, religious calendars, and others. Some of the purposes in the Mesoamerican context, however, reveal particular interests and concerns of Mesoamerican philosophies of time.

One prominent feature of the connection between the 260-day and solar year calendars and the Long Count calendar in the Maya tradition is the connection of human time to divine time, or to use more contemporary terms, "deep time."[11] The idea of deep time is that there are certain time periods far beyond human experience within which events unfolding along a much vaster amount of time take place. Geological and astronomical processes, for example, take place in a much longer span of time than even human collective memory can span. The entirety of recorded human history has taken place in about 5000 years. The entirety of human *existence* has been roughly 200,000 years. Geological processes, in contrast, take millions of years, and astronomical processes often stretch billions of years. If we think in terms of collective human consciousness, cultural awareness, and a sense of the moment or era, we cannot even think in a small fraction of the 5000 years of recorded history. Who thinks of themselves and their time as continuous with the origins of the civilization of the "fertile crescent" of Mesopotamia 6000 years ago? The collective memory and sense of "present" of any given time will generally stretch back no more than about 50 years (as it is dependent on the memory of the people alive at the time). In the US today, the presidencies of Bill Clinton or Ronald Reagan are still very much a part of the collective memory, but

---

[10] Rice, *Maya Calendar Origins*, 12.
[11] Mircea Eliade's concept of "sacred time" is what I have in mind here. See Eliade, *The Sacred and the Profane*, 64; Soud, *Divine Cartographies*, 20.

those of JFK or Dwight Eisenhower are somewhat less so, and those of Abraham Lincoln or John Adams are relegated more to the category of history than to our collective sense of present. We can see this by watching discussions of politics on the news – people will still refer to things that happened in the administrations of Clinton or Reagan as if they are part of the contemporary landscape, while more distant figures like Lincoln or Washington will only be invoked as historical figures.

The purpose of the Long Count calendar seems to be to tie the events of collective memory, the collective present, to this deeper divine time. We see the association of events in the calendar on memorial stelae with corresponding divine time events giving them context and significance. Through these accessible events in a recognizable human time, we gain access (via substitution) to divine time events, to a vast timeline seen as somehow standing outside of or separate from the time of individual or even human experience.[12]

Lars Pharo discusses this in connection to Classic Maya stelae from a number of different sites, connecting the activities of rulers to divine events or those of past recurrences of a date in the Long Count. Discussing Copan Stela C, Pharo writes:

> ...[T]he inscription on Stela C (south side), Copan narrates that the anniversary of 6 Ajaw of the 260-day calendar, of a previous Long Count computation, was celebrated on the same date (e.g. 6 Ajaw) of the present Long Count calendar. There is a count of 11.14.5.1.0 from 6 Ajaw 13 K'anasiiy of the unknown former Long Count to 9.14.0.0.0 6 Ajaw 13 Muwaan of the current Long Count. A wrapping or binding of a stone (*k'altun*) was conducted on the date ? 13 'Kalabtun' 6 Ajaw 13 K'anasiiy. This undertaking on the date 6 Ajaw of the 260-day calendar was commemorated by the Copan lord Waxaklajun UBaah K'awil on 9.14.0.0.0 6 Ajaw 13 Muwaan (December 3, 711 AD), when he erected or set up a banner stone. Moreover, on 1.11.4.12.9.0.0.0 1 Ajaw 8 Saksihom, a date of a former Long Count, there was a stone binding or wrapping (*k'altun* ritual) conducted by an obscure deity according to Stela N, Copan (East and West side). K'ak' Yipyaj Chan K'awil performed, on the same date of the 260-day calendar (9.16.10.0.0 1 Ajaw 3 Chakat), a not recognized action. Hence,

there is another example where a 'period-ending date' of the contemporary Long Count calendar is associated with a mythical *k'altun*-ritual conducted by a supernatural being within a previous Long Count. We see (again) that there is a correspondence of the position of the day Ajaw (e.g. 1 Ajaw) of the 260-day calendar in a previous Long Count with the present Long Count.[13]

Consider the time frame in which geological and astronomical events happen. We each have a sense of the length of 50 years in experiential time, even if we have not lived 50 years. None of us has an experiential sense of one million years, however, or even one thousand years. These broad times are useful to understand processes that unfold over a much longer time than the processes of human life or existence. In contemporary understandings however, we generally do not link deep time with the more "human time" of our experience. We do not think of Halloween or Christmas 10 million years ago, or the celebration of the new year 1 billion years into the future. In Mesoamerican calendars using the Long Count, we find links between these vast distant times and the regular human cycles of the 260-day ritual calendar and the solar calendar. This situates human life and activity within expanse of continual creation, the infinitely unfolding timeline stretching into the past and future.

Barbara Tedlock stresses the sense in which the 260-day cycle takes on new features in each of its repetitions. While each recurrence of a day brings with it the associations of previous instances of that day, new essences are added to the day as new associations are connected to it in new recurrences. Here, as in so much else in Mesoamerican philosophy, we see an aggregative conception of the generation of what is new. What is new is constructed of and embedded in what is old or already existing. Tedlock writes, discussing the divining work of the *ajq'ij* working with an individual "client":

> From the point of view of the 260-day cycle and the blood movements, time and events certainly repeat themselves, but when the day Junajpu or a movement on the back of the body points to the deed of an ancestor, as they have pointed out many times before, the questions next asked will be directed toward discovering the uniqueness of that deed and the actual name of the ancestor.[14]

---

[13] Pharo, *The Ritual Practice of Time*, 58.
[14] Tedlock, *Time and the Highland Maya*, 203.

We find numerous references to certain distant periods of time in discussions of calendric origins, and connections between different cycles. The date of August 3114 BCE[15] (13.0.0.0.0 4 Ajaw 8 Kumk'u) that begins the Long Count calendar is connected to creation mythology, but this is understood in the context of ongoing creation, rather than an origin point. The origin of cycles in the distant past is related to the creation of things in the present. One hint of this is that many of the astronomical alignments connected to the 3114 BCE date turn out to be lined up with objects as they appeared during the Classic Period (when the alignments were made) rather than the way they appeared in 3114 BCE. This cannot have been the result of a lack of knowledge that astronomical objects would have appeared in different places over the years due to the long process of procession of the equinoxes (which was known in this period). Linda Schele hypothesized that such alignment was explained by the concerns of the Classic Period Maya to center creation in their present. She wrote that "the Maya, or perhaps their predecessors the Olmecs, would have wanted the astronomy to work with the myth when they could see it, rather than in a mythological past."[16]

A number of scholars argued that the Long Count calendar and its cycles represented ritual renewal of creation of the cosmos. While there is debate over the issue of whether the world is understood as destroyed and remade,[17] complete discontinuity in terms of destruction or disordering is not necessary, or particularly consistent with what we see in Maya sources concerning death and rebirth and cyclic renewal. The *Popol Vuh*, for example, shows us gods and heroes who are cycled and renewed, against the backdrop of a continually changing, independently cycling world. There is no catastrophic or large-scale destruction followed by renewal of the cosmos at once – rather, all things are undergoing renewal at all times, on different scales, cycles, and timelines.

The connection between human time and deep time is made manifest by ritual and the continual establishment of new calendric cycles, in

---

[15] The Gregorian equivalent to the date in the Maya Long Count calendar beginning the cycle which people in the Classic Period understood themselves to be within.

[16] Friedel, Schele, and Parker, *Maya Cosmos*, 96.

[17] Pharo, *The Ritual Practice of Time*, ch. 1.

terms of the Long Count as well as the other calendars. Floyd Lounsbury discussed connections between Long Count dates prior to the 3114 BCE origin date and the Long Count as recounted in the Classic Period.[18] Dates in the Classic Period Long Count are meant to be counterparts to these dates from earlier iterations of the count in more distant periods, connected more intimately with the cultural memory and the ritual of those to whom the newer dates were present. Lars Pharo writes of this that "the use of corresponding dates creates a model for contemporary human (and ruler) behavior by imitating exploits of the deities in 'Great Time' or 'Deep Time'."[19]

Reductionism and Time

This all leads us to a consideration of the issue of fundamental explanation and reduction as connected to time. Mesoamerican traditions avoid the kind of reductionism found in Western and Middle Eastern philosophical and religious traditions, in which one single thing is often appealed to as a foundation to explain everything else. This is behind the ever-present attempts to understand the world in terms of one fundamental kind of entity, one fundamental theory, etc.

Some scholars of Mesoamerican thought, most prominently Miguel Leon-Portilla, proposed that in numerous metaphysical systems in Mesoamerica (particularly for the Maya), time played the role of fundamental constituent of nature, akin to the role of *atoms* for the ancient Greek naturalists, or *dharmas* for the Buddhists of the Abhidharma school(s).[20] Things and events are linked to and explicable in terms of periods of time, particularly the *k'in* (day). All things can thus be understood as having the day as their fundamental component. Leon-Portilla seems to derive this to some extent from the parallel between *k'in* and the Nahuatl term *tonalli*, which stands for "day" as well as "spirit/soul." *K'in* does not clearly have this sense, however. Leon-Portilla correctly points out that the sun god, K'inich Ajaw, includes this concept of the sun, and that this is linked with kingship in the Maya region. This leads Leon-Portilla to conclude:

[18] Lounsbury, "A Rationale for the Initial Date of the Temple of the Cross at Palenque."
[19] Pharo, *The Ritual Practice of Time*, 56.
[20] Leon-Portilla, *Time and Reality in the Thought of the Maya*, also Knowlton, *Maya Creation Myths*.

K'in, aparece, en resumen, como el meollo cambiante, cargado de connotaciones religiosas y de sinos buenos y malos, inherentes a la realidad cíclica del universe y muy problablemente también a la esencia de la divinidad misma.

[K'in appears, in short, to be the changing core, full of religious connotations and good and bad fates, inherent in the cyclical reality of the universe, and also very probably also in the essence of the divine itself.][21]

Time, in the form of this most basic element of the day (*k'in, tonalli*), is taken as not only constitutive of longer periods of time in the calendar, but as fundamentally constitutive of all aspects of the cosmos. The day can be understood in this sense as the basic and fundamental constituent of reality, of which other things are composed.

We have good reason, however, to reject such a temporal reductionist view. First – such a reductionist view would be very odd and out of place in Mesoamerican thought given the focus on the interchangeability of things. That is, we don't find appeals in texts or oral tradition to reduction or to explaining phenomena in terms of any more basic entities. When we do find explanation of why certain activity in the world is as it is, there is appeal to correlative entities. We know that these explanations are not reductive in nature because the very entities used to explain can themselves be explained in terms of the entities they are used to explain. Explanations are made in terms of related activity, essence, and other parts of the world. Likewise, these things can be explained in terms of the original entity.

James Maffie explains that for the Aztecs, time is *relational* rather than *substantial*, which expresses this correlative nature of time.[22] There can be no reduction of time because each time period is manifest and explained in terms of its connection with other time periods. Time then appears as the key and basic example of correlativity. The correlativity of time is such that particular instances of time are not only connected with other instances and periods, but places, gods, people, and a host of other things in the world. Depictions of days and months of the Aztec calendars in some of the codices shows a link of time periods with particular directions.

---

[21] Leon-Portilla, *Tiempo y realidad en el pensamiento Maya*, 45.
[22] Maffie, *Aztec Philosophy*, 420.

Leon-Portilla discusses what he calls "al espacializarse el tiempo" (the specialization of time) in discussing the account of Bernardo de Sahagun on the grouping of years as organized by spatial connections – connections to the directions, particular regions, and realms (such as the realm of the dead). There were also directional associations made in groupings of days within the 260-day calendar to create four "directional" months in the 260-day calendar. There were four groupings of five days each (adding up to the 20-day sign days), each corresponding to one of the cardinal directions[23].

The Character of Time

Numerous Mesoamerican traditions present correlative views of time, in which periods of time are associated with a number of other features of the world, and have their own character and features, just like other aspects of the world. Periods of time carry with them certain associations, moods, energies, and other characteristics.[24] While there is today sometimes a tendency to exoticize this aspect of Mesoamerican thought, this idea is not at all foreign to other traditions, including those of the modern West. Consider the character of our own calendar year, its dates, and its associations. Are there certain associations and feelings you connect to December 25th? October 31st? February 14th? The very notion of having a day or period commemorating some event or associated with some idea is the same correlative human impulse that is behind the correlative associations made with time in Mesoamerica. Even if the specific application is different, the association of time with particular characteristics of the world, particularly human characteristics that we can call *character*, seems to be universal.

Consider the holidays I mentioned above. In late November of every year, as the sun continues to recede in the northern hemisphere moving toward the winter solstice, many of us shift toward a season focused on family, gift-giving, hearth and home, and hopes for the future. We put up decorations in our homes and towns, the music we hear when we go into

---

[23] Leon-Portilla, *Filosofia Nahuatl*, 121–2.
[24] Maffie, *Aztec Philosophy* 419.

stores changes, we plan to meet family and shop for gifts. Even without particular actions, the dawning of this season almost always causes certain changes in our minds, associations, and feelings. There is nothing essentially different about the final week of December, one might say, that gives this time period particular characteristics that couldn't be associated with any other time. But this would miss the point. December, as such, does not exist in nature mind-independently. Before humans created the Roman calendar (from which the modern day Gregorian calendar descends), there was no December. Before humans existed, there were no months or days. Calendrics are among the more clearly conventional aspects of the world. This is something Mesoamerican traditions generally recognized. Humanity has an important role to play in constructing the world as we find it, as we experience it. We in fact experience the world in terms of days, months, years, etc. But we don't do so strictly because of features of a world independent of us. The mind-independent aspects of the world provide only one component of what is necessary to construct the cosmos we experience. As the Maya *Popol Vuh* and other texts stress, the construction of the cosmos is a joint project of nature or the gods and humanity. The calendars we create are a good example of this. If we were different kinds of animals, or even if we were differently inclined as humans, we could have constructed calendric systems completely differently than we have. Or we could have discarded them altogether. The fact that we see so many different calendric systems throughout history and in different regions demonstrates the variable and conventional nature of time as such. Time, and our experience of it, is mind-dependent – it is linked inextricably to the human mind and its characteristics. This is a fundamental insight of Mesoamerican traditions.[25]

[25] I am here not making a distinction between mind-dependent and mind-independent such that what is mind-dependent is completely unconstrained by mind-independent features of the world. The mind itself is constrained by mind-independent features of the world, and as such, nothing, no matter how fully mind-dependent, can ever be independent of constraint by mind-independent features of the world. Thus, to call something mind-dependent is to say that it relies on conceptualization or other forms of mental construction, not to say that it is independent of nature. Conceptualization *is* ultimately a natural process, and we ourselves are part of the unfolding of the patterns of nature.

The *relationality* of time is also a key insight in Mesoamerican traditions. We create and mark time based on certain regularities in human life, such as the daily pattern of sleep, seasons of agricultural growth, menstruation and gestation, and other cyclical aspects of human life. These human cycles and activities are also generally connected with particular deities and activities in religious life, which generally marks these periods of human life. This is the case in Western and other systems no less than in Mesoamerican ones. While in modern life the liturgical calendars of Christianity have by and large fallen by the wayside, even the most secular of people in our society recognizes and follows days connected to religious figures, deities, saints, etc. The days of the week in English enshrine ancient gods associated with the planets – our word "Thursday" derives from "Thor's day," commemorating the ancient Germanic god of thunder, associated with the planet Jupiter (*Iovis* in Latin, thus the rendering in Romance languages, such as *jueves* in Spanish, *jeudi* in French, etc.). Gabina Pérez Jiménez and Maarten Jansen discuss these connections between Mesoamerican and Western conceptions of time, writing:

> The calendar establishes a symbolic connection between days and divine Identities: in Mesoamerica through the 20 deities of the day signs, the 13 deities of the day numbers, the 9 deities of the nights, the 20 deities of the 13-day periods etc., and in the Christian calendar through the link of days with patron saints. Similarly, religious narratives are acted out in rituals connected with the passage of the seasons: the Christian liturgy projects events from the lives of Christ and the saints onto the year (Christmas, Easter etc.), while Mesoamerican religion pivots on the remembrance of ancestors (now the Days of the Dead) and the prayer for rain and the renewal of life on occasion of the sun's first zenith passage (now the Day of the Holy Cross).[26]

We see in Maya day names and numbers clear associations with gods and aspects of nature. The glyphic depiction of a word or idea often contains images of other associated entities. The same is the case with Nahuatl day signs – depictions of the entity associated with the day. These entities are associated not only with the concrete thing depicted, but also with the correlatively associated features of the world. This is where a correlative

---

[26] Jansen and Pérez Jiménez, *Time and the Ancestors*, 562.

approach shows us the depth of what is going on in Mesoamerican traditions. On *reductionist* views, things in the world are ultimately explained by some constituent feature to which things can be reduced, such as explaining objects and change in terms of atoms and their physical properties – the kind of physical reductionism we see in much of contemporary thought. On such a view, if atoms and their physical properties ultimately explain every phenomenon that exists, then every one of those phenomena must ultimately be reducible to atoms and their properties. Thus, things such as psychology or art might on their face appear to be about something other than atoms and their physical properties, but they must ultimately be understood in terms of these, if this kind of physical reductionist view is correct. This kind of view has been challenged in numerous ways by philosophers today, who generally maintain some kind of commitment to what they would call "naturalism," without embracing physical reductionism.

The dominant metaphysics in Mesoamerica is not reductionist, but *correlativist*. That is, events and things are not understood as reducible to certain fundamental components that explain everything. Rather, events and things can be translated to or connected with other events and things in ways that explain them, but not at a more fundamental level. A thing or event can be explained by its correlated entities, while those correlated entities can also be explained by it. A correlative system is not generally understood in relations such as constitution, but there are a number of different ways such systems might work. A correlate is explained by the various things it is linked to – it's oppositions, reciprocals, place in a cycle, etc. Thus, hot is explained by cold and vice-versa, tall by short and vice-versa. Comparative concepts such as these are good example of correlativity. One of the unique and interesting features of Mesoamerican correlative thought is that correlativity can also be understood in terms of constitution and identity. It is not just that a thing is explained by other things to which it is related, but also is explained by other things with which it could be identified, of which it can be constituted, and that it has been or can become. While we will see further examples of this in Chapter 4 in consideration of identity, this view can be found in Mesoamerican conceptions of time as well.

Take, for example, the associations of day signs in Maya and Aztec thought. The Aztec tradition associated the expansive concept of *tonalli*, life essence, spirit, soul, with days. This term was used for "day" as well as the human spirit. (*q'ij* in K'iche' seems to have a somewhat similar association, between day and spiritual essence). The association of both of these entities is made through the root of the term in *tona*, expressing "light" and "heat" that is associated with both the day (via the sun) and the human life essence (via the heat of the living being and its motion). The concept of *tonalli* as such has even more associations than these, seemingly connected to this sense of *heat*, including summer, character, face, and even fate.[27] The sun god Tonatiuh is associated with such heat and motion as well. (This may have been how Leon-Portilla came up with the day- *k'in*- as fundamental unit in Maya thought – a view I think is wrong). Each day is associated with a god, as well as with the particular features of that god, in a way that fixes characteristics, *nahual* associations, rituals, and other aspects of the cosmos.

Maya day signs linked with the [360-day] calendar including months also show association between particular days and correlated days and months. The final days as well as the first days of a given month are associated with the adjacent month as well as the one in which those days are included. The term "*chum*" (seating) is connected to this fixing of days and months. The final day of a month was understood as the transitional "seating" of the next month, and the god associated with the coming month would be established on that day, rather than the first day of the next month. The concept of *chum* was connected to the accession of rulers as well, the "seating" of a ruler in the royal mat (throne). This correlative connection between seating of rulers and months had ritual significance, as new rulers were often installed on the seating day of a particular month.[28] This points out the overlap between the identities of these different periods of time, the sense in which they are not just associated with one another, but contain one another. As with the case of the *k'in* glyph, the images representative of a word often suggested such

---

[27] Maffie, *Aztec Philosophy*, 424.
[28] Bassie-Sweet and Hopkins, *Maya Narrative Arts* 92; Whitmore, 516–519.

Figure 3.2 k'in *glyph – the image of a* plumeria rubra *flower in the center, with the "tail" on the bottom*

correlative links. The *k'in* glyph depicts a plumeria rubra flower (Figure 3.2). We see there is a chain of causal connectivity here that connects this to the concept of the day. A flower relies on the sun for its existence. The sun is closely linked with flowers, because it is only during times of greatest brightness that they bloom. And the day itself is determined by motion of the sun. A number of languages contain terms for "day" that refer to the sun. The Maya glyph for day, then, goes one step further and depicts a day through what is *brought about* by the sun – an effect of the sun, thus contained in it. The glyph represented not just a play on associations between the sun as determinant of day and as key component necessary for the growth of a flower, but a claim of interconnectivity of essence. The flower, and the day, contain the sun as part of their explanation and their essence. If we think about what things in the world the flower requires for its existence, what is correlated with it in the way hot is correlated with cold, the sun is one of those things. But in this sense the sun can be understood as a *component* of the flower. The sun as creator is contained within the flower – the flower is constituted by the sun. While this is only suggestive in looking at the character of glyphs, we see a number of passages in Mesoamerican texts and claims of Mesoamerican people that make this more explicit. The K'iche' Maya *Popol Vuh* discusses biological descent as constitution and thus continuation of the essence of an original (a view I discuss in much more detail in Chapter 4). A relevant passage from the *Popol Vuh* reads:

> [H]is son is like his saliva, his spittle, in his essence, whether it be the son of a lord or the son of a craftsman, an orator. The father does not disappear, but goes on being fulfilled. Neither dimmed nor destroyed is the face of a lord, a warrior, craftsman, orator.[29]

The days themselves, then, also have the kind of correlative associations with one another that they have with other things and events in the world. This correlative system of time is continuous with the correlative metaphysics we find throughout Mesoamerican traditions, emphasized in every area discussed in this book. The metaphysics of precolonial Mesoamerica is for the most part not one of reduction, but of correlation. Correlative systems of metaphysics are no less explanatory than reductive systems. Both are understood as offering *explanation* for the phenomena we observe, as well as enabling prediction.

Ages and Creation

Time has the correlative features that it does at least in part through the (collective) act of human construction through creativity. This is a key aspect of Mesoamerican metaphysics – the sense in which the world is dependent on the creative completion of human beings. There are correlative associations between things independent of human conceptualization, such as the connection between an animal or plant and its biological successors, but there are also correlative associations between things on the basis of our conceptualization of them in a certain way. The distinction between hot and cold, for example, is based on human perception. Calendrics and the existence of time itself, according to numerous Mesoamerican sources[30], is dependent on humans. This does not, however, suggest that time lacks reality, or is less real than aspects of the world that are mind-independent. There is no metaphysical distinction between humanity and the rest of nature as we find in some other traditions. The features found in humanity are found in nature, and the correlations between these explain both. Precolonial Mesoamerican traditions recognized what has taken thinkers in the West until relatively recently

---

[29] *Popol Vuh*, Tedlock trans., 99.
[30] *Popol Vuh* and accounts of the *Florentine Codex* being the most prominent.

to recognize (and many still don't) – that the world as we experience it is in large part a construction of the mind, through things such as perception and conceptualization. We do not find prominently in Mesoamerican thought the question of what the world mind-independently looks like, as on this view there would be no facts of the matter about such a world – it would not be the world at all. Such a question would be ill-formulated. To separate the world into the phenomenal and noumenal would suggest that there could be a cosmos that could be experienced separately from the experience of it.

The creation accounts of various texts in Mesoamerican traditions do seem to suggest that there was some time (in the sense of changes, events happening, etc). at which humanity did not exist, but at those times the gods existed as perceiving and constructing entities (and still exist), and the other aspects of nature itself also are seen to have this perceptual constructive ability. There is no conception of the world as existing independently of conceptualization and the experiences of things in the world, as such conceptualization and experience is a fundamental *part* of the world. This does not entail that Mesoamerican traditions were largely idealist in their ontology. It was not that only mind exists, but rather that the world as such can only exist as a combination of mind and non-mind. Neither can exist "in-themselves" as such. We are returned to the correlative nature of Mesoamerican thought – what James Maffie refers to as "agonistic inamic unity" in the Aztec tradition. We can take the conscious and non-conscious as opposed but not fully independent aspects of the world that require one another for their existence and (in the correlative sense described above) can be understood as inclusive of one another. Maffie writes:

> Aztec metaphysics sees these paired opposites as interdependent, interrelated, mutually engendering, and mutually complementary *while at the same time* mutually competitive and antagonistic. Neither opposite is conceptually or temporally prior to the other.... these paired opposites are dual aspects or facets of *teotl*.[31]

Here we see again something very different from a reductionist explanation of the numerous kinds of things in the world. We have mind and

[31] Maffie, *Aztec Philosophy*, 137–138.

non-mind in the world, and though we have a monistic system in which these are both ultimately understood as one, they are not understood as such via reduction of one to the other, but rather in terms of the ability to understand them as aspects of one another, as aspects of the cosmos itself.

This is also behind the focus in creation stories throughout Mesoamerica on the *dual* as the fundamental creative unit. Rather than the world emerging from a *one*, as we find in Abrahamic traditions, or a one originally grounded in a nameless transcendent nothingness, as in certain traditions in East Asia like the Daoist tradition, origin and change always happens with originating pairs in Mesoamerican texts and traditions. We see this in numerous context. The *Popol Vuh* begins with the god pair of the "framer and shaper" (*Tz'aqol* and *B'itol*) and a number of other pairs associated with creation. The Aztec story of the creation of the cosmos in the *Historia de los mexicanos por sus pinturas* begins with a pair of creator gods representing the dual aspect of male and female, Tonacatecuhtli and Tonacacihuatl. The traditional Aztec story of the origins of the calendar refers to an origin creator pair of Cipactonal and Oxmoco, a man and woman created by the gods, who originate humanity and go on to construct the calendar and its ritual purposes.[32]

The Human Role in Time

As in the *Popol Vuh* and other texts, this activity of humans was seen as essential, in aiding the gods in construction of the cosmos. Creating and fixing the calendar is not understood as something conventional separate from the world and connected with mind, but rather as part of the process of completing the world, part of the creative process that leads to the existence of the world as we experience it. We begin to see why Mesoamerican traditions stress human activity as necessary for construction and maintenance of the world. As is emphasized most clearly in Aztec thought, human ritual activity plays a necessary role in continual creation and maintenance of the integrity of the cosmos. If humans cease to play their necessary role in terms of ritual creation (including essential tasks such as

---

[32] We find different accounts of the two in different texts, as is common in Mesoamerican traditional stories. In the *Florentine Codex*, for example, the genders of the two are given, while in the *Historia de los mexicanos por sus pinturas*, the genders are reversed.

keeping the days), the world as such cannot exist, and will collapse. This also shows us the centrality of the idea that the world is not given, inert, and stable. Creation is an ongoing process – the cosmos is continually unfolding, rather than having been created fully at some point and subsisting thereafter. If creation does not thus continually happen, there can be no cosmos, as the cosmos is best understood as an *activity* rather than as a static object such as a "substance." The various Mesoamerican creation stories, then, are not understood as historic events of the past, but as continual and ongoing creation unfolding at every moment. Through certain types of ritual, such as performances or enactments of this sacred history, we become able to witness this continual creation.

In the *Popol Vuh*, the creation of the calendar, the "keeping of the days," is a key event in the creation of humans. Early in the text, there is an account of the numerous attempts of the gods to create beings with the ability to use language to honor them and to keep their days – associated with both worship of the gods and the construction of the calendar, as the ritual significance of the calendar. The gods first create nonhuman animals, asking the animals to worship them, to "keep their days" (*kojiq'ijila'*). The animals fail to do this, as they are unable to speak as "people" (*winaq*). The conceptualization necessary for language is connected to that of calendrics and the worship of the gods. A critical bit of the passage reads:

> "Speak! Call upon us! Worship us and keep our days!" they were told. But they did not succeed. They did not speak like people. They only squawked and chattered and roared. Their speech was unrecognizable, for each cried out in a different way. When they heard this, the Framer and Shaper said, "their speech did not turn out well." And again they said to each other: "they were not able to speak our names" … They were therefore told: "you shall be replaced because you were not successful."[33]

The gods then created successive beings of mud and then wood, but each of these failed in the same way and was destroyed, before the gods finally hit on the correct formula and created humans, who could speak and worship and keep the days in the requisite ways. The keeping of the days of the gods was connected to their being spoken of, remembered, revered. This activity of humans is essential in that it keeps the gods present.

---

[33] *Popol Vuh*, Christenson trans., modified.

The Aztec story of the ages, or suns, likewise presents a view of human-ity as playing an essential role in determination of the calendar and (linked to this calendric process) the continuation of the world. The central Aztec myth concerning the world was that there had been four previous "suns" and that the current age was that of the fifth sun. Each of these previous ages was inhabited by its own beings, which were destroyed at the end of the age. Each of these ages was represented by a distinct Sun deity, with a new one taking the role in each defining age. In the beginning of the fifth age, a dual deity marks the creation, also associated with the city of Teotihuacan, one of the most important sites in Mesoamerica. This city, the remnants of which stand today just outside Mexico City, was a cultural center that influenced almost all of the peoples in Mesoamerica, and is quite possibly the source of many of the ideas discussed in this book.[34] The gods sought a volunteer to become the new sun, which would require an act of self-sacrifice, by jumping into a fire prepared by the gods (one of the many symbolic representations of sacrifice and rebirth throughout Mesoamerican traditions). The gods choose two among themselves, the arrogant Tecuiztecatl and the humble Nanahuaztin. Originally Tecuiztecatl was to become the sun because of his power and energy. He looked for-ward to the chance to bring himself further honor. Nanahuatzin was to become the moon, and prepared himself through blood auto-sacrifice and acceptance of his duty. When it came time to enter the fire, Tecuiztecatl froze in fear and couldn't bring himself to jump into the fire. The gods cast him aside and asked Nanahuatzin to enter the fire. Nanahuatzin calmly prepared himself and jumped into the fire. Finally, his courage roused by Nanahuatzin's act, Tecuiztecatl followed and jumped into the fire. Nanahuatzin, though originally selected for the inferior position, became the superior – his courageous act of sacrifice making him the new sun, transforming into the new sun, while Tecuiztecatl became the moon (the sun is associated with Tonatiuh, "movement of the sun" who is identified with Nanahuatzin in some accounts and not in others).

The creation account of the fifth sun continues with the formation of the original human pair, Cipactonal and Oxomoco, male and female

[34] Sanders and Evans, "Rulership and Palaces at Teotihuacan," in *Palaces and Power in the Americas*, 270–274.

representatives of the original human. The story associates with this pair the origin of other humans as well as central features of the human cultural realm, particularly the calendar. A traditional story recounts that Quetzalcoatl, the well-known culture hero (associated with learning and the arts among other things) and grandchild of the original pair, suggested the day signs as his grandparents constructed the calendar, selecting the days of the 260 day ritual calendar. The order of the creation of the calendar and the work of Quetzalcoatl (who is also responsible for writing in the Mixtec tradition) was necessary for the foundation of the human world. These ancestral humans give us the creative and active roles proper to humanity. Cipactonal, the man, is represented as the first daykeeper priest in addition to the first man – his name, "Alligator Day", stresses this aspect of his role. The alligator – *cipac* – is the first of the day signs in the ritual calendar, so Cipactonal's name translates more figuratively to "First Day", stressing his connection to calendric origins as the work of men. The woman Oxmoco is likewise linked to what is seen as the fundamental creative work of women. Her name, associated with either pregnancy or midwifery,[35] stresses her role in the origins of human procreation. These two acts, daykeeping and procreation, are themselves essentially linked. To keep the days is a *creative* act of humanity, not a mere descriptive recounting. The nature of fostering the round of continual creation of new human beings through procreation is similar to that of assisting in the continual creation of the days through daykeeping. According to Janes and Perez Jimenez, "both roles are complementary and overlapping: activities such as divination, codex writing and healing were explicitly related to that primordial couple."

In Maya tradition, the human role in organizing or structuring time is additionally suggested by certain ritual timekeeping practices also associated with the terminology of the Long Count. The 360-day solar year in the calendar is marked by the term *tun*, whose glyphic image is a stone (a shared meaning of the term). *Tun* as referring to a stone is an earlier use of the term than its reference to the year, with the latter arising around the late Preclassic Period, just before the Classic Period, marked (in part)

---

[35] Jansen and Perez Jimenez, *Time and the Ancestors*, 21, also *Codex Cihuacoatl* identification as *diosas de las parteras*.

by the rise of the culture of stela erection throughout the region.[36] Stones
were used to mark the passage of time likely before the rise of stela culture in the Classic Period. The terms for different periods of time – collections of years – in the Long Count calendar are not only multiples of the
tun (stone), but *bindings* of stone. A number of scholars discuss the "stone
binding" (*k'altun*) ritual practiced in the Classic Period, associated with
the ending of *k'atun* (20-year) periods. This ritual involved the wrapping
or binding of stone representative year-markers (stelae or other objects)
with cloth or paper. The creation of sacred bundles through the binding of
objects was a common practice throughout Mesoamerica, and the binding
of years is likely associated with this. The significance of binding, in the
case of the general practice, may have been multifaceted. David Stuart
suggests that binding was a way of protecting the sacredness of the bound
object(s) – in the case of the *k'altun* ritual, "to protect and contain the
divine essence held within the stones that embodied time and its movement."[37] One aspect of the human role in "keeping the days", then, would
be to contain or bind the essence of things in such a way as to mark them
or render them useful or significant for the community. The binding of
years marks off a period and makes it discrete. This binding happens at
the ending of a particular period, marking a period as within the cycle and
completed.

This notion of binding as *completion* is also tied to the human role in
construction of time (and the cosmos). An incomplete time period, one
that has not yet been fully associated with events, persons, and things, is
undergoing creation. The binding of these years also then suggests their
completion, their filling, or their fulfillment. The years can now be bound
or tied because there is no longer anything more to put within the bundle.
It has been completed. This conception of construction and completion
seems to have been on the minds of Maya thinkers in the Classic Period.
The concept of *tz'ak* ("complete," "ordering," "whole") refers to this. The
term is used mainly as a verb, the act of completion or ordering, and can
also adjectivally refer to a whole, a thing that is completed or ordered. The
idea of being complete is connected to that of being fulfilled, finished, or

[36] Justeson and Mathews, "The Seating of the Tun," 587; Rice, *Maya Calendar Origins*, 172.
[37] Stuart, "Kings of Stone," 157.

at an end. The English term "complete" shares this connotation – something is complete when it has all of its essential parts and features, and is complete also when it is concluded. The latter sense is connected to the former – an event can only be said to have all of its proper parts and features when all parts of the event have taken place, which is for the event to be concluded.

The ordering or completion of a period of time is something that must be done or facilitated by humans through ritual. Time cannot bind itself, it cannot be fulfilled or completed on its own. Why is this? Because time is linked closely to the events, persons, and things contained in it. It is characterized by and identifiable with these things. Presumably this is why we see periods of time rendered in glyphic form by the images of heads of gods and other correlative markers (just as we see with the representation of the day as a plumeria rubra flower). Time governs our experience and our world, but the human community also plays a key role in organizing and completing time.

Further Reading

For more on time and calendrics in Mesoamerica, see Leon-Portilla, *Tiempo y realidad en el pensamiento Maya* (Time and Reality in the Thought of the Maya); Rice, *Maya Calendar Origins: Monuments, Mythistory, and the Materialization of Time*; Aveni, ed., *The Measure and Meaning of Time in Mesoamerica and the Andes*; Pharo, *The Ritual Practice of Time*. Full publication details for all of these works can be found in the bibliography.

4   Identity, Self, and Personhood

Persons and Selves

The topics of personhood and selfhood are tricky aspects of metaphysics, as they are linked with so many other philosophical issues. They involve unusually complicated issues, even for philosophy. We generally mean many different things when we use terminology like "self" and "person," and each one of these can (and often does) serve as the basis of philosophical reflection. Because this area is so multifaceted, I will try to be clear here about just what we have in mind in this chapter when we discuss selfhood and personhood – two major topics in Mesoamerican Philosophy. These concepts do not necessarily easily map on to the traditional distinctions and debates in Western, Chinese, or other philosophical traditions.

There are three major topics related to issues of persons and selves that early Mesoamerican philosophical systems deal with: 1) social personhood, 2) selfhood and essence, and 3) performative identity.[1] While this list is not exhaustive, and there are many other issues concerning the concept of self in Mesoamerican traditions, the central concerns of many Mesoamerican systems revolve around these three common themes.

One important difference that we find between the distinction of topics concerning the self in Mesoamerican traditions and other traditions is that there is no clean distinction drawn between metaphysical and moral concerns involving the self. The metaphysical and moral self, if we can maintain such a distinction, run together in numerous ways, and the distinguishing of the two (even in contemporary philosophy)

---

[1] The dominant view of performative identity in Mesoamerican traditions, which I cover in the fourth section of this chapter, is that of embedded identity.

can only ever ultimately be for expediency and purposes of analysis. There are, however, different ways of making distinctions concerning senses of the self, such as those listed above common to Mesoamerican traditions. What we would generally discern as metaphysical and moral issues run together in many of these traditions. But likewise, what Mesoamerican thinkers would discern as issues of essence and issues of identity tend to run together in many of our own contemporary discussions of the self. We cannot fault early Mesoamerican thinkers for "failing to see" the distinctions between metaphysics and morality any more than they could fault us for failing to see the distinction between essence, identity, and character activity. The guiding concerns of ancient Mesoamerican philosophers concerning personhood and the self were simply different than those of most contemporary philosophers. These questions were tied to social systems (as in our own case), ritual and religious contexts, familial and lineage concerns, dynastic considerations, and reflection on the rise and fall of cities and wider political and religious-cosmic systems. Modern questions concerning the person and self originate in very different cultural and historical sources, embedded within different institutions and social contexts, and should thus be expected to be very different in their nature. To claim that the questions of today's philosophers concerning the self and the distinctions they make on the topic are the *correct* ones is a mistake, akin to assuming that certain social and cultural situations are the proper ones, that a certain situatedness in the world is the normatively correct one, even while vicissitudes of nature and human cultural difference, rather than any reliable mechanism for tracking the truth, brings about those questions and distinctions.

In the sections below, I offer a broad overview of the dominant views of personhood and selfhood in ancient Mesoamerica. Beginning with the conception of social personhood, I then turn to the issue of essence and selfhood, finally culminating in the "embedded identity" theory of personal identity that relies on these previous views. One fundamental difference from philosophy as we find it in ancient Mesoamerica and in other traditions is that we will not, for the most part, find explicit argument of schools, traditions, or thinkers against one another in formative philosophical texts.

Social Personhood

The concept of the person is familiar to us, although we generally take it to be a number of related things. When someone asks you who you are, how do you generally respond? You may offer your name, maybe your family, likely certain facts about your appearance and physical features, your character, your attitudes and preferences, and the kinds of things you tend to do, whether your profession, hobbies, or other activities. These responses are key to understanding a central aspect of Mesoamerican views of personhood.

In a number of Mesoamerican traditions we find the view that one does not become a person until one gains a social context. As Markus Eberl says, "for the Aztecs, biological birth creates a body devoid of essential human characteristics,"[2] and that a person must be gradually created through the contextualization of the individual into a web of interrelations between other individuals and communities. The Aztecs thought of this in terms of "shaping and polishing," a process in which the gods are intimately involved. In the Mixtec codices, we find a similar view of personhood, in which particularities of the personhood of certain members of society, such as rulers, were constructed on the basis of their performance of rituals and the other responsibilities of their offices.[3]

In numerous Mesoamerican philosophical traditions, the person is centrally linked to social context and interaction. Fundamentally, many of the concepts associated with personhood, such as role, responsibility, authority, and agency (among others), are linked with communal context. The intrinsic sociality of personhood is not, for Mesoamerican traditions, limited to human relations with other humans. Rather, multiple aspects of the world form to create layered nexuses of relationships. These include relationships between nonhuman animals, other living beings, and even inanimate objects such as artifacts and natural objects. All of these entities can be and are in continuous relationship with human beings and human society. The concepts of the *way* in Maya thought and the *nahual* in Aztec thought, for example, link the human to a nonhuman counterpart

---

[2] Eberl, "Nourishing Gods: Birth and Personhood in Highland Mexican Codices."
[3] Jansen and Pérez Jiménez, *The Mixtec Pictorial Manuscripts*, 224.

or co-essence. Likewise, in texts such as the *Popol Vuh*, we find interaction between humans, the gods, and nonhuman animals. All things in the world can be in relationship with one another because all things in the world can be said to be *living* and capable of communication. Contemporary Maya daykeepers understand their roles as in part communicators with non-human aspects of the world, possible because these aspects of the world themselves are living. Two contemporary daykeepers in Quetzaltenango, Guatemala discussed this with Daniel Fitjar:

> It's the contact with the energies and the contact with the *nahuales,* with the Maker and Modeler … I rely on the *nahuales,* the spirituality, the energy, with the sacred fire…
>
> How would I define life? I couldn't define life at all. I wouldn't try to reduce it at all … Time itself has life. Part of that is because time is in movement, it's not static, it's not fixed, it's not still—and that's how it's able to be counted by a calendar or a clock. Certainly, the cosmic elements of the universe, let's say—whether we're talking about the Milky Way, or Venus, or the Sun, or they Moon—and whether we're talking about the shifting patterns of carbon, or quarks. They're all part of things which are in movement, in flux, and therefore can be said to have life.[4]

How can human persons be related to nonhuman objects, and how does this link such objects to personhood? Given that personhood is primarily understood in terms of role occupation and performance and communal integration, the attitudes, inclinations, feelings, and other states of members of the community can be directed at or affected by a large range of things, going beyond the human. A human infant, who has few to none of the capacities of a fully agentive adult, can have a communal context and a clear position and role within a community. Likewise, buildings, homes, and ritual objects (among other things) can have relationships with humans akin to those we can have with each other. Consider your connections to those objects, places, and nonhuman animals that play important roles in your lives. You likely have a very different relationship with the building in which you live than you do with other buildings in your neighborhood, and a different relationship with either of these than you do with

---

[4] Fitjar, *Balancing th e World*, 46.

buildings in other towns you've seen once or twice, and buildings you've never seen. Part of this relationship has to do with familiarity – you have intimate knowledge of the details of your own house, with a dramatically lower familiarity with these other buildings. You may recognize the outer features of your neighbor's house, features of their lawn, and perhaps even a few details about the inside of the house. You may recognize particularly striking features of houses further afield, without as intimate a grasp. And you will know nothing at all of certain buildings, those outside your town that you've never seen, for example. You will recognize some famous buildings, like the White House or the Taj Mahal, even if you have never seen them in person. These relationships are much like those we have with other people. Certain close intimates, such as family members, are people whose features we know very well, while others we may recognize but don't know much about, and certain famous people we will know certain things about, even though we have never met them.

And the parallel to human relationships does not end with familiarity. Certain objects have the power to create in us particular responses, emotions, memories. The building in which we live generates responses much like those generated by family members. We have very different relationships with our hometowns than we have with the places to which we migrate or visit. We may think that in a relationship with an inanimate object such as a house, the relational effects are all in one direction. That is, we might believe that the house can have certain effects on us, but that we cannot have effects on the house. This, we might, think, is an important disanalogy between human relationships and relationships we might have with nonhuman objects or animals. We find a very different view in Mesoamerican traditions. Objects in the world, whether human or nonhuman, have effects on other objects, and these effects can be discerned in our interactions with the objects in question. We clearly recognize the ways in which nonhuman objects such as houses can have important effects on human beings, but humans can also have reciprocal effects on houses, rocks, dogs, or plants. This need not be thought of in terms of magic – think about the scuffs, scars, and individual markings of place you leave in your home, for example. The building in which you live is changed by your living in it, by your leaving signs of your presence that alter the material itself, by shaping and molding the place. We can truly say that not only are you familiar with your house, but your house is familiar with you.

This is all part of what is included in the relational conception of personhood found in Mesoamerican traditions. And it is part of the reason that not only humans, but also nonhuman animals, artifacts, and other objects can be considered persons or closely associated aspects of personhood. As we will see below, artifacts and nonhuman objects can become representative of individual persons because of their relational features, such that they can come to carry the *essence* of a person in ways relevant to personal identity.

The Maya concept of the *uinik* (person)[5] is that of such an interrelated and extended social entity. The *uinik* is a communally contextualized individual – a *person* – with an actualized role in society. While having a communal context is necessary for personhood, development of a fuller sense of personhood requires more skillful and deeper integration into the community. The *uinik*, in terms of the particularly human person, is one who plays a central role in the community. The term, in the Yucatec Maya context, was attached to the concept of the *halach uinik* (true person) during the late Postclassic and colonial period in the Yucatan. Such a person was the main ruler of a Maya city-state. Earlier precedent for the social relatedness of the ruler in particular can be found in the Classic Period Maya practice of association of the ruler, *ajaw*, with the particular city-states they ruled through the use of emblem glyphs. Emblem glyphs were representations of the name of a particular Maya city-state, such as Copan, Tikal, or Calakmul.[6] The city's name comprised *one* part of the emblem glyph, with the other sections representing the ruler of the city. Consider the emblem glyph shown in Figure 4.1, representing the city of Tikal (called *Mutul* in the Classic Mayan).

---

[5] Also commonly spelled "*winik*." "*uinik*" is a term found in multiple Maya languages, including Yucatec Maya. There are close equivalents to this term in other Maya languages (such as the K'iche' term *winaq*), but the Yucatec Maya form is the most widely used in Mayanist literature.

[6] These are all later names for the cities, not the same as those of the emblem glyphs of the respective cities.

Figure 4.1 *The emblem glyph of the city of Tikal*

This glyph is comprised of three elements – the leftmost section that resembles an eye from which a necklace of pearls descends is the word *k'uh* (holy, revered). The most prominent section, in the bottom right of the glyph, represents a tied bundle, and is the word for the city itself, *Mutul*. The section on the top right, comprised of two circular components, is the phonetic rendering of the word *ajaw* (ruler). So the emblem glyph literally reads: "The holy ruler of Tikal." This glyph representing the ruler, however, also represented the city-state itself. The emblem glyphs appear in texts to represent the cities themselves. The identities of the ruler and the city here are interchangeable. This is in part understood in terms of relationality – the city of Tikal and the ruler of Tikal have a fundamental and intimate relationship. In the Classic Period, a Maya ruler also had the ritual responsibility of sustenance of the city and its people. The relationship was so close and essential that in an important sense the ruler could be thought of as a manifestation of the state, and vice versa (I discuss in the fourth section of this chapter the related idea of "embedded identity").

Similar marking relationships can go back even to infancy and birth. The Aztecs incorporated individuals into wider communities first through rituals at birth. Interestingly, these rituals were forward looking – not integration of the infant *as such* into the community, but an integration of the infant into his or her future roles in the community.[7] The socialization in terms of inhabiting of roles transforms the individual human being into a person. As I explain further in the next section on essences, part of the picture in Aztec thought is the emergence of the essence, or *tonalli*, and the connection of this general essence to individual essence. This essence does not on its own construct and sustain the person. Human activity, including rituals and the contextualization of the individual into

---

[7] Eberl, "Nourishing Gods: Birth and Personhood in Highland Mexican Codices," 455.

the community, are necessary to strengthen the essence of the individual, and to complete the construction of the person.

Part of the link of the individual human being to the wider community that constructs personhood is the link of the individual to nonhuman aspects of the cosmos. As we saw above, persons can be of many different kinds in Mesoamerican traditions, not limited to human individuals. The primary and essential feature of a person is that it is a thing that can have an essence, can stand in influencing relations with other members of a broader community, and can have an influential effect on that community and the operation of the cosmos, through performance of roles. Persons can thus be understood as combinations of roles and essence. This will turn out to have important implications for the view of personal identity we will see in the Section Four of this chapter.

We see that in numerous Mesoamerican traditions, including the Maya and Aztec, there is a strong sense of the essential human role in the construction of personhood. We are not born persons. Rather, we are provided with a kind of raw material and essence that we then shape into persons. This is not only the case for persons. In the Maya and Aztec views, humans assist the gods themselves in their act of creating the cosmos, which includes the creation of human (and nonhuman) persons. According to Mesoamerican traditions, ritual and interconnection between things not only builds community, but also creates a world of objects as they come to be understood in this communal context. Just as clumps of stone, wood, and straw only become a house when constructed and lived in *as* a house, an individual only becomes a person when connected to the community (both the human community and the wider cosmos).

Part of the contextualization into the wider cosmic community that constructed a person was the connection of the individual to particular gods, days, and characteristics. The individual role in the community as well as characteristics of these individuals were tied to associated features of other central aspects of the world, including particular gods, days, numbers, and co-essences (such as the Maya *way* and Aztec *nahual*). Calendrics played a major role in Mesoamerican societies not only in determining growing season, festivals, and other important events, but also in contextualizing human individuals in the wider cosmos. One's birth date (according to the central ritual calendars) was thought, in both Maya and Aztec traditions, to confer properties corresponding to particular positions in the community.[8] Markus Eberl writes, of the Aztec birth almanacs:

> The birth almanacs ... foreground the calendar in the form of the twenty-day count and correlate it with activities, patron gods, and discrete symbols. This enabled the diviner to interpret the supernatural forces that acted on a child born on a specific day. The twenty day signs spell out a defined set of social identities and personality types.[9]

Calendric correlation also plays an important role in Maya conceptions of person construction. Naming conventions among certain Maya groups even today contain reference to one's birth date according to the 260-day ritual calendar.[10]

For the Aztecs, human effort during life could establish personhood in degrees. Like the Maya, the Aztecs saw the human soul as not singular, but composed of a number of different parts, all of which could be understood as essences of a kind. They distinguished between the impersonal life spirit or animating energy, *tonalli,* and more social and individually possessed *teyolia* (as I explain further in the next section).[11]

The general and impersonal nature of *tonalli* is suggested by its etymology, from *tona,* which refers to warmth radiated from the sun – also related

---

[8] Weeks, Sachse, and Prager, *Maya Daykeeping: Three Calendars from Highland Guatemala,* 5–12.

[9] Eberl, "Nourishing Gods," 468.

[10] Sharer, *Daily Life in Maya Civilization,* 117.

[11] There has been discussion concerning the etymology of the term *teyolia* and its relationship to the related terms *yolia* and *toyolia.* Sometimes these appear to be identical, and in certain cases *teyolia* or *toyolia* refers to human soul or heart in particular (as opposed to the heart/soul of other things). David Carrasco claims that *teyolia* is a specific form of *yolia,* connected to humans. (*City of Sacrifice,* 180). *Teyolia* has also been suggested as a general version of *yolia,* although this conflicts with certain uses of the term *teyolia* as well. It is not altogether clear whether the term is *te-yolia* or *to-yolia* (both of which can be found), and whether the *te-* prefix refers to *te-* (human), *to-* (our), or something else (see Furst, *Natural History of the Soul in Ancient Mexico,* 15). There is no consensus on this, and it may be used in different ways across texts. Some scholars (see for example Berdan, *Aztec Archaeology and Ethnohistory,* 208; Laack, *Aztec Religion and Art of Writing,* 96) use them interchangeably for this reason. I use "teyolia" rather than "yolia" or "toyolia" here due to its familiarity (it appears to be the most widely used form in the literature) and for consistency.

to the current sun deity of the 5th age, Tonatiuh.[12] This kind of vital energy was associated with heat, a key feature of the sun. It is also used to refer to the day and day sign. The day sign associated with an individual's birthdate is an important determining feature of characteristics associated with the individual.

Teyolia was linked to the individuating features of a person, their character, and their unique social connections. Miguel Aguilar-Moreno points out that this energy was understood as augmentable through the performance of exemplary social activity.[13] One builds one's *teyolia* through the excellent performance of role activity that binds one ever more closely to the wider community. We see here a demonstration of the idea that nonhuman things can be persons as well – *teyolia* was said to belong to any object that had the power to have relationship with and effect on other aspects of the world, particularly the human. Thus, "cities, mountains, lakes, plants, people, and any objects that held power" possessed *teyolia*, according to the Aztecs.

The human relationship with the gods and other aspects of the cosmos was understood both in terms of completion and in terms of reciprocity. One of the relationships that makes a human individual a person is that between the individual and the cosmos, represented by the gods. For the Aztecs, the original fashioning of the human being by the gods (see Figure 4.2) is understood as properly repaid through both proper social activity and through sacrifice. This sacrifice is not only the "heart sacrifice" well known in the west, involving the ritual execution of human and nonhuman animal victims, but more broadly the sacrifice involving willful foregoing of one's own interests on behalf of the wider community (including the gods) – a conception of sacrifice shared by the Maya, and found in many global traditions.[14]

The widespread Mesoamerican practice of autosacrificial bloodletting, in which rulers and nobles pierced their own body parts (generally the penis for men and the tongue for women) was meant to ritually symbolize the commitment of the ruler or noble to the community, and his or her willingness

---

[12] Aguilar-Moreno, *Handbook to Life in the Aztec World*, 171.

[13] Aguilar-Moreno, *Handbook to Life in the Aztec World*, 172. Also see David Carrasco, *City of Sacrifice*, 180.

[14] For the Maya view, see McLeod, "Sacrifice: A Maya Conception of a Misunderstood and Underappreciated Component of Well-Being."

Figure 4.2 *The Aztec god Tlaloc, presenting a formed child.* Codex Borgia

to take on pain, suffering, and distress on behalf of this wider community. As with similar autosacrificial rituals elsewhere in the Americas, such as the well-known "sun dance" of the Lakota, such rituals bound the sacrifice more closely to the community, thereby increasing and strengthening their personhood, and their importance to society. Sacrifice, in its multitude of senses, was seen by numerous Mesoamerican traditions as required for the continual maintenance of the human community and the cosmos (connected to the doctrine I refer to as "continual creation"). Individuals within the society each have a responsibility, based on their role, to contribute to this maintenance, a task that necessarily involves sacrifice. Such acts as bloodletting and fasting were connected to the idea of renewal, with the genital perforation of men connected to potency and fertility. Such sacrifice also had a shamanic component, with the powerful essence of nobles and rulers enabling contact with unseen aspects of the world during sacrifice (such as the gods and ancestors). Even the gods themselves were sometimes depicted as engaging in such autosacrificial bloodletting,

Sacrifice is one among many activities and rituals that can tie the individual more closely to the community, strengthening one's personhood. At the limit, the power of one's person pervades the entire community, as in the case of the ruler. Maya imagery from numerous sites demonstrates the centrality of the ruler in the identity of the city-state. A good example of this can be seen in the stelae of the ruler Waxaklajuun Ub'aah K'awil[15] at Copan. The ruler is depicted on the front of the stela known

---

[15] Previously understood as "18 Rabbit," a name still used, even though today our understanding of the glyphs associated with his name translate the name as "18-the-images-of-K'awil." See Restall and Solari, *The Maya: A Very Short Introduction*, 23.

as "Stela A," while the sides and back contain a glyphic text describing the four directions and other important cities, implying (on one interpretation) the ruler's centrality to the organization of the city and its relations to other important regions. Aztec rulers, like Maya rulers, were associated with the sun, with its power to both provide life and make visible one's world. These are similar images to those we find in other historical cultures that developed a conception of an all-powerful, nearly transcendent ruler, such as Akhenaten's Egypt, Constantine's Rome, or the France of the "Sun King" Louis XIV.

The "sociocentric" conception of personhood that we find in ancient Mesoamerican traditions[16] does not preclude a conception, alongside it, of essences, which play essential roles in characterizing a person, causing features of individuals that allow them to become persons, and sustaining life. There are a number of different kinds of essence that each individual possesses, according to many Mesoamerican traditions, and understanding the self requires understanding these essences.

Selfhood and Essence

Mesoamerican philosophical systems have a number of interrelated concepts that are important to explore in order to understand their views on selfhood and personhood. This is crucial, because a number of these concepts are very foreign to concepts that readers without a knowledge of Mesoamerican traditions may have seen before. The structures of self and person are built on the foundation of these concepts, which I outline in this section. Aztec and Maya concepts in particular are useful, in their application and similarity to other concepts discussed throughout Mesoamerica.

For the Aztec, individual human beings contained three essences, each of which had wider reach than just the individual. The first, and widest reaching, of the three is *tonalli*. *Tonalli* for the Aztecs was a generalized essence or power, a kind of vital life-force. *Tonalli* is a feature of all things that possess vitality and power, and can be thus understood as an animating force. James Maffie writes:

---

[16] To use the wording of Monaghan and Just, *Social and Cultural Anthropology*, 135–136.

Tonalli includes solar head, energy, or power; solar radiation; life force sensed and transmitted as heat; day; day sign; day name; a person's fate, destiny, or birth-merit as determined by her day sign; personal and calendric name; animating energy, soul, spirit; and vigor, character, or temperament.[17]

Given that this life force animates the individual and in some important sense powers them to be able to play the roles constitutive of their person, it is also tied to a person's destiny or fate (an association linked to the characteristics of the day sign associated with one's date of birth). The outcomes of one's life are explained by *tonalli*, both its level and kind.[18] *Tonalli* is associated with heat – the heat of the sun, the heat generated by life and motion. When that heat is possessed, it emanates from an object. Thus, the more *tonalli* things possess, the hotter they will be. The sun as central purveyor of *tonalli* exemplifies this. Humans receive *tonalli* from the sun, according to the Aztec view (notice the tie to organizational role of the ruler), and it is concentrated in specific places in the body. The head, in particular head hair, was thought to be a central location of *tonalli*. This explains practices such as taking the hair of defeated warriors in battle, as a way of capturing their *tonalli*. The blood is another location of *tonalli*, with important implications for bloodletting sacrifice – both auto-sacrificial bloodletting and the more widely known "heart sacrifice" ritual executions practiced by the Aztecs. *Tonalli*, while it is contained within and animates the human, is not an individual possession, and can be gained and lost. It is a fully general feature of the world on which humans and other beings rely for their lives, but is recyclable, just like energy in general. *Tonalli* is gained and lost, and ultimately at death, the *tonalli* of an individual recycles into other things in the cosmos. As bearing facts about one's fate, *tonalli* itself will determine the pattern of this rise and decline of *tonalli* in the individual.

The second essence of the individual human being is *teyolia*, which to some extent overlaps with *tonalli*, in that it plays a role in animation and energy for the human being. Unlike *tonalli*, however, *teyolia* is more individual-specific, rather than a generalized force. For this reason, *teyolia* is

---

[17] Maffie, *Aztec Philosophy*, 214.
[18] Reminiscent to some extent of *qi* 氣 in early Chinese philosophical traditions.

associated with the individuated essence of a particular person, and the aspect of the person that remains representative of that person after their death. It is the *teyolia* that can enter the other realms and lives on (individually) after death. As such, it is associated primarily with individuating features of a given person. *Teyolia* is, of course, still a feature of nonhuman aspects of the cosmos, as we have seen above that there are nonhuman persons as well for Mesoamerican traditions.[19] The Aztecs thought human *teyolia* to be based primarily in the heart.

The third essence of the individual human being, *ihiyotl*, was associated more specifically with breath. This echoes a common theme throughout global intellectual traditions, associating breath with animating spirit or life essence. We see the concepts of *qi* in early China, *atman* in India, and *pneuma* in ancient Greece, all of which originally refer to breath, and come to have the sense of spirit or life force. The liver was thought to be the seat of *ihiyotl*.

Maya conceptions of the animating essences of human beings are somewhat similar, but we also see some key divergences. We find similar views that there are numerous essences in each individual (a common Mesoamerican position). One of the most important of these is *itz*, which is associated with resin, sap, or other liquids seen as possessing potency, such as milk, tears, and semen. *Itz* is an essence associated with shamanic power, with the "Itzam" (seer, sage) understood in the Yucatan as a person who had the power to manipulate or control *itz* beyond the normal human ability. Thus, gods associated with *itz*, such as the god Itzamna (a major god in Classic and Postclassic Maya thought), were seen as governing "writing, divination, and other esoteric lore."[20] Even more broadly, the Maya thought of *itz* as a concept expressing the unification of different aspects of the world, seen and unseen. It pervades the cosmos, and is manifest in persons – in humans particularly as *ch'ul*, which is associated with blood. As the essences of persons can be understood in terms of their links to other things in the world, *itz* helps explain these connections, not only between humans and other elements of the world, but between all things that form the basis of our unified experience and a unified cosmos.

---

[19] Maffie writes: "Teyolia is present in humans, animals, and plants as well as mountains, wind, rivers, and towns." *Aztec Philosophy*, 194.
[20] Karl Taube, *Major Gods of Ancient Yucatan*, Issue 32, p. 40.

For the ancient Maya, the concept of "co-essences" also played a major role. Other aspects of the cosmos, such as nonhuman animals, or natural phenomena such as rain, wind, or lightning, can share fundamental relationships with human beings, including the latter being representative of the individual human as an essence, in much the way the impersonal essences such as *tonalli* for the Aztecs (or the Maya *ch'ul*) are related to the individual.

The best-known Maya concept of co-essences is that of the *way*, which Stephen Houston and David Stuart describe as "a companion spirit, a supernatural being with whom a person shares his or her consciousness."[21] As is the case with other essences, nonhuman persons also possess *way* co-essences. The idea of the co-essence further emphasizes the necessary connection between persons and other elements of the world. The community into which the person is contextualized is not only the human community, but the community of the wider cosmos, in which the human and the nonhuman alike have significant roles to play.

We can see that the concepts of essence and co-essence discussed in this section are connected closely to the issue of social personhood. While essences can individuate in ways that personhood does not always individuate, the two are intertwined closely. The Mesoamerican ideas on these issues lead to the fascinating and unique view of personal identity described below.

Embedded Identity

We now have enough of a background in Mesoamerican theories of personhood and the self to understand one of the central and unique insights of these traditions – specifically, the doctrine I refer to as *embedded identity*.

The issue of personal identity is one discussed in almost every philosophical tradition, going back to the earliest ones. We observe the constant change of the person from moment to moment, day to day, throughout a lifetime. The features one has as an infant are different in almost every

---

[21] Houston and Stuart, "The *Way* Glyph: Evidence for 'Co-Essences' among the Classic Maya," 1. I also argue that *itz* has the sense of "truth" in Maya philosophy. See McLeod, *Philosophy of the Ancient Maya*, 117, and McLeod, "Itz and the Descent of Kukulkan: Central Mexican Influence on Postclassic Maya Thought."

way from the features (both mental and physical) one has as an adult. How do we make sense of the endurance of a self through time and change? The problem of making sense of personal identity led numerous traditions to adoption of concepts such as that of an unchanging and eternal soul (the *psyche* of the ancient Greeks, or the *atman* of certain Indian traditions). We find different answers to the question in other traditions, with some holding that there are no enduring substantive selves, and that selfhood across time is properly understood as a matter of the proper relations between different mental and physical complexes (whether via memory, biological continuity, or some other relation).

In ancient Mesoamerica, the self was associated primarily with a substantive *essence*, understood in somewhat different ways across different Mesoamerican traditions. As pointed out above, there are numerous different essences associated with individual persons, rather than a single representative essence with which a person is identified, such as a "soul." This can make it somewhat difficult to translate and explain Mesoamerican essence concepts. But it also (along with other important features) allows for an interesting and unique conception of personal identity, in which there can be both *partial* identity between person stages or instances, as well as cross-temporal and cross-spatial identity. This conception of embedded identity is one of the most unique features of Mesoamerican traditions. It is tied closely to the notion of ritual constitution of person-hood and the link between essences and communal location.

While we find the view of embedded identity throughout Mesoamerican traditions, it is most clearly developed in ancient Maya sources, on which I rely most heavily for the following account (with some assistance of Aztec concepts).

The concept of *k'ex* (substitution) in the Maya tradition offers us an accessible starting point for making sense of embedded identity. *K'ex*, according to the Maya view, is based in both performance and essence. An individual, through ritual performance, can enact the identity of certain persons, such that they take on the essence of the person enacted, and thus *become* the portrayed person, rather than only representing them. This may happen in a number of ways. Performances of important cultural stories through dance, oratory, and ritual can enact personhood, as can adoption of characteristic roles or positions. A *k'ex* is a substitution of the essence of the enacted person for that of the enactor. Thus, a dancer who is portraying a particular god in a ritual performance can take on the essence of this god, such that they become a *substitute* for the god, sharing its essence. The dancer is then (as enacting the role) *identical* with the god in question.

There has been a great deal of discussion of *k'ex* among Mayanist scholars, both of the concept in ancient Maya thought and contemporary manifestations of it. Much of what we know about the ancient concept of *k'ex* comes through contemporary ideas in Mesoamerica that scholars believe are linked to these earlier ideas and practices (evidence for which we find in both Postcontact texts such as *Popol Vuh* and precontact texts and imagery).

We have seen in sections above that characteristic activity in terms of communal role is what determines and defines a person – thus for there to be the *same* person in any two instances is in large part for there to be the same characteristic activity and role in these two situations. Given that essences are closely connected to communal location and activity, an essence can then be transferred on the basis of the transfer of roles. This is one way of understanding the concept of *k'ex*. However, there is more to it than just this. A passage from the K'iche' Maya text *Popol Vuh* demonstrates an aspect of substitution as embedded identity.

This passage follows a description of the birth of the Hero Twins, Hunahpu and Xblanque, from the head of One Hunahpu (which is also the head of his twin Seven Hunahpu), which impregnated a woman from the underworld, Xibalba, by spitting into her hand. The text explains that this saliva can be understood as carrying the essence of One Hunahpu (and Seven Hunahpu), such that his children can be understood not only as new entities derived from One Hunahpu, but as literally the continuation, the *substitution*, of One Hunahpu himself.

> After that, his son is like his saliva, his spittle, in his essence, whether it be the son of a lord or the son of a craftsman, an orator. The father does not disappear, but goes on being fulfilled. Neither dimmed nor destroyed is the face of a lord, a warrior, craftsman, orator. ... "So be it," said the head of One and Seven Hunahpu—they were of one mind when they did it.[22]

---

[22] *Popol Vuh*, Tedlock, trans.

Notice a few important features of this story. First – substitution entails not just relation, but identity. Second – identity can obtain between one and many. That is, in this story, One Hunahpu's substitution is not only a single person, but *two* people, namely the Hero Twins. Third – identity can obtain on the basis of sameness of mind or thought (as in the case of One and Seven Hunahpu). What makes the head of One Hunahpu identical to that of Seven Hunahpu is that they "were of one mind." How can we make sense of all of this as a theory of personal identity?

Identity between One and Many

It may seem that identity of personhood can only obtain between entities or stages in different times – for example, between a thing considered at time 1 and another thing considered at time 2 (where the two things are often related mental and physical complexes). But let's consider what this view of personal identity commits us to. If person A and person B are qualitatively distinct – perhaps person A has different mental and physical features from person B – then holding them to be identical persons commits us to a view that two things can be identical while qualitatively distinct. Consider a person at 10 years old and that same person at 20 years old. The 10 year old and 20 year old are qualitatively distinct in a number of ways. The 10 year old is identical to the 20 year old insofar as the two persons can be taken as identical. So we are already violating a seemingly basic principle of identity, commonly known as "Leibniz' Law" (identity of indiscernibles), which holds that any things that share all of their features must be identical. There is a related principle (indiscernibility of identicals) holding that any identical things must share all of their features.

Most views of personal identity are already committed to such a violation (and seemingly cannot avoid it). So what more do we lose if we accept the possibility of qualitatively distinct entities that are temporally continuous? That is, if qualitatively nonidentical things can be identical if they exist at different times, why can't qualitatively nonidentical things be identical existing at the *same* time? Much of our resistance to this idea relies on intuition. Consider the famous "Ship of Theseus" case for identity of artifacts through time. An original ship sets out to sea, and over the years as parts go bad, the parts are removed, thrown overboard, and replaced with new parts. Eventually, many years later, all of the original parts have been replaced by new parts, and the new Ship of Theseus is completely distinct from the original. We might be inclined to say that, functionally, this new Ship of Theseus is identical to the original ship, even though it is made of numerically distinct parts. But we can complicate this picture. Unbeknownst to us, scavengers have been following the Ship of Theseus over its years at sea, and every time a piece of the ship was discarded overboard to be replaced with a new one, the scavengers collected it. Many years later, the scavengers finally had enough pieces to construct a ship from the original parts of the Ship of Theseus, numerically identical to the original Ship of Theseus. Should we say this scavenger-reconstructed ship is identical to the original Ship of Theseus, or should we say the functionally current ship playing the role of the Ship of Theseus is identical to the original Ship of Theseus?

Notice that the view that there is indeed a problem here relies on the intuition that there cannot be more than one thing at a given time that counts as *the* Ship of Theseus. But why should we find this any more problematic or difficult to understand than the existence of two qualitatively distinct but identical objects existing at different times? Indeed, the fact that to many of us, the identity of the Ship of Theseus seems unproblematic until the newly constructed ship is introduced and there is a "competitor" seems to show that we are relatively unfazed by failures of Leibniz' Law in identity, unless it involves co-temporal objects. But Leibniz' Law is violated either way – how can we justify its co-temporal violation as any more unacceptable or nonsensical than its cross-temporal violation?

Thus, it seems we have no reason beyond intuition for resisting the idea that there might be identity between numerous co-temporal persons. On the Mesoamerican view of embedded identity, persons can co-temporally exist, such that two or more simultaneously existing persons might be identical to some single previous person. To return to the Ship of Theseus example, the Mesoamerican intuition here would be to take *both* ships as identical to the Ship of Theseus. This intuition is additionally justified in the case of persons (which a ship can be!) if we recall that role and communal context are conditions for personhood. Two persons may play an identical or near-identical social role, having the same connections with other members of the wider human and nonhuman community. In certain cases of this kind, it can be correct to call these two persons *identical* persons.

Playing identical or near-identical social roles is not in itself sufficient for personal identity between co-temporal things. These two things must also share the same essence in other senses. The concept of *k'ex* applies mainly to continuation not only in terms of role, but also in terms of ancestral or biological continuity. To substitute a particular entity, one must be ancestrally related. This has differing implications for different kinds of substitutable entities. Certain nobles and rulers can substitute past rulers, and a wider range of people can substitute the gods, who have ancestral relationships with humanity as a whole. Agricultural imagery is useful here, and also often used by Maya thinkers and scholars of Maya thought. Robert Carlsen writes:

> *K'ex* is the process of making the new out of the old. At the same time, just as a single plant produce multiple offspring, *k'ex* is change from one into many.[23]

While we tend to see offspring, in the case of plants and humans, as creating the new from the old, the dominant view in Mesoamerica is that while we can understand offspring as in some sense new, there is a transmission of essence through the creation of offspring, which, combined with the right kind of person-making activity, can render an offspring (even *multiple* offspring) substitutions of original bearers. Any descendent of a person, according to the Mesoamerican embedded identity view, is *potentially* identical to that person. Such descendants share one essential essence of the original person. However, given the necessity of social location and role performance in personhood, such a descendant must also have the same communal context as the original person to qualify as a substitute and thus identical person. For example, the grandson of a great ruler, independent of his activity and social context, always has the *potential* for identity with the grandfather. Once the grandson adopts the proper role, social context, and characteristic actions, however, he becomes a substitute for the grandfather, and thus becomes identical with the grandfather.

---

[23] Carlsen, *The War for the Heart and Soul of a Highland Maya Town*, 51.

One question we may ask here: Why think that this is not simply a point about *roles* rather than a point about personhood? We recognize that multiple people can potentially play a particular role in the community at different times. For example, a given person can achieve the role of Secretary-General of the United Nations, and a different person can later take that role, succeeding the previous one. We do not, however, take this to demonstrate shared personhood. It is not that Kofi Annan, Ban Ki-moon, and Antonio Guterres, who held the role at different times, are the same *person*, rather they are distinct people who successively held the same role. If we consider why we make such a move, however, it is because we don't define personhood on the basis of roles and essence. If roles are partly constitutive of personhood, then two persons occupying the same role (who also meet the other conditions, in this case sharing of descended essence) will count as the same person. So the reliance of personhood on roles turns out to be a key feature of this Mesoamerican view of personal identity.

We find a number of textual references and contemporary practices connected to the concept of substitution. Naming conventions in a number of Mesoamerican regions take children to be named after grandparents, with the understanding that the grandchild is a substitution (or potential substitution) for the grandparent. There are also numerous stelae from the Maya Classic Period depicting individuals as substitutes for earlier persons, mainly gods and rulers. An example of this from Palenque is the ruler K'an Hok' Chitam (490–565 CE), who was described on a panel as the substitute (*k'exol*) of an early ancestor, in the guise of the god Chak Xib Chak.[24] Classic Period rulers in general were understood as substitutes for gods, thus understood as identical to these gods.

We have seen above that personhood, for Mesoamerican traditions, is not limited to humans, but that a variety of nonhuman things can be persons as well. This has important implications for embedded identity, as well as generates a potential problem. Substitution (*k'ex*) can take place between a human person and a nonhuman person. That is, a nonhuman animal or artifact can substitute a human person, such that it attains identity with that human person. We see examples of this throughout Mesoamerican

---

[24] Schele and Miller, *The Blood of Kings*, 274.

literature. In the K'iche' Maya *Popol Vuh*, there are two important examples of such substitution. In the first case, the woman of Xibalba, pregnant with the Hero Twins, is ordered by the lords of Xibalba to be executed, and in place of the woman's heart, a ball of sap is substituted, with the idea that this sap ball *becomes* the heart of the woman. Another example later in the text is the replacement of the head of Hunahpu (who loses his head in the underworld) with a gourd, until his head can be retrieved.[25] We see in these cases partial substitution – that is, the substitution of person *parts* with other things, rather than a whole person, as we see in other cases. This is another unique feature of embedded identity – the idea that a person has parts that can be interchanged with other parts, and that do not need to be temporally or spatially continuous.

To explain this, we can look back to the idea of personhood as emerging from communal relations and context. Just as a person becomes such through occupying a particular position, playing particular roles, and interacting with a community in certain ways, the parts of a person become what they are through playing a structural role in constituting an individual who can perform these broader social roles. Thus, the head of Hunahpu is that through which he can speak, hear, etc. in the ways that allow him to interact with the world in the way a person must. The gourd *becomes* the head of Hunahpu when it is removed from its context of being a gourd and placed into the operational context of working with all of the other parts of Hunahpu to perform the role of the thing through which Hunahpu sees, hears, etc. While this may be a mythical example (and the authors of the *Popol Vuh* certainly intended it as such), it also teaches us important features of this theory of personhood found throughout Mesoamerica.

As with much of the content of the theory of embedded identity, we might be less inclined to reject this idea as nonsensical if we think about examples closer to home.

Take the artificial limbs of an amputee, for example. A person who has lost a leg in war can be fitted with a prosthetic that can help them to

---

[25] This is also surely intended to be reminiscent of his father Hun Hunahpu's head being removed and placed in a calabash tree, which then generated the hero twins by spitting into the hands of the woman of Xibalba.

perform many of the functions the person performed before losing that leg. This artifact that previously was just plastic, steel, and other components becomes in essence a functional leg, and working in tandem with the other parts of the person's body, becomes not only a leg, but the leg of *that person*, rather than your leg or my leg. The identity of any given part of a person is fixed by its role and relationship to other parts of the person. And the person as a whole can be understood as made such by the person's role and relationship to other parts of the community. Embeddedness and identity must be understood within this part-whole communal context.

Embedding

The "embeddedness" component of the embedded identity theory comes from the idea that a given person can take on new identities, such that they do not lose their former personhood, but take on the personhood of another in addition. That is, persons can be *embedded* within other persons. Say that, given the requisite ancestral connection and communal activity, Ruler B comes to substitute previous Ruler A, and thus becomes identical with Ruler A. Ruler B does not thereby lose their personhood as Ruler B and become wholly Ruler A. Rather, Ruler B is now *both* Ruler B *and* Ruler A. This is the sense in which we can understand embedding. Essence and activity that can *multiply constitute* particular persons. One way of putting this is that persons can be *co-constituted*. The same mental and physical stuff, or the same role performance, can constitute multiple persons.

This view of course seems to run into a difficult problem right away. That is, if persons can be co-constituted by individuals and activities, then in cases of embedding, the conditions for being person P are exactly the same as the conditions for being person P* (at some given time). But if this is the case, how do we avoid the conclusion that person P and person P* (during whatever time the conditions for P-hood and P*-hood are the same) are themselves identical? The view of embedded identity clearly seems to want to keep them distinct – person P and person P* are not identical, even though one may be embedded in the other. There are a number of ways we might make sense of this. Perhaps the most obvious solution is to make identity successive rather than embedded – holding that one can be person P at one time and person P* at a second time, then revert (after the completion of the P making substitutive action) to being person P at a third time. But such successive identity doesn't seem to be consistent with the evidence we have about the view in ancient Mesoamerican texts as well as contemporary practices related to these early views.

A better way to solve the apparent problem, while retaining the distinction between embedded persons P and P*, and one more consistent with broader features of Mesoamerican views of persons, is to consider particular traits or parts as multiply constitutive or owned. A good way to think of this for purposes of understanding is in terms of familial features. Most of your physical or mental features are reminiscent of those of various ancestors, and you have likely had certain of these features pointed out to you by family members as similar to others, if you've not noticed it yourself. Your mother may tell you that your eyes look exactly like your great grandfather's, or your uncle may say that you've got the same bellowing laugh as your grandmother. Most of the features we have we share with ancestors (the exceptions being environment-based features, such as language and accent – and much of these we share with close ancestors as well). The eyes that look like those of your great grandfather are not *yours* only, but they are also his. The laugh that you share with your grandmother is not yours only, but it is also hers.

We can use this insight to understand multiply constitutive traits on the view of embedded identity. At certain times, a person is constituted by a number of different traits, actions, etc., most of which they share with some others (ancestors and community members), and some of which are unique to the individual. Not all of an individual's traits and actions will be relevant to their personhood, particularly given that personhood is understood primarily in terms of role and communal context. A person's accent, for example, is generally not a relevant feature of their personhood. And this entails that one's accent can change while one remains the same person.[26] For those features central to personhood, however, when these features all obtain, every person constituted by those features exist in embedded state. There are still of course a number of difficulties

---

[26] Notice, however, that one's social context can only change in a very limited sense consistent with sameness of personhood. An accent may change because of changed social context, in which case there may indeed be a break in personhood.

faced by this view. How, for example, do we make sense of the continued existence of person P through time independently of person P* if the constitutive features of P can at any time be the same as the constitutive features of P*? It should be the case, we might think, that P and P* should then *always* be identical, rather than only at certain times when P is substituting P*. The view of discussed above, that a person who can substitute another always has the *potential* to be identical with the substituted person even in the lack of actualized identity, might go some way in responding to this worry, but absent an adequate account of potentiality and actuality in connection with this, the problem remains outstanding. This, of course, is not a demerit of Maya views of personhood. Every theory of personal identity has its difficulties, and the ongoing job of philosophers is to try to resolve these difficulties, or alternatively to try to show that they are irresolvable.

Further Reading

For more on personhood, the self, and identity in Mesoamerica see Houston, Stuart, and Taube, *The Memory of Bones*; Hinojosa, *In This Body: Kaqchikel Maya and the Grounding of Spirit*; Scherer, *Mortuary Landscapes of the Classic Maya: Rituals of Body and Soul*; Furst, *The Natural History of the Soul in Ancient Mexico*. Full publication details for all of these works can be found in the bibliography.

5   Creation and the Gods

Creation Stories and the Nature of Being

In most philosophical traditions across the globe, the issue of creation is at the heart of understanding the nature of the cosmos. What is the fundamental structure of the cosmos? In order to answer this question, we also have to know how things come to be, and how are they maintained in existence. All of these questions are at the core of metaphysics in philosophical traditions across the globe, including Mesoamerican traditions.

The fundamental nature of the cosmos and its maintenance are central issues in Mesoamerican philosophy. The correlative metaphysical systems of Mesoamerica, with their focus on interdependence, transformation, and continual creation, rely on particular views about the nature of the world and its operation that we look at in this chapter. We look here at the development of key concepts connected to creation and change, as well as to the particular ways these are developed in creation stories across Mesoamerica. Creation stories serve an important purpose in Mesoamerican thought. They should be thought of not as *only* myth grounding the overall tradition and system, but also as discussions of the nature of being, change, and continual creation.

One of the fundamental differences between Mesoamerican creation stories and those found in some other traditions, such as Abrahamic traditions for example, is that Mesoamerican accounts are not primarily historical in nature, but rather offer explanation of ongoing change. Mesoamerican creation accounts give us accounts of the unfolding structure of nature that double with origin stories. Unlike other origin stories, however, they are not contained in an original past – rather, they explain (through symbolic language) how processes of change happen presently and continually, every time. The creation stories then are metaphysical explorations rather than only accounts of the origins of the world. Numerous scholars have pointed out that in the wide array of Mesoamerican accounts of creation, we do not find anything like *creation ex nihilo*, but rather we find the notion of creation of shaping through transformation.[1] This is a theme we will see throughout this section concerning creation – it is linked with transformation, and is something that is ongoing. There is no original point or time of creation in Mesoamerican accounts, rather there is a stress on the ways in which creation is ongoing. The process of constructing and engendering the cosmos continually unfolds, and requires the cooperation of nature, the gods, and humanity. Thus, we cannot take for granted the existence of the cosmos as such, the orderly and structured world within which we move and change, as this world requires maintenance to continue. Observation of our world shows the connection between creation and regeneration. Our creation of artifacts happens through the reshaping and transformation of preexistent things in the world. New concepts and organizations are placed on parts of the world that always existed. If we think about things like computers, for example – all of the material in the world that goes into making up the computers we use today was also in the world 1000 years ago, it is just that 1000 years ago humans did not have the knowledge and ability to shape these things from those materials. We've brought no new material into the world, we've simply reshaped what was already here. Everything in the computer I used to type this, the computer you may be using to read it, was here on Earth 1000 years ago, a million years ago. Creation of this computer, and the idea of computers in general, is *transformation*. Another key example of creation available to us (and one of the most basic) is procreation. Both in the case of creation of new humans, and our observation of renewed creation in the world – procreation of animals, the growth of new plants, etc. In all of these cases, there is generation of a new organism from the old – a transformation of the body of one organism to create another, its duplicate. We recognize this in the human case not only because new humans literally come from the bodies of former humans, but in the offspring we recognize the features of the parents and ancestors. This is clearly a transformation of what is there – a combination and

---

[1] Oswaldo Chinchilla Mazariegos, *Art and Myth of the Ancient Maya*, 54.

a blending into something new through reorganization of the parts of the old. Continued identity is understood in terms of continuation and transshipment of essence through change. Creation, in Mesoamerican traditions, is ongoing, assistive, and facilitated through conceptualization and other forms of human activity.

As we see in Aztec views of creation, this leads to a fundamental concern with ritual – the rituals need to be kept on, or there is a danger of the collapse of the cosmos as such. Thus, we see that the concept of ritual takes on an enormous importance. We find in Mesoamerican traditions a recognition of the key role that ritual plays in shaping our world and creating the basic conditions of the cosmos we experience. Humans are not separate observers of an already constructed cosmos. Rather, we play an active role in its construction and maintenance, and the tool we use for this creative activity is ritual. Because we often fail to recognize the significance of ritual in the modern world, we often allow our processes of ritual to be guided by individuals, institutions, and cultural patterns that do not have our thriving as their aim, such as corporate institutions driven by profit generation. Humans are always engaged in ritual, consciously or not, and we gain our rituals from our cultural background, from the patterns with which we are raised and learn to experience the world. We can reflect on our rituals, we can choose them or endorse them or change them, but they can also become part of our lives that become automatic and unconscious, such that we engage in them unreflectively and mechanically. Often in the modern world, we don't even realize what the rituals we follow are or why we follow them – largely because we have abandoned the consideration of ritual and its place in human life. We have largely abandoned a truth that the Mesoamerican traditions understood well, that ritual shapes our world and our experience. As we will see, ritual is a central aspect of creation stories in Mesoamerica.

Ritual performance in precolonial Mesoamerica often surrounded the enactment of accounts of creation. The *Popol Vuh*, one of the most important complete texts we have on the topic, is *wholly* about creation. The centrality of creation and origin stories in Mesoamerica is in part connected to the notion of the legitimization of and ritual coherence of the community – similar to what we find in a number of other traditions – although in the *Popol Vuh,* the story of the origins of the K'iche' people is contained in the back half of the text, with the vast majority of the text devoted to creation more generally.

Mesoamerican creation stories differ in their focus, and some of the same elements can be found across the stories, but one common feature of these stories is the focus on the cyclicality and continuity of creation. There are many versions of creation stories throughout Mesoamerica, both across and within traditions. Roughly shared versions of creation stories were performed and told across Mesoamerica, with a number of versions making it into text. While well-known versions such as that of the K'iche' Maya *Popol Vuh* or the Aztec codices are most commonly associated with Mesoamerican views, these stories should not be taken as orthodox or definitive, but rather as representative of a larger variety of Maya and Aztec *types* of creation stories. What is fortunate in our situation with the *Popol Vuh* and the Aztec codices' accounts is that in these we have complete textual accounts that give us a coherent structure to study. There are, however, oral traditions and other sources of creation stories that should not be neglected. In the overview of creation accounts and their philosophical significance in this chapter, while I use the well-known textual accounts as frameworks, I also occasionally refer to other creation accounts outside of these texts. This is particularly important given the nature of our most common sources. The texts written down by Spanish missionaries, while we know they are in many ways faithful to the original versions they document, sometimes clearly diverge from native accounts. This happens to greater or lesser extent across texts. Of course, this problem does not disappear when we use oral tradition from contemporary sources or consult precolonial text and imagery. This is because contemporary oral tradition is influenced by the same material we read documented by Spanish figures, and the changes and biases they may have had have also influenced the ways contemporary people of Mesoamerica understand these traditions. Also – the precolonial glyphic texts (particularly in the case of the Aztec, Mixtec, and Zapotec material, but also to some extent for the Maya) do not always determine a specific reading, thus we must rely on later texts such as the Spanish rendering of performances and oral tradition in Latin script, as well as oral tradition documented by ethnographers.

Popol Vuh and Other Accounts of Creation

Probably the most robust and organized creation story we have in textual form from all of the Mesoamerican traditions is the K'iche' Maya text *Popol Vuh*. This text gives an in-depth account of creation, from the first work of the gods to the origins of the K'iche people. The earliest written version we have dates to 1701, based on earlier versions. The earliest extant written version is the text of the Dominican priest Francisco Ximénez, who produced a volume including the K'iche rendered in Latin script, as well as Spanish translation. It is unclear (and a matter of ongoing scholarly debate) whether Ximénez relied on an earlier K'iche written version or whether he was the first to render the K'iche' *Popol Vuh* in Latin script directly from oral sources. Regardless, the *Popol Vuh* certainly documents the K'iche' performance as it was in the seventeenth century, with roots in earlier versions.

We know that the *Popol Vuh* account contains at least some information from the sixteenth century after the arrival of the Spanish, as Christianity is referred to numerous times, and there are some passages that seem to demonstrate Christian influence. The nature of this Christian influence on the text, however, has sometimes been overstated. Allen Christenson points out that we do not find *direct* Christian influence in the text, even though the way some of the stories are structured and interpreted demonstrate parallels.[2] This is clearly not a text meant to render Christian ideas in a Maya guise, or containing fabricated ideas inserted by Ximénez or some other Spanish source.

Many of the stories in the *Popol Vuh* correspond to imagery and texts from the precolonial period, although we have no complete glyphic account of the text in the way it is rendered in the modern K'iche' version. The central stories and themes of the *Popol Vuh* – the creation of humanity from maize, the travails of the hero twins Hunahpu and Xbalanque, the theme of sacrifice and rebirth – we find these in Classic and Postclassic Period imagery.[3] The fleshed-out account we find in the *Popol Vuh* gives

---

[2] Christenson, *Popol Vuh*, 24–25.

[3] The Classic Period equivalents One Ajaw and Yax Bolon are depicted on a number of Classic Period vases, for example. Bassie-Sweet and Hopkins, "The Family of Ancient Creator Deities," 111.

us context for these early images, and ties them together into a coherent whole. This whole should not be understood, as pointed out above, as the *only* account of these stories given in Maya history – like aspects of language, these stories had a family resemblance but could vary sometimes quite radically from one region or traditional version to another.

The creation story of the *Popol Vuh* hits on all of the major philosophical topics covered in this book and seen as central in Mesoamerican traditions. In the account here, I focus on the connection between creation and the nature of the cosmos, as other philosophical issues connected to the text are discussed in other chapters. Creation, as such, is perhaps the central theme of the *Popol Vuh*, to which all other philosophical issues are connected. When the *Popol Vuh* discusses any philosophical issue, it is always connected to creation and the nature of the cosmos. This nature is fundamentally linked to change, to growth and decay, and to becoming rather than static being. A key feature of Mesoamerican views of creation, and that offered in the *Popol Vuh*, is that creation is continual – a process of construction, transformation, and decay, rather than something relegated to an origin point in the past. The process of creation is continuous with and requires that of change. Mesoamerican traditions recognized the extent to which creation happens always and continually within an already existing cosmos of other changing things. A new human being, a new plant, a new home, ritual, or nation – all begin in the context of a wider cosmos that is itself continuously changing. Precolonial Maya astronomy was one of the most developed systems in the world – the Maya astronomical almanacs, such as the extant Dresden Codex, chart the planetary movements, so precisely that they recognized the cycles of Venus in its morning and evening appearances, and a number of other planetary patterns. Even this most seemingly changeless aspect of the world, undergoes changes, though on a scale broader than those in which we live as individuals and communities. Maya thinkers recognized this. Creation, insofar as it requires cooperative effort between humanity and the gods/nature, also requires understanding of the fundamental changes and patterns of change happening in the world.

The *Popol Vuh* is a difficult text to summarize, as its imagery and the incidents discussed in it are so enormous in scope. The text begins with an account of the ordering of the cosmos by the early gods, who are shown already in existence and collaborating with one another to bring about or refashion the cosmos. In their creation, they attempt to fashion humans, to worship them and keep their memory, but the gods continually fail to create adequate beings. They engage in a number of rounds of creation, including the creation of nonhuman animals and the creation of effigies of wood, but in each case these beings fail to have the ability to carry out the most important of tasks the creator gods intend them to perform. At this point, before the story of the origin of humanity continues much later in the text, the story shifts to discussion of the origins of many other aspects of the world. Behind each of these, most connected with astronomical objects, there are a host of created characters – most centrally the famous Hero Twins, Hunahpu and Xbalanque, who descend to the underworld, Xibalba, ultimately defeat the lords of death through their own sacrifice and rebirth, and ascend to the heavens as the sun and moon. After this, the narrative returns to the origin of humanity, with the gods' successful attempt to create beings to keep their days, constructing them from maize (the staple food crop of Mesoamerica). After this creation, the text then tells the story of the origin of the K'iche' people, from the first place of Tulan, the breaking apart of nations, and a migration from this Tulan to the current homeland of the K'iche' (in modern day Guatemala).

We find accounts of creation in the Yucatec *Chilam Balam* books as well. Chapter 10 of the *Chilam Balam of Chumayel* gives an account of the creation of the cosmos[4], linked with the date K'atun 11 Ajaw – another sign that the creation these texts discuss is something ongoing in a perpetually changing cosmos, rather than a point at which things come to be *ex*

---

[4] The account of the *Chumayel*, as is common in colonial period Mesoamerican texts, begins with a caveat that all of the views discussed should be abandoned in exchange for Christianity. Unlike the integration of Christianity in texts such as the Aztec *Florentine Codex*, however, which is much more antagonistic to native religion, the position in this portion of the *Chumayel* takes the older views as a kind of first stage, which has been eclipsed by Christianity. The old gods, according to the text, were once effective, but because these gods were "perishable," they were temporary, and Christ's resurrection superseded these old gods. The text reads: "…[T]he first gods were perishable gods. Their worship came to its inevitable end. They lost their efficacy by the benediction of the Lord of Heaven, after the redemption of the world was accomplished, after the resurrection of the true God, the true Dios, when he blessed heaven and earth." *Chilam Balam of Chumayel*, Roys trans., 50.

nihilo. Creation happens within an already established and already chang-ing backdrop of time.[5] As we see in numerous other Mesoamerican texts, in this account of the *Chumayel*, the creation of the world begins with the destruction of a previous world.

> ...the green tree of abundance was set up in the center of the world as a record of the destruction of the world. [...] The world was not lighted; there was neither day nor night nor moon. Then they perceived that the world was being created. Then creation dawned upon the world. During the creation thirteen infinite series added to seven was the count of the creation of the world. Then a new world dawned for them.[6]

A number of Aztec texts recount creation stories as well. The *Florentine Codex* is one of the best-known accounts of Aztec thought at the beginning of the colonial period. In the mid to late sixteenth century, in the early years of contact between Mesoamerica and the Spanish, the Franciscan priest Bernardino de Sahagun (1499–1590) compiled, with the help of native Nahua students, an account of Aztec history, belief, and society that he called *Historia general de las cosas de la Nueva España*, better known today as the *Florentine Codex*. It is here we gain much of our knowledge of precolonial Aztec views, as the text was written over 50 years during the earliest part of Spanish involvement in Mesoamerica, with cultural diffu-sion still happening.

The *Florentine Codex* is a massive encyclopedia-like text of Aztec cul-ture, and was produced in 12 volumes, on different aspects of Aztec cul-ture from accounts of the gods and creation to daily practices and rituals. The primary volumes dealing with creation are Book Three, on the ori-gin of the gods, and Book Seven, on the sun and moon, with parts of the numerous other volumes also informative. In Book Three, we see an origin account of the gods and humanity most similar to the structure seen in the *Popol Vuh*, suggesting a shared origin story through the wider Mesoamerican region. In this book, we see an account of the origins, after

---

[5] This view of creation is Plato's account of creation as requiring preexisting material and is certainly not limited to the Mesoamerican traditions. In the *Timaeus* of Plato, for example, the world is understood as being created from a pre-existent chaos by the Demiurge.

[6] *Chilam Balam of Chumayel*, Roys trans., 52.

which follows a story of the human emergence from and movement out of Tula/Tollan, the mythical or semi-mythical origin place discussed in a number of different Mesoamerican origin stories, including this one and that of the *Popol Vuh*.[7] In other texts, we find accounts of an "Aztlan" from which the Nahua people emerge – this is the origin of the most well-known name associated with this group: "Aztec," "the people of Aztlan." This name was not used by the Nahua themselves, who instead used "Mexica" (although the Mexica were just one of the numerous Nahua groups in the region).

One interesting feature we see of many of the colonial accounts of early Mesoamerican origin stories, particularly those written in native languages in Latin script, is their often stated rejection of the truth or value of the old stories and the old gods, along with endorsements of Christianity. Perhaps the exception to this is the *Popol Vuh*, in which we find mention of Christianity without the kind of pro-Christian rejection of earlier Maya religion that we see in other sources, such as the *Chilam Balam of Chumayel*, which instructs its Maya readers to "turn your hearts away from your old religion."[8] Some of the colonial period texts were compiled by Spanish missionaries, such as the *Florentine Codex* of Bernardino de Sahagún, and it is thus not surprising that we find this evangelistic message in parts of that text. In other cases, it is unclear who is responsible for the Christian messages oppositional to native thought. In some of these cases, it could be done for purposes of throwing Spanish authorities off the scent. The Spanish had the goal of Christianizing Mesoamerica and eliminating traditional religion. The authors of texts such as the *Chilam Balam* texts would have been educated at least to some extent in Spanish methods, as these texts are in native languages rendered in Latin script. Whether or not they held to the view of the superiority of Christianity and the need to do away with older religious practices cannot be known. The fact that they wrote down all of this precolonial knowledge suggests that they actually did

---

[7] The origin city referred to in these texts is not likely to be the site today known as Tula, in central Mexico. It may be a hybrid, an idealized reference to earlier cities, or a reference to Teotihuacan, which had a major influence on the wider Mesoamerican region in the Preclassic Period. See Kowalski and Kristan-Graham, *Twin Tollans*, 24.

[8] *Chilam Balam of Chumayel*, Roys trans., 51.

think it was important and, despite the claims, that they didn't want this knowledge to disappear.

Other texts dealing with creation from this region include a number of pictorial texts from the beginning of the colonial period or just before, such as the text known as the "Selden Roll," the Codex Mexicanus, and the Codex Boturini, as well as translated texts such as the Codex Magliabechiano, a copy of an earlier Aztec glyphic text, with Spanish accompanying text. In almost all of these texts, origin stories and accounts of the history and development of a particular people (whether K'iche', Aztec, or Mixtec) is connected with the work of the gods, and the history of these gods. The origins of the gods, time, humanity, and other aspects of the cosmos are interrelated, and these originate through time as the unfolding of continual creation (which can be made visible or accessible through ritual).

A Means for Seeing

An account of creation, then, is not a historical account of some bygone time, but an account of a continually unfolding process that goes on in nature even as we encounter the story of the text. The K'iche' Maya *Popol Vuh* is understood in this way. This is why the authors refer to the text as a tool for seeing (*ilb'al*). The *Popol Vuh* refers to itself numerous times in the text – in discussing the nature of the text, *Popol Vuh* is understood as something used to see the nature of reality, truths about life and the world, and their continual creation. A passage from the opening of the text reads:

> *Xchiqelesaj, rumal maja b'i chik ilb'al re Popo Wuj, ilb'al saq petenaq ch'aqa palo, u tzijoxik qa mujib'al, ilb'al saq k'aslem, chuchaxik.*

> We bring it forth because there is no way to see the *Popol Vuh*. The way of seeing clearly that came from across the sea, the account of our obscurity, and the means of seeing life clearly, it is said.[9]

Likewise, the final passage at the closing of the text stresses the issue of seeing (*ilb'al*), and how the written text, in this case, is the only remaining

---

[9] *Popol Vuh*, Christenson trans., modified.

means to see the continual creation recounted in the *Popol Vuh* and the origins of the K'iche' people:

> *Xere k'ut u k'oje'ik K'iche'. Ri' rumal maja b'i chi ilb'al re. K'o nab'e ojer kumal ajawab'. Sachinaq chik.*

> This is now the being of the K'iche', because there is no longer a way to see it. It was with the lords at first, but now it is lost.[10]

The seeing (*ilb'al*) discussed here is connected to a number of different things. First, the *Popol Vuh* itself is something that can be (or rather in the past could be) seen. The author here says there is no longer a way to see the *Popol Vuh* because originally it was not a text in this sense at all, but rather a ritual performance. This performance is intimately connected to the other sense in which seeing is connected to the *Popol Vuh*. It is a means of seeing clearly particularly because it reenacts, or rather enacts in real time, the act and process of continual creation. While the Ximénez manuscript is the earliest extant version of *Popol Vuh*, there were doubtlessly earlier written versions, including precolonial written versions in Maya glyphic script. Despite this, the *Popol Vuh* the author here refers to is not the written text in either the current Latin script or the earlier glyphic versions, but rather the *performance* of the *Popol Vuh* as a living ritual. One way to understand this is to think about the distinction between a book intended purely for reading, such as a novel or a book of philosophy such as this one, and something like the script of a play or film, or even better the libretto of an opera. Both kinds of text can be read, but in the case of the latter, the written text is more like a blueprint or a guide for something else. The novel or the philosophy book *is* the written text one can hold. The play or the opera, however, is the performance, and the written text is a guide to the performance – instruction for the performers, and an assistance for the viewers.

The *Popol Vuh* discussed here, which can no longer be seen, is the performance itself, rather than the textual guide. The *Popol Vuh*, like other important ritual texts, was performed. In its performance, meaning was imparted through enactment of the events of creation. This should not be understood as *reenactment* in terms of the duplication of some event in

---

[10] *Popol Vuh*, Christenson trans., modified.

the past, as when a group reenacts a famous historical battle – but instead as a direct representation of the ongoing process of creation continually unfolding in the world. The *Popol Vuh* itself is thus a means for seeing more clearly this process of creation. The first passage above expresses this, that the *Popol Vuh* is "the means of seeing life clearly." Features of the world not generally visible to people in our daily lives become visible through the performance of these acts of creation by ritual performers. When these performers take on the role of gods and other characters in the *Popol Vuh*, they are not, like actors, merely imitating these gods, but literally *becoming* them, in an act of "substitution" (*k'ex*). Contemporary Maya ritual and practice bear this out, as we find this understanding of ritual still in the Maya region. Particular individuals can perform rituals that serve as means for seeing the gods and otherwise invisible aspects of the continual creative process of the world. Allen Christenson recounts a ritual he observed in Guatemala:

> In Santiago Atitlán, a priest extracts certain garments that once belonged to the ancestors and wears them as he dances to the four cardinal directions to recreate the limits of the cosmos. Following the performance of this dance in 1998, the priest sought me out to ask if I had seen "the ancient nuwals [revered, powerful ancestors] giving birth to the world." He explained that they had filled his soul with their presence as he danced, guiding him in his steps, and now everything was new again. In the eyes of the priest, the dance was not a symbol of the ancestral dance, but a genuine creative act in which time folded inward on itself to reveal the ancestors themselves.[11]

The *Popol Vuh* and other such performed rituals, then, are means for seeing in the sense that in their performance, we witness the creation of the world. The creation of the world, then, is something ongoing but otherwise unseen. The *Popol Vuh* discusses how humans lost the ability to see this unfolding creation of the world, through angering the gods with their complete knowledge and vision of the world. The texts says: "[T]heir knowledge of everything that they saw was complete – the four corners and the four sides, that which is within the sky and that which is within

---

[11] Christenson, *Art and Society in a Highland Maya Community*, 24.

the earth."[12] The Framer and Shaper were upset by this omniscience of the humans they had created, as it put them alongside the gods, and thus the gods took away from humans this ability to see clearly, and left them with the ability to see only what was right in front of them. This was achieved through a blinding, a dimming of vision, to use the imagery of the text. The text connects this to operation of the gods on the human "essence" (k'oje'ik). The essence of humans became such that there were many aspects of the world that we could not see. Yet through certain ritual, and particular kinds of people, we can secondarily access some of these aspects of the world, in much the same way we gain the ability to see distant objects using a telescope, or features of things too small to see, with the aid of a microscope.

The theme of vision in creation can be found throughout Mesoamerican creation literature and related imagery. Seeing was associated not only with special kind of consciousness, but with creative agency, in terms of its efficacy on transformation of things. The *Florentine Codex* calls the eye "the mirror, instrument for seeing, that by which all live" (*totezcauh, tlachialoni, nemoani*)[13]

Notice also from the above quote that the focus on not only substitution, but *renewal*. A common theme of the *Popol Vuh* is the continual renewal of the world through the unfolding creative process. This continual and cyclic process of creation can be found in numerous Maya texts and traditions. Stories of creation in the Maya region and throughout Mesoamerica often begin not with a *creation*, but with a *destruction*. The Yucatec Maya *Chilam Balam* texts recount such creations. In the *Chilam Balam of Chumayel*, the origins of the well-known Maya "world tree" are in an initial destruction by the gods:

> Then the sky would fall, it would fall down upon the earth, when the four gods, the four Bacabs, were set up, who brought about the destruction of the world. Then, after the destruction of the world was completed, they placed a tree... [...] Then the green tree of abundance was set up in the center of the world as a record of the destruction of the world.[14]

---

[12] *Popol Vuh*, Christenson trans., 185.
[13] *Florentine Codex*, Book 10, Dibble and Anderson, 103.
[14] *Chilam Balam of Chumayel*, Roys trans., 51.

After this destruction, the gods create anew, bringing about the ordered world as we know it. This also happened *in time*, with the date K'atun 11 Ajaw given as the time of this initial destruction. Here, we find a clear conception of the creative process as something happening within an ongoing cosmos. Creation is fundamentally a *reorganization*, a transshipment of essence from one thing to another. As Stephen Houston writes, in discussing substitution (*k'ex*) as "cyclic replacement": "Truly new things may not exist; their essence could be transshipped, however."[15]

At the beginning of the *Popol Vuh*, we find the gods *Tzaq'ol* and *B'itol*, (Framer and Shaper), along with a host of other gods, including others whose names are connected to renewed birth and creation, including the Xpiyakok and Xmuqane, who are described as *I'yom* and *Mamom* (which Christenson translates as "midwife" and "patriarch"), and "Protector" and "Shelterer." The Framer and Shaper along with the other gods formed the conditions for the arising of humanity, which is also discussed in the text as if it already existed prior to its "creation" by the gods. All of this happens very much *in medias res*, despite the seemingly Christian influences of certain early parts of the *Popol Vuh*. An example of this influence is the creation of the Earth from the "word" (*tzij*), an idea that does not seem to correspond with precolonial Maya text and imagery. The identity and work of the Framer and Shaper demonstrate a link between creation and transformation. The work of framing and shaping is to modify what is there, rather than to bring completely new things into being. The stuff of the cosmos can be shaped and reshaped, taken apart and put together in new ways. This can happen in terms of physical construction as well as in terms of conceptualization. Not only can the same physical stuff be divided and combined in new ways to create new things, but the same physical stuff can be conceptualized in new ways to create new things, just as when we use a stone for grinding spices and it becomes a pestle.

The account of the creation or beginning of the gods themselves in the Aztec *Florentine Codex* also presumes the prior existence of the cosmos, and an unknown period or situation prior to the beginning of the relevant gods, who appear to have created themselves or at least arisen from a transformation of earlier gods. The text associates the origins of the gods with

---

[15] Houston, *The Life Within*, 72.

the city of Teotihuacan, and, like the Maya texts, associates their beginning with an original destruction. Creation here begins in destruction, the transformation of some prior thing. The death of the gods allowed for the rebirth of a new sun – following a general theme connecting creation to rebirth and renewal. A key passage of the *Florentine Codex* reads:

> How the gods had their beginning, where they had their beginning, cannot be known. This is plain: that there in Teotihuacan, they say, is the place; the time was when there still was darkness. There all the gods assembled and consulted among themselves who would bear upon his back the burden of rule, who would be the sun. (This has already been told in various places.) But when the sun came to appear, then all the gods died there. Through them the sun was made to revive. None remained who did not die (as has been told). And thus the ancient ones taught it.[16]

The sacrifice and destruction of the gods here is seen as a necessary part of the coming to be of the sun, and thereby the conditions for the cosmos, in a continuing unfolding cycle. Note the connection here to vision and knowing (which we will look at much more closely in Chapter 7). Humans cannot fully know the origins of the gods, and must rely on what figures of the past said and what can be gleaned from the understanding of those who have special access to particular truths about the world through their unique vision (the shamanic vision as discussed below). The time before this beginning we can comprehend was in "darkness," a place that cannot be seen. Maya and Aztec imagery focuses on the extension of seeing through ritual or the abilities of certain people. Sight is connected to distance and clarity.

Seeing is associated not only with creation in Mesoamerican texts, but also with destruction, as the two are inextricably linked. As we see the creation stories in numerous traditions begin with a primordial destruction, Maya and Aztec imagery also associates sight with the dead. In the Maya *Dresden Codex*, one of the five remaining Maya codices, we find images of the god of death surrounded by eyeballs, each with the power of vision, as marked by the lines emanating from the eyeballs.

Houston, Stuart, and Taube point out a number of connections between sight and creation in Maya texts and imagery. The images of vision in the

[16] *Florentine Codex* Book 3, Dibble and Anderson trans., 1.

Dresden Codex, they point out, share similarity with words for birth, and the idea of "projection" from the body. They suggest that to have sight is to be a "co-creator," in the sense we have seen in texts such as the *Popol Vuh*, in which humans help the gods to establish the cosmos through the keeping of days. They write:

> What is crucial here is that the eye is *procreative*. It not only receives images from the outer world, but positively affects and changes that world through the power of sight—in short, it behaves as an "emanating eye" that establishes communion between internal will and external result. For example, among the Yucatec Maya, ethnography tells us that sight had an "agentive quality" through "willful acts."[17]

The text, creation story, and ritual performance as *means of seeing*, then, is also the means for creation itself, and the human participation in and co-creation of the cosmos.

Sacrifice, Destruction, and Creation/Rebirth

Performances of ritual reveal the unfolding of continual creation because they are *part* of continual creation. This explains also why certain ritual performances were seen as socially fundamental and necessary for the maintenance of the cosmos as such. Aztec forms of such ritual are well known (if often misunderstood). The ritual of human sacrifice (as well as autosacrificial bloodletting) was connected to the need to continually assist the unfolding creative process that maintains the cosmos. The key here was in the power associated with blood, which was seen as holding the sacred "essence" that enabled the abilities of humanity (*chalchiuatl* in Nahuatl).

The *Codex Chimalpopoca* account of sacrifice associates it with creation, describing the autosacrificial act of Quetzalcoatl, which itself generated new creation. An account reads:

> And as soon as he [Quetzalcoatl] was dressed, he set himself on fire and cremated himself. And so the place where Quetzalcoatl was cremated is named Tlatlayan [land of burning], And they say as he burned, his ashes

---

[17] Houston, Stuart, and Taube, *The Memory of Bones*, 167.

arose. And what appeared and what they saw were all the precious birds, rising into the sky. They saw roseate spoonbills, cotingas, trogons, herons, green parrots, scarlet macaws, white-fronted parrots, and all the other precious birds. And as soon as his ashes had been consumed, they saw the heart of a quetzal rising upward. And so they knew he had gone to the sky, had entered the sky. The old people said he was changed into the star that appears at dawn. Therefore they say it came forth when Quetzalcoatl died, and they called him Lord of the Dawn.[18]

Although it offers this positive view of sacrifice and rebirth (a common theme in Mesoamerican texts), we also find in the same text a negative view of the kind of human sacrifice often associated with the Aztec, claiming that "the first Quetzalcoatl" (a god and semi-divine culture hero who made different appearances through history) disapproved of the practice, and it was only with later corrupted rulers that the "devils" started and perpetuated this practice.[19] While there may be some aspect of Spanish revulsion of the practice represented here through influence, we can see that Aztec views of this form of sacrifice were complex. Certainly the most common form of blood sacrifice, both in Aztec and Maya contexts, was the autosacrificial bloodletting ceremony, in which a ruler, nobles, or other important members of society would draw their own blood as a way of contributing to the renewal of society and the world. The same thing may have happened in the Mesoamerican context as happened in that of early China – the practice of burial of servants with a deceased ruler was mainly stopped as it was seen as unsavory and cruel, and the servants began to be replaced by replicas, such as the famous "Terracotta Warriors" of the tomb of the first emperor of Qin at Xi'an. There is evidence that the kind of human sacrifice most associated with the Aztecs, who have the most infamous reputation for it, was less prominent in other parts of precolonial Mesoamerica where it existed.

As we saw above in the origin of the gods passage from the *Florentine Codex*, the destruction and sacrifice of the gods was seen as necessary for the creation of the sun. The maintenance of the this world, in the Aztec tradition, required the continual sacrifice of individuals in society, in mirroring

[18] Bierhorst trans., 36.
[19] Bierhorst trans., 40–41.

of the act of the gods. Blood sacrifice, most often autosacrificial drawing of one's blood through piercing of key body parts such as the penis and tongue, was just one of the forms of sacrificial offering aimed to ensure the continual creation of the cosmos. Sacrificial offerings of other precious goods such as flowers and resin, through burning, as well as ritual performances such as the "reenactment" of creation of the *Popol Vuh*, were intended to have this effect. Creation, as we have seen, was closely linked to transformation, ritual, and the maintenance of the cosmos. Creation was not a single specific act, but an ongoing communal process requiring effort and sacrifice on the part of all, but particularly on the part of those leading the community – rulers, priests, and nobles.

A common theme of Mesoamerican texts on creation is the link between generation and the decay of some former thing. In origin stories, this usually involves some form of willful sacrifice on the part of heroic characters, pointing again to the central human role in generation of the cosmos. The creative human role is also a sacrificial human role – not only in the sense of the ritual execution that has received intense attention in the West from colonial times onward – but also (and more importantly) in the sense of offering aspects of oneself, from one's strength, time, and movement to one's life itself at the limit, to ensure the continual creation of the cosmos and thus the continuation of the community We will see more on this point in the final chapter of this book.

Principle of Dual Creation

Generation and decay, sacrifice and rebirth – these are examples of a very common metaphysical principle found throughout Mesoamerican philosophy – the *principle of dual creation*. Creation and change cannot happen from the activity of one thing alone. Every transformation (and creation is fundamentally a transformation, as discussed above) requires a dual source. The feature of duality in general is central to Mesoamerican thought, particularly with respect to creation and origins. In the *Popol Vuh*, we find a variety of dual gods and heroes associated with origins. The "Framer and Shaper" of the beginning of the text are the most basic creative forces among the gods. The "original" creation, according to the text, is a refashioning of things, a renewal of the old. Any point of creation can then be understood in this way – the reconstitution of things as a cooperation between two interacting entities. This is why at the very beginning of the *Popol Vuh*, a litany of god pairs are discussed, with these preexisting pairs responsible for the creation of all things as they are. The text instructs us that "[the god pairs] gave voice to all things and accomplished their purpose in purity of being and truth."[20]

The two sets of hero twins at the center of the most prominent stories of the *Popol Vuh*, Hunahpu and Xbalanque, and their dual fathers One Hunahpu and Seven Hunahpu, also show us the duality of creation. The creative activity of One and Seven Hunahpu is primarily in bringing about the later set of hero twins. While the mother of the hero twins Hunahpu and Xbalanque is a single woman of Xibalba, they have essentially two fathers. The specific activity of their generation was done by the head of One Hunahpu, but as the text points out, One Hunahpu and Seven Hunahpu at that point are of one mind, and thus are identical. The head of One Hunahpu serves as both representation of One Hunahpu and the substitution of Seven Hunahpu. Early in the story of One and Seven Hunahpu, Seven Hunahpu is referred to as "secondary" and playing a merely supportive role. The duality here is not one of equality. One Hunahpu is the dominant, visible, and active element, while Seven Hunahpu is the recessive, invisible, placid. It is worth noting here that a number of other traditions have taken such principles to be necessary for change – a combination of an active and a passive principle. The *yin* and *yang* of the Chinese tradition, for example, is understood in just this way. In the *Popol Vuh*, these features are expressed in roles of the characters representative of these principles. While One Hunahpu is married and has his own (two) children, the text explains: "Seven Hunahpu had no wife. He was merely a companion, merely secondary. By his nature, he was like a servant to One Hunahpu. They were great thinkers, for great was their knowledge. They were seers here upon the face of the earth."[21]

The lords of the underworld, Xibalba, who come to oppose the hero twins and represent a kind of constructive antagonist in the text, are also understood dualistically, named One Death and Seven Death. The

---

[20] *Popol Vuh*, Christenson trans., 53.
[21] *Popol Vuh*, Christenson trans., 99–100.

numbers one and seven here, in the case of Hunahpu (one ruler) and death, are connected to origination. One and Seven Death along with the other god pairs of Xibalba set out to defeat the hero twins, in response to the vitality of their activity. The twins engage in the famous Mesoamerican ballgame, likely a symbol of life and human activity, which angers the lords of Xibalba. We see the struggle established between life, growth, and vitality on one hand, and death, decay, and destruction on the other. This fundamental opposition is established in the conflict between the original heroes, One and Seven Hunahpu, and the original "villains," One and Seven Death. As the *Popol Vuh* goes on to demonstrate, however, understanding these opposed pairs purely in terms of protagonist and antagonist would be incorrect. The lords of Xibalba turn out to be necessary to the development and transformation of the hero twins, even through their sacrifice and rebirth. One and Seven Hunahpu are summoned to Xibalba by its lords, and are sacrificed by the lords of death, who behead One Hunahpu and place his head in a calabash tree, where it returns to life to impregnate a woman from Xibalba with the hero twins Hunahpu and Xbalanque.

In this discussion of sacrifice and rebirth, decay and regeneration, we see a view emerge of immortality in the Maya tradition. The immortality suggested in the *Popol Vuh* is not a kind of persistence of the individual and separate self, but rather a continuation through substitution, through the sense in which an individual is manifest in that which they help to bring about. Having foresight, One and Seven Hunahpu recognize they must go to Xibalba when they are summoned (which means they will ultimately be killed). Their mother cries for them as they prepare to leave, and One and Seven Hunahpu respond: "[W]e must go, but we will not die. Do not grieve."[22] This statement of deathlessness can be understood in a few different ways. Given the survival of the head of One Hunahpu in the calabash tree, there is in some sense a continuation. But more importantly (and this is likely the central allusion here), One and Seven Hunahpu attain deathlessness by their continuation in the second set of hero twins they bring about. The new hero twins are referred to as "substitutes" of their dual father. The mother of the twins, before their birth, explains: "These that I am carrying belong to One Hunahpu. One Hunahpu and Seven Hunahpu

---

[22] *Popol Vuh*, Christenson trans., 106.

are alive. They are not dead. That which they have done is merely a man-ifestation of their light ... Thus you shall see it. You shall see his face in these that I am carrying."[23]

In the creation and activity of the second set of hero twins, we also see the principle of dual creation at work[24]. In many ways mirroring their dual father, Hunahpu and Xbalanque are likewise summoned to Xibalba, where the lords of death attempt to defeat the twins. This time, the twins defeat the lords of death through a number of tricks, and finally overcome them completely through the ultimate act of sacrifice and rebirth. The twins sacrifice themselves in Xibalba by willingly entering into a fire pre-pared for them in an oven (we can see similarities here to the Aztec story of the origin of the fifth sun with the self-immolation of Nanahuatzin and Tecuciztecatl). They are resurrected in a number of different forms, which shocks the Xibalbans. In each of these new forms, the twins sacrifice them-selves and are again reborn. The lords One Death and Seven Death, the dual antagonists, admiring this ability to be sacrificed and reborn, ask the twins to sacrifice them. The twins do so, but refuse to bring the Xibalbans back, thus leading to their final defeat. After this, the hero twins are trans-formed one final time, into the sun and moon. This is presented as a final manifestation not of the twins themselves, but of their dual father, One and Seven Hunahpu, who is continued through this transformation.

Robert Sharer describes another aspect of the principle of dual creation in the *Popol Vuh*:

> The myth of the Hero Twins ... highlights the dualistic theme that permeates Maya ideology. This can be seen in the eternal struggle between the powers of good and evil, day and night, life and death. The benevolent forces, bringing thunder, lightning, and rain, fructify the corn and ensure plenty. The malevolent powers, characterized by death and destruction, are responsible for drought, hurricanes, and war that ruin the corn and bring famine and misery. This eternal contest is depicted in the codices, where Chaak, the rain deity, is shown caring for a young tree; behind him follows the death god, who breaks the tree in two.[25]

---

[23] *Popol Vuh*, Christenson trans., 121.
[24] There are a number of other dual or twin characters skipped over here, such as One Batz and One Chouen.
[25] Sharer, *The Ancient Maya*, 730.

While Sharer is right about this notion of oppositional forces connected to duality, it is not always the case that these forces are antagonistic, or that one is benevolent and the other malevolent. As we have already seen, destruction is necessary for creation, given that things cannot be created from nothing – thus death, decay, and ruin play an essential role in the ability of things to be generated. This is why we find stories of creation accompanied by stories of prior sacrifice – the Hero Twins are sacrificed to become the sun and moon, just as are Nanahuatzin and Tecuiciztecatl in the Aztec story, and Quetzalcoatl in the *Codex Chimalpopoca* account described above.

Notice that all three of these accounts of sacrifice and rebirth involve fire. This imagery of fire likely has its own significance that also tips us off to the fact that death is not understood as a manifestly negative and malevolent thing. Fire destroys what it touches, but we know it is also one of the most essential tools humans have for survival. We can cook meat with it to kill dangerous bacteria. We can use it to burn crops to clear fields for planting and fertilize the soil with the remaining ash. Such "slash and burn agriculture" was a key technique for the precolonial Maya, and the image of fire would have had important association with fertility of the land. Fire both consumed living plants, and made it possible for new ones to grow. Without this fertilization through creation of swidden fields by burning, the soil would not retain sufficient nutrients to allow crop growth, and the field would become barren. This association of fire with fertility would have been clear to precolonial Maya and other Mesoamerican groups. The association of death and sacrifice with fire, then, also shows their necessity for the generation of new things.

In Aztec thought, we also see the duality of creation represented in a number of ways. The creator deity Ometeotl ("Two Teotl") is fundamentally dual in nature. The centrality of duality in some Aztec stories of creation is even more explicit than in Maya sources. The dual, through the number two (*ome*) is connected with the places and deities of creation. Ometeotl, which is itself understood in terms of two other dualistic deities, Ometecuhtli and Omecihuatl, resides in "the place of duality," Omeyocan. Duality itself here seems to be the fundamental creative force. Miguel Leon-Portilla was the primary proponent of this view, which placed Ometeotl as the central creator god of the Aztecs.[26] While there has been

[26] Leon-Portilla, *Aztec Thought and Culture*, 84–85.

scholarly debate over the role or existence of this dual god in the Aztec tradition, there is clearly a concern with duality as creative principle, just as we see in Maya thought. Whether or not Ometeotl is understood as central, or whether explicit reference to duality is made as Leon-Portilla argued,[27] we clearly see a stress on dual gods in creation in the same way we find in Maya texts. The *Historia de los Mexicanos por sus pinturas* discusses the creation of Oxmoco and Cipactonal, the original human pair responsible for the creation of human culture.[28] The dual deities Ometecuhtli (Tonacatecuhtli) and Omecihuatl (Tonacacihuatl), also envisioned as a male-female pair, were taken as creative as well.

Part of the stress on the duality of creation is likely due to the key example of human (and animal) procreation, requiring pairs for generation. Male and female deities and elements of the world suggest this (although we do not always find duality gendered in this way, for example in many of the cases from the *Popol Vuh*). Creator deities are sometimes referred to in both male and female form. Michael Lind discusses the Zapotec god Cozaana, creator of animals and fish, and god of hunting, as in at least one instance female, though generally referred to as male, and connected to birthing.[29] The Zapotec god of children and procreation, Huichana, is likewise referred to as both male and female. Creation stories of the Mixtec also begin with two gods responsible for creation. In an early seventeenth century account from Spanish priest Gregorio García reportedly based on a Mixtec book in precolonial Mixtec writing, there is a discussion of the creation of things by a primordial god pair. García wrote:

> In the year and day of obscurity and darkness, before there were days
> or years, the world being in great darkness, when all was chaos and
> confusion, the earth was covered with water. There was only slime and
> mud on the surface of the earth. At that time, the Indians imagine, a God
> who had the name of 1-Deer and the surname of Lion Serpent, and a very

---

[27] See Haly, "Bare Bones: Rethinking Mesoamerican Divinity" and Maffie for criticism of this view.

[28] Phillips, trans., "History of the Mexicans as Told by Their Paintings," *Proceedings of the American Philosophical Society* XXI, 617–618.

[29] Lind, *Ancient Zapotec Religion*, 16–17.

attractive and beautiful goddess named 1-Deer, whose surname was Tiger Serpent, made themselves visible. These two gods are said to have been the origin of all the other gods that the Indians possessed.[30]

Suspicious similarities to the Christian story of creation aside, this reference to two original creator gods was certainly something common across Mesoamerican traditions, and which would not have appeared as an obvious part of a creation myth to a Christian writer such as García. Notice also in this account that both the male and female god share the name 1-Deer. This suggests the kind of combination of duality and unity we find in Maya and Aztec sources – a common feature of Mesoamerican metaphysics, and accounts of creation in particular. Mixtec creation accounts also refer to pairs of twins, similar to what we find in Maya texts such as the *Popol Vuh*. With every generation, there is a new pair that creates the next. The Mixtec *Codex Vindobonensis* contains pictorial description in the Mixtec writing system of these various pairs, and accounts of their generation. In a part of the story reminiscent of the birth of the Maya hero twins from the head of One and Seven Hunahpu in the calabash tree, a male and female emerge from a tree, at the base of which is a disembodied head from which the tree appears to emerge. The tree appears to be anthropomorphized as also the body of a human from which the pair is born. Kevin Terraciano notes that the tree is dual-gendered, "[containing] both male and female symbols."[31]

On Christian Influence and "Centering"

While this principle of dual creation is found more or less across Mesoamerican traditions, we also find a number of elements of Mesoamerican creation stories that seem sometimes surprisingly close to parallel creation stories in Christianity. Given that the sources of many of these stories are colonial texts written often in Latin script during the period of heavy Spanish influence, it is natural to wonder to what extent these stories are influenced by Christianity, and include elements that

[30] In Terraciano, *The Mixtecs of Colonial Oaxaca*, 255.
[31] Terraciano, *The Mixtecs of Colonial Oaxaca*, 257.

were not present in earlier precolonial Mesoamerican creation stories. While there is certainly *some* new invention, there are a few reasons that I don't think there is very much, and that most of the material with a striking resemblance to Christianity in Mesoamerican texts actually does have precolonial Mesoamerican roots. First, much of the material with which there seems to be resonance with Christian ideas is documented in precolonial sources. Images like the Maya world tree, which becomes associated with the Christian cross in the colonial period and later, can be found in the Classic Period. The image of creation of the cosmos from an initial watery state from which things arise, found in the Book of Genesis, is also seen in Aztec creation mythology, with the god Tlaltecuhtli, representing the earth, arising from the waters of the ocean. Second – the influence of ideas from other cultures, even when imposed as in the Spanish colonization of Mesoamerica, hardly ever works through the imposition of completely new ideas and displacement of the old. In every area where we find cultural exchange, we find systems in which new ideas are presented *through* the old, in which resonances are found within the traditions and emphasized. This happens even in our own time and place. Think about how we encounter ideas from other cultural contexts and the ways they influence our preexisting culture. We tend to find aspects of these other cultures that connect with the concerns and ideas we already have, and emphasize those. Look at what happened to Christianity in its movement from the eastern Mediterranean to Greece, Rome, and Western Europe. It did not displace earlier views and practices, but rather centered certain preexisting views and practices, and gave them different interpretive framework. The idea of salvation and redemption from earlier Jewish contexts was understood through Platonic conceptions of the liberation of the soul. The idea of sexual fidelity in earlier Jewish contexts was read through concepts such as that of the vestal virgin in Rome. Christianity in Europe did not so much transform earlier modes of thought as *center* certain aspects of earlier thought and organize them in a different way. This is the same thing we find in Mesoamerica. This is also why Mesoamerican Christianity often looks very different than European Christianity or Asian Christianity, even though they are all supposed to be the same thing. The substrate of Christianity, in whichever form it is brought to a place (in this case medieval Spanish Catholicism) is interpreted and understood through a framework of preexisting cultural ideas. Any person can only make sense of something *from the place in which they already stand*. Intellectual movement and discovery can certainly happen, but we always move from where we are, and with the intellectual language we already possess, which will reveal itself in our movement and the places we end up. Just as there is biological descent, and genetic features of individuals can be found in their descendants, the intellectual features of one's cultural background can be found in one's own thought. This cultural background is never as black-and-white as we often make it seem, "Western" or "Mesoamerican" or "Chinese," just as biological descent is never that way. Our constructed categories that are meant to capture certain biological features, such as race, often badly miss the mark – yet inherited features are certainly found in our intellectual systems, as they are in our bodies and minds. And just as it is a mistake to understand many inherited genetic features in terms of race, it is also a mistake to understand inherited intellectual features in terms of large-scale cultural constructs such as Christianity.

The aspects of Mesoamerican creation stories resonant with Christianity that we find in colonial accounts, then, are most likely not inventions or borrowings from Christianity, but are rather due to the *centering* of aspects of earlier Mesoamerican thought. It may well be that aspects of the colonial creation stories that are central in those stories did not play such a major role in precolonial accounts. The arising of things from water in Aztec accounts, for example, may have been a less prominent or important aspect of Aztec creation stories before the influence of Christianity and was perhaps elevated into a new position because of the similarities between that story and ones from Christian scriptures. Similarly, we find centering of aspects of Mesoamerican traditions as exchange happens between cultures within Mesoamerica itself. For example, in the Maya Yucatan in the Postclassic period, we find a greater focus on gods such as Itzamna, Kukulkan, and origin stories more similar to those of central Mexico. These figures and stories can be found in earlier material as well, but the new connections between the Yucatan and central Mexico during the Postclassic likely centered the aspects of Maya thought already resonating with that of central Mexico, making preexisting aspects of Maya thought more prominent.[32]

---

[32] See McLeod, "The Descent of Kukulkan."

Further Reading

There is an enormous literature on creation and the role of the gods in Mesoamerica. Some of the best places to start are: The classic K'iche Maya text *Popol Vuh* (Allen Christenson and Dennis Tedlock both have well-known translations); Knowlton, *Maya Creation Myths*; Book 3 of the *Florentine Codex*, on the "Origin of the Gods"; Vail and Hernandez, *Recreating Primordial Time*. Full publication details for all of these works can be found in the bibliography.

6   Being and Worlds

The Concept of Being and the Basic Stuff of the World

The concept of being is sometimes seen as a purely "Western" construct, one that requires certain linguistic features inherent to Indo-European languages such as Greek, Sanskrit, or English to formulate.[1] Even if this were true, of course, it would mean the idea could extend much further than what we call the "West," as the ancient Indo-European languages with the relevant structure stretch from India, Persia, and North Asia to the end of Europe. Their expansion to the Americas, Africa, and Oceania happened only late in history with European colonialism.

The linguistic hypothesis concerning the concept of being is badly flawed, however. The structure of language does not limit the human ability to conceptualize the world and our experience. Language, while certainly influencing thought, is not determinative of the ways we can conceptualize. If this were the case, no new concepts could ever arise than those already determined by a language at present stage, which would also make the growth and change of language impossible, nor could one ever learn a new language after acquiring one. We know that these two things are not the case. Languages develop via processes of change resembling those of biological evolution. Usage, conceptualization, new ideas, accents – these all form to turn one language over time into others. This is why, for example, there are so many different Indo-European languages, Maya languages, Sino-Tibetan languages. Language families are created from a common ancestor, from which these languages diverge over time through the natural processes of language change that eventually results in distinct languages. From the one language of Proto

---

[1] See A. C. Graham, *Studies in Chinese Philosophy and Philosophical Literature*, 330–331.

Indo-European descend languages that are mutually unintelligible today, including English, Russian, Hindi, Persian, Greek, and many others. The same is the case for Maya languages such as K'iche', Yucatec Maya, Ch'orti', etc. This process is only possible if conceptualization is not completely determined by language. Not to mention that it is possible for a speaker of a Sino-Tibetan language like Mandarin Chinese to learn an Indo-European language like English and vice versa. Moreover, one who knows both languages can *translate* the meanings of one language into the other. Thus, even if certain features of a language suggest or make natural particular concepts or even views, the conceptual apparatus of one language cannot be inaccessible to speakers of another, even if that apparatus necessarily has to be explained differently in each language (otherwise they would not be different languages at all!). Learning the Spanish language, for example, was not necessary for understanding the very different ideas that the Spanish people took with them to the Americas, even if these ideas were not naturally suggested by features of native languages.

The concept of being, as such, is dealt with in Mesoamerican traditions in very interesting ways that *in some senses* resembles what we find in other global traditions. Concepts such as *itz'* and *teotl* are concepts of a kind of "basic stuff" of the cosmos determining its nature. It is not quite right to call these *constituents* of reality, in the sense of a material such as atoms that make up the world in physicalistic systems, but rather the nature of reality itself, that is, *being* itself. All that exists is being, has the nature of being, and being can be understood as that which both is and underlies, is prior to, and sustains all things. What it is to be, to exist, is a particular quality for precolonial Mesoamerican thinkers just as it was for those in ancient Greece, India, and elsewhere in the world.

In Mesoamerican systems, there are fundamental aspects of reality associated with being that are appealed to as explanation for the world, its existence, and its changing patterns. In Maya thought, the concept of *itz* comes close to this, although it is a complicated issue, as we will see below. Miguel Leon-Portilla, as we saw briefly in Chapter 3, argues that the concept of *k'in* (day) plays something like the role of "being" in Maya thought. I discuss this further in this chapter. The Aztec concept of *tonalli* has some overlap with this concept (and with *itz*), and there is a key connection made in both of these traditions between the power of the sun and the essence or power of the individual. While *k'in* is not being itself, there were certainly good reasons for Leon-Portilla's reading, and key aspects of the concept do offer us something close to parts of a concept of being.

One of the things we have to contend with here is the idea that we should expect a one-to-one match for terms in English and Mesoamerican languages. It is sometimes argued (in work on numerous traditions) that to find a concept of X in any given tradition, we need to find a single term that corresponds to X in the language or tradition that is our frame.[2] In this case, with English as the frame, this would entail that we need to find a single term expressing a concept of being in Mesoamerica. This argument belies a lack of engagement with numerous languages. There are hardly ever any simple one-to-one correspondences for concepts across different languages. The same concepts are expressed in different ways across linguistic systems – with some things that are expressed with a single term or idea in some languages expressed in multiple terms or ideas in other languages. The concept of being is much this way in Mesoamerican thought. There is a *cluster* of terms and concepts in Mesoamerican traditions expressing the idea of being, not a single one. This is not only the case in one direction, however. If we take something like the Maya concept of *k'in* and look to find its corresponding concept in contemporary American thought, for example, we can find it, but we require a cluster of terms and concepts "sun," "ruler," "essence," etc. If it were not the case that we could explain the concept of *k'in* in this way, then it would have to remain permanently and hopelessly opaque to us as English speakers.

One might object here that just because we can *express* a particular concept in English (or Maya languages, or whatever) does not mean that people in that philosophical tradition theorized with or thought about such a concept. The concept of *k'in*, for example, while it can be expressed in English terms and a concept cluster, was not theorized as such in English-language philosophical tradition. Does the lack of a single term, then, show not that a concept cannot be *expressed* in a language, but that the tradition in question

---

[2] A number of scholars refer to this as the "lexical fallacy." It pops up not only in philosophical contexts, but also in history, theology, and other areas. See for example Osborne, *The Hermeneutical Spiral*, 84; Van Norden, *Virtue Ethics and Consequentialism in Early Chinese Philosophy*, 22.

did not operate with or theorize about such a concept? I don't think it can. While investigation of a tradition can show whether or not that tradition had a concern with a particular concept, language alone cannot. We know that pre-Columbian Mesoamerican thinkers had a concern with concepts such as time, for example, even though there is no single term in any Mesoamerican language corresponding to the English "time". I use the example of time here intentionally – of all concepts, it would be most absurd to deny that pre-Columbian Mesoamerican traditions lacked a concept of time, as it is clearly one of the most apparent aspects of extant Mesoamerican texts as well as oral traditions and contemporary traditional practices. We learn about whether a tradition has philosophical concern with a particular concept by investigating the tradition, not by looking at features of the language in which the relevant philosophical tradition is conducted.

K'in and Tonalli

As we have seen in previous chapters, many of the extant Mesoamerican texts, both precolonial and later, deal with time and calendrics. Time was clearly a major concern of Mesoamerican philosophy. Part of the explanation for this concern with time, however, is that the concept cluster of time also included conceptions linked to being and the nature of the cosmos more broadly. Leon-Portilla picked up on this in his discussion of *kin* in the Maya tradition, clearly influenced by his understanding of the role of *tonalli* in Aztec thought.

In Aztec thought, *tonalli* signifies not only the day, but also a kind of life-essence. The connection between the two is based on the understanding that humans gain their vital essence, spirit, or ability to think and move from the sun. There is also an analogy drawn between solar heat and the heat of motion, of the living human body.[3] *Tonalli* animates the individual, but its particular quality (which differs by individual) also determines the extent to which the individual possesses energy, talent, force, etc. *Tonalli* was understood as manifest in heat of the body (thus the connection to the sun), and could be determined by its effect on generating changes in the body. Changing features of the human body, such as its growth in size, as

---

[3] Carrasco, *Religions of Mesoamerica*, 89–90;

well as growth in peripherals such as hair and nails, was taken to demonstrate *tonalli*, as being the effects of *tonalli*. The source of *tonalli* in humans was connected to the blood (similar to the *k'ul/ch'ul* of Maya tradition). Because blood bore *tonalli*, the offering of blood in ritual autosacrifice was understood as a kind of transfer of *tonalli*, an offering of the substance to the gods. We can see how features of blood and bloodletting would naturally support such a view. Circulating blood, like breath, is a key feature of living human beings (which also explains the focus in other traditions like those of China and India focusing on breath as the source of something like *tonalli*). As anyone who has donated blood or lost blood knows, losing blood will lead to a decline of the features generally associated with the energetic living person – one will become lightheaded and weak as the body is deprived of the oxygen carried by the blood until more can be made.

Tonalli, while it belongs to individuals, is not *limited* to those individuals. This distinguishes it from the other Aztec concept connected to spirit and vital essence, *teyolia*. Because it is a more general feature of the world (again the link to the sun is relevant), *tonalli* can be transferred between things and individuals, in ways life-essence cannot, according to views in other traditions. Ritual bloodletting is one way *tonalli* can be transferred between the individual and the gods. Individuals an also claim or give *tonalli*. It can enter and leave the body, and through means such as the imagination of dreams or even the emission of semen (certain views of *qi* in early China mirror this). The relevant connection here to a concept of *being* is that *tonalli* is general and not distinct by individual, but rather a pervading aspect of the cosmos. James Maffie points out that *tonalli* exists in everything and everywhere, and that its transformation and movement is a matter of degree rather than of presence vs. absence. Maffie writes:

> Tonalli is a fully general and impersonal force. It is unique neither to individual humans nor to human beings as such. It resides only temporarily in any given human and upon death recycles into the cosmos. Tonalli is absorbed by animals and plants as well as fire, statues, gemstones, brilliantly colored bird feathers, animal skins, and warriors' costumes. Humans are able to perceive (e.g., by sight and touch) the tonalli contained within things. In sum, tonalli diffuses over the earth's surface and it inhabitants, and in doing so energizes and influences them.[4]

[4] Maffie, *Aztec Philosophy*, 272.

This general vital essence is then a feature of the cosmos more properly, and explains the connection between *tonalli* and a general conception of being. The *tonalli* was associated particularly with the head, and understood as emanating from the Sun, from which it was transferable. As we have seen, the Sun itself held a crucial place in Aztec conceptions of the cosmos, in terms of its creative power and its representation of the cosmos itself. The created, organized world was understood in terms of the current Sun providing things with their energy.

A number of scholars, including Alfredo López Austin, have noticed the similarity between many features of the Aztec concept of *tonalli* and the Maya *k'ul* or *ch'ul* (the former being the Yucatec pronunciation). Sharing association with the blood, in the Maya context, the feature of divinity and spirit is also suggested, with the term often translated as "holy". Both *tonalli* and *ch'ul* are connected to vital energy – all things with life and motion are animated by them. It is not quite right to link them to the concept of life as we generally understand it today, however, in which we distinguish living from inanimate things. Not only do living things in our biological sense contain *tonalli* or *ch'ul*, but all things in motion, that perform activity – the cosmos itself. There is no heavy ontological distinction drawn between things such as animals and plants that move, grow, and act, and other things in the world that do such, including rivers, clouds, and all other aspects of the world continually in motion. From this perspective, all things in the world can be seen as "living" things in some sense, but not in the sense we generally understand the term "living". It is not that all things are biological organisms, but rather that all things contain the vital energy that allows them to move, transform, and act as they do. We recognize that rocks contain energy, which explains their movement down a hill, but we do not understand this energy and movement as self-generative or living. Mesoamerican traditions tend to hold that the activity of humans, dogs, plants, and the like, does not have a different source than that of other moving and transforming things in the world. The concept of *life* in Mesoamerican thought should be thought of as something like *animation* or *vitality*. As such, it is a feature of all energetic aspects of the world, and the world itself as moving and changing thing.

The emanation of *tonalli* from the Sun (as well as to a lesser extent from other animate things in the world) leads to a natural association of this vital energy with the Sun (although it is hard to know which sense of *tonalli* was earlier. The root *tona* is connected to "heat," but the sun's heat and the heat of vitality and movement are both connected to this). Given that *tonalli* is a vital energy responsible for motion and change, the sun is the natural object most clearly and abundantly possessive of it. Even today in the industrial and technological world we live in, nothing in our experience comes close to the power, regularity, and dynamicity of the sun. How much more so would this have been in a time where there were no modern machines. The closest things to the Sun in their vital power would have been volcanoes, storms, earthquakes. And none of those approach the power and regularity of the Sun. Although the Sun of course does far more than we recognize through our direct experience of it alone, even what we gain through such experience sets the Sun apart in our world as a source of vitality and power. The Sun defines the day by brightening the entirety of the "world", erases the stars and planets when it is above, provides intense heat such that it can change the temperature, start fires, or create drought, defines the seasons by its changing position through the year, and makes possible the growth of almost all of the vegetation that covers the Earth. Anyone who has stood out in the noonday Sun on a clear summer day recognizes the powerful effects of the Sun on everything it touches.

The *tonalli* as day, then, is closely connected to *tonalli* as vital energy. The correlative metaphysics of Mesoamerican traditions is here on full display. An identity is drawn here between the light and heating power of the Sun and the vital energy that powers movement and life in humans and the rest of the cosmos. Though *tonalli* may take different forms, present in the heat of the Sun as much as in the movement of a person, or the growth of hair or plants, it is this underlying source manifest in different forms. This is very close to a more general conception of *being*, which plays much the same role in traditions like those of Indo-European cultures. This also helps us see how nothing that *is* can also fail to be *living*. To be is to have the kind of vitality that allows at least for the maintenance of existence.

For Mesoamerican traditions, being cannot be static, but rather is understood as a continually unfolding process (maintained by the continual creation discussed in the last chapter). Thus, a concept of vital energy can play a very similar foundational role to that of being in other traditions.

If the cosmos is most fundamentally a *process* rather than a *thing*, then the fundamental question of ontology is not Quine's "what is there?", but instead "what *does* there?" Being, in Mesoamerican traditions, is being in motion, being in process.

We see now some of the reason one might take the Maya concept of the day and time, *kin*, as roughly equivalent to the Aztec concept of *tonalli*. This is indeed what Leon-Portilla does. And while his reading is problematic, it is not without merit or justification, and there are important ways that the concept of *kin* overlaps with a more general concept of processual being expressed by *tonalli*.

K'in expresses both the day, the Sun, and that which the Sun makes possible. This is graphically and elegantly expressed in the Classic Mayan glyph for *kin*, depicting a Plumeria Rubra flower. Here we see a flower as representative of the sun that causes the flower, and the Sun as symbol of the day. There are numerous levels of signification at play here, as well as a statement of identity. It is not just that the Sun *causes* the day and the flower, but that the Sun is contained in the flower, such that a depiction of a flower is *at the same time* a depiction of the Sun. In this way the flower can be understood as the substitute (*k'ex*) of the Sun. The concept of substitution is not limited to human activity. A substitution is a transshipment of essence through activity, relationship, or response, and given that all aspects of the cosmos are fundamentally of the same stuff (just as general features like *ch'ul* or *tonalli* are impersonal and everywhere), any part of the cosmos can substitute any other, through manifesting its essence.

The concept of *k'in* in Maya thought is connected also to the forms of rulership connected to ritual and religion that formed in the Classic Period. The title *k'inich ajaw* was often used, with the term for the Sun attached to the ruler (*ajaw*), making a Maya lord a "sun king," suggesting his power and reach. The image of the Sun has been a powerful symbol for rulership throughout human history. For the same reasons discussed above in association of the Sun with vital power, the hegemony of the Sun in the world represents the kind of omnipresence and control the ruler ultimately strives to achieve over the people. A ruler like the Sun is one who not only controls the society, but sustains it, is necessary for its continued existence, and gives it life. These are associations rulers throughout history knew well and used to their advantage, including the ancient Egyptian pharoah Akenaten's association of himself with the Sun (*aten*), the Roman emperor Constantine's association of himself with the god Sol Invictus (the unconquered Sun), the traditional Japanese view of the emperor as a descendant of the Sun goddess, *le roi soleil* Louis XIV, and many others. Priests in Postclassic Yucatan held the title *aj k'in*, connected to their role as keepers of days – a key role of humanity we see discussed in the *Popol Vuh*.

Because of the ubiquity of *kin* in extant Maya texts, Leon-Portilla locates in it a concept of being, arguing that time itself, in the form of *kin*, pervades and supports the cosmos. Leon-Portilla writes:

> *Kinh*—sun-day-time—was not an abstract entity but a reality enmeshed in the world of myths, a divine being, origin of the cycles which govern all things. Many are the faces of *kinh*, but its essence is always divine. Time permeates all and is limitless. ....*kinh* appears, as the heart of all change, filled with lucky and unlucky destinies within the cyclic reality of the universe and most probably inherent to the essence of divinity itself.[5] (Leon-Portilla, 33)

We can look to the texts and practices here to evaluate Leon-Portilla's claim, clearly influenced by the Aztec view of *tonalli*. A number of other scholars see *k'in* as a metaphor for the cosmic order more generally, given its connection to all aspects of the cosmos. The Maya calendars were understood as ways of organizing *k'in*, and the idea of "keeping the days" of the gods was understood as necessary to maintain the cosmos in its form. Leon-Portilla [and others'] speculation about the connection between *kin* and this organized cosmos, then, is not completely off the mark, even if *k'in* is not ultimately the fundamental constituent of reality these scholars claim.

Sun imagery and association of certain gods and heroes with the Sun is prominent in Maya, as in Aztec, traditions. In the *Popol Vuh*, the hero twins Hunahpu and Xbalanque are transformed after their self-sacrifice in the realm of the dead into the Sun and Moon – a story that seems to have important parallels with the Aztec story of the origin of the fifth sun. The day and its link to the Sun certainly carries important connotations of power and rulership, as well as organization of time, in the Maya context.

---

[5] Leon-Portilla, *Time and Reality in the Thought of the Maya*, 33.

To find a more general concept expressive of *being* as a quality of the cosmos, we have to look to concepts such as *ch'ul* and *itz*.

Ch'ul and *Itz*: A Link to Being

Both of these concepts are generally discussed in terms of a power, potency, or vitality associated with the individual, and their essence, or features of the individual as individual. The concept of *ch'ul* (*k'ul* or k'uh in Yucatec Maya) has a better claim to something in the realm of the concept of being as such than concepts like *kin*. *Ch'ul* is often translated as "holy" or "sacred"[6], and is connected to a vital energy, as in the case of the Aztec *tonalli*. Maya sources discuss different parts or aspects of the human soul, with *ch'ul* being the general, shared, and continuing aspect of the individual – a general vital energy that can be transferred between things, and is connected to a kind of revelatory power through blood sacrifice, such as the autosacrificial bloodletting of rulers and nobles. Schele, Friedel, and Parker describe *ch'ul* as a general power animating the cosmos.[7] It is a vital essence properly belonging to the cosmos itself, as well as to individuals. The connection between individuals (persons, things, etc.) and the cosmos is not one of *reduction*, however. Thus, we cannot say that individuals possess *ch'ul* in a secondary or derivative way. Given the general nature of *ch'ul* as transferable vitality, as well as the fact that each thing in the cosmos is individuated not on the basis of separable substance, but on the basis of activity and essence, this shows that *ch'ul* must play an important role in making things as they are, in defining things as such. That is, *ch'ul* is here playing the role of being as such.

Ch'ul/k'ul has an important connection to the gods and to rulers, with Classic Period glyphs representing rulers as *ch'ul*. Erik Book translates the term as "god-like," linking the concept to the divine.

In Maya traditions, there is a further complication. A related concept, *itz*, seems to be playing much the same role as *ch'ul* in parts of the Maya tradition, particularly in Yucatan and Postclassic imagery and texts. The concept of *itz* is in some ways more fleshed out than that of *ch'ul*, and we have a number of sources referring to or discussing the concept.

---

[6] See Macri and Looper, *The New Catalog of Maya Hieroglyphs*, Vol. 1, 70.
[7] *Maya Cosmos*, 402.

The origins of *itz* seem to be in connection to a liquid essence, the gum or resin of a living being connected with its vitality or life, including secretions such as dew, milk, sap (particularly of the rubber plant, which is widespread and important in the Yucatan), and semen. *Itz* comes to take on connotations connected to magic and shamanistic ability.[8] Rituals of sacrificial offering to the gods involved offering of *itz* sap along with blood drawn in autosacrificial bloodletting, burned together as an offering of vital essence to the gods. From this, we can see that *ch'ul/k'ul*, connected to blood, and the vital power of *itz* became at some point related concepts. Schele, Friedel, and Parker call them "fundamentally related substances – magical and holy stuff."[9] While there is clearly some connection between these two concepts, what is less clear is whether these were separately developed but ancestrally related concepts that came to overlap in ritual during the Postclassic in Yucatan, or whether these concepts were developed separately to flag different aspects of the world.

The centrality in Postclassic sources of the god Itzamna/Itzamnaaj also suggests this role for the concept of *itz*. Itzamna is one of the central gods of creation, and is associated with the 3114 BCE origin of the Long Count calendar – although as numerous scholars point out, this event was not seen as the beginning of the cosmos, but rather a key reorganization. The role of Itzamna as creator is linked to his role as representative of artists and sages. Creation, in this context, is not the kind of construction of a cosmos from nothing that we find in Abrahamic contexts, but rather a conceptual creativity linked with art, writing, and knowledge – the kinds of subject that would be linked to scribes, daykeepers, and other framers of ideas. The model of creation centered in Mesoamerican thought is that of intellectual and artistic creation, rather than physical construction. The cosmos as such is conceptualized and designed continually, and the work of the scribe, sage, daykeeper, and artist is a continuation and extension of the work of Itzamna. In this sense, those with these roles can be understood as *substitutes*. Itzamna is also connected to the sky and to the creation of rituals – two other key aspects in the human-god co-continual-creation of the cosmos, as we have seen above.

---

[8] Barrera-Vasquez and Rendon, trans., *El libro de los libros de Chilam Balam*, 29.
[9] *Maya Cosmos*, 211.

The figure of Itzamna is likely linked to central Mexican influence in the Yucatan, and thus the concept of *itz* that is centered in the rise of this figure likely tracks the earlier concept of *ch'ul/k'ul*, as a different version of the same.[10] One of the key features of *itz* relevant to our discussion of being is its connection to the ability to see and communicate with other unseen aspects of the world. This is potentially connected to a meaning of *itz* in Nahuatl, "to look" or "to see" (according to the seventeenth century *Diccionario de l'arte de la lengua mexicana* of Horacio Carochi). The god Itzamna is often associated with the glyph for *akbal* ("darkness" or "blackness") in Postclassic Maya imagery, and this suggests his association with vision through the symbolism of black obsidian, which was used for mirrors in Mesoamerica. Lynn Foster writes of the *akbal* glyph:

> [T]his may represent the polished black surface of an obsidian mirror. The polished black surfaces of such mirrors were important devices that allowed shamans to see past and future events. As an attribute of Itzamna, the obsidian mirror suggests and important function of the god.[11]

The power to see the unseen aspects of the world exists through possession of *itz*. The vital power of *itz* seems to increase with those with the ability to mold and structure it, the *itzam* ("sage," "shaman," or simply "one who manipulates *itz*"). The acts of construction of the cosmos, connected to the continual creation enacted through ritual, keeping of the days, and construction of texts (among other activities), rely on *itz* and the human power to manipulate *itz*. We can see that *itz* is truly a fundamental aspect of reality, associated with being itself, in its continual unfolding and vitality.

Transformation and motion are central to the concept of being in Mesoamerican traditions. Being is continually *becoming*. For this reason, the concept cluster surrounding being involves vital essence, power, and energy. For Mesoamerican traditions, to be is to be in motion, active, in *performance*. This of course is mirrored through the rituals demonstrating and enacting this performative being – to bring about or make visible

---

[10] See McLeod, "*Itz* and the Descent of Kukulkan: Central Mexican Influence on Postclassic Maya Thought."

[11] Foster, *Handbook to Life in the Ancient Maya World*, 166.

some aspect of the world, it needs to be enacted, put into motion, or revealed as in motion. Being, in short, is *vitality*.

Given this, how do we understand the seeming separation of worlds in Mesoamerican traditions? There are at least two different planes of existence discussed in these traditions – the realm of the living and that of the dead. In the Maya tradition, there is the world above, and Xibalba, the world of the dead. Xibalba has rough equivalents in other Mesoamerican traditions, such as Mictlan for the Aztecs. While these realms are not generally accessible or visible in the normal run of life, as traditional stories suggest, living humans can access them. This happens primarily through ritual, including the autosacrificial bloodletting ceremonies. These unseen aspects of the world, then, are accessible and should not be understood as separate in substance or nature. They are part of the same process of the cosmos, continually created. While humans must generate certain kinds of knowledge and ability to access and understand these aspects of the world (as discussed further in the next chapter), they are nonetheless part of the same single continually changing, continually unfolding cosmos. These aspects of the world are fundamentally linked to one another, as we have already seen in many of the foundational myths of Mesoamerica.

Teotl

While the concept of *ch'ul* clearly has parallels to the Aztec *tonalli*, a more commonly compared concept is that of *teotl*. A number of scholars[12] have drawn the comparison between the two concepts, in terms of association with gods, a sacred vital essence or power, and vitalistic source of being. Like *ch'ul*, the concept is associated with gods or the divine, perhaps translatable as "god" or "god-like" (following Boot's translation of *ch'ul*). The most developed contemporary discussions of *teotl* in the Aztec tradition are found in the work of Miguel Leon-Portilla, Alfredo López Austin, and James Maffie, which we will see below.

Through investigation of the *Florentine Codex* of Sahagun, Molly Bassett has located five features of *teotl* that suggest it as a more general concept

---

[12] Including James Maffie, David Stuart, and Stephen Houston.

of being. Through investigating semantics in the *Florentine Codex*, Bassett argues that *teotl* was thought to have:

> [A]xcaitl (possessions, property) … has a *tonalli* (heat, day sign, fate, fortune, privilege, prerogative) … has a *neixcahuilli* (an exclusive thing, occupation, business, or pursuit) … is *mahuiztic* (something marvelous, awesome, worthy of esteem) … is *tlazohca* (valuable, beloved).[13]

The *Florentine Codex* use of *teotl* refers to gods or a specific god (there is a plural form of the word as well, *teteo*). The gods are described as *teotl* in the text, but objects in the cosmos are also described as *teotl*, which seems to distinguish them from normal objects, attributing to them some greater level of power or vitality. As with *itz*, *teotl* seems to have been associated with darkness or blackness, also potentially a connection to obsidian mirrors and the concept of vision. Vision and knowledge are possible through the vital energy of *teotl*.

The work of Arild Hvitfeldt in the 1950s seems to have inaugurated the reading of *teotl* as a general energy pervading the cosmos, akin to the concept of *mana* in the native traditions of Oceania.[14] A number of later scholars begin from this position and advance more worked-out philosophical positions. As some have pointed out, however, this interpretation does seem to conflict with some of the evidence in Aztec texts concerning *teotl*, such as the fact that individual gods are referred to or named as *teotl*, and the fact that there is a plural form of *teotl* (*teteo*) that refers to groups of gods. If *teotl* is a general *mana*-like vital energy, the term also seems to have another sense, linked to a different concept. Anastasia Kalyuta argues that Hvitfeldt's conclusions concerning *teotl* were flawed, and based on only a limited number of primary texts to which he had access, primarily Sahagun's *Florentine Codex*. And as she points out, even the *Florentine Codex* includes material that would problematize this interpretation.

James Maffie's book *Aztec Philosophy* is largely organized around the concept of *teotl*, which he argues is the fundamental metaphysical concept in the Aztec tradition. Maffie defines *teotl* as a "continually dynamic, vivifying, self-generating and self-regenerating sacred power, force, or

---

[13] Bassett, *The Fate of Earthly Things*, 91–92.
[14] Hvidtfeldt, *Teotl and Ixiptlalti*.

energy,"[15] and argues that the Aztec view of the world is a monist view in which ultimately only this *teotl* exists. All things in the cosmos, and the cosmos itself, are not only infused with and animated by *teotl,* but ultimately reduce to *teotl.* Maffie connects *teotl* to an impersonal and non-agentive energy, more than to the concept of a god or gods. He focuses on its dynamicity, and says that Aztec thought understands being thus as *becoming.* *Teotl* is the Aztec concept of being as such, but understood as a dynamic becoming, rather than a static "is-ness."[16] This seems to me not so much a rejection of a concept of being as a link of being with activity. Being, in Mesoamerican thought, is generally associated with activity, with energy, with becoming. This is why creation is continually unfolding – things do not exist in some static way after an origin point or construction – rather, activity is the only thing that keeps things in existence. There is no being without activity, without continual becoming. This makes *process* more fundamental than substance in Mesoamerican thought. While the process metaphysics of the Western tradition might be some parallel in terms of ways of thinking about the most fundamental reality, we should not stretch the claim of the theoretical similarity of these views too far.

Maffie understands the Aztec dynamic metaphysics as in opposition to the "metaphysics of being" found in much of Western thought reaching back to the ancient Greeks. While there are certainly differences between Aztec (and other Mesoamerican) metaphysics and those of the ancient Greeks, I'm not convinced that those differences are quite as stark as Maffie presents them. A metaphysics of being as we find in Plato and Aristotle, Maffie writes, is the view that "to be real is to be permanent, immutable, static, eternal, and at rest,"[17] while a metaphysics of becoming "identifies the real with the constant flux of things."[18]

Maffie argues that the Aztec view of *teotl* is a monist view, arguing against the positions of Leon-Portilla and Lopez-Austin, which both accept a kind of dualism. I think the right view here is that the Aztec position on *teotl,* like Maya and other Mesoamerican views, is best seen not through

---

[15] Maffie, *Aztec Philosophy,* 22.
[16] Maffie, *Aztec Philosophy,* 25.
[17] *Aztec Philosophy,* 26.
[18] *Aztec Philosophy,* 25.

the frame of thinking about a fundamental stuff of the world, but in terms of accepting the reality of numerous different kinds of things that exist. That is, we don't find a *reductionist* metaphysics in Mesoamerican thought. All things exist – that is, the correct ontology is one that includes everything over which we can quantify, whether abstract, imagined, solid, etc. – and the fact that these things are *also teotl* does not entail that they are *only teotl*, any more than the fact that an individual who is performing a ritual such that they substitute a particular god is *also* that god entails that they are *only* that god. In such a case an individual remains both the individual they were and also the substituted god. The evidence suggests we should think of *teotl* in the same way. The singular *teotl* and plural *teteo*, and their ability to coexist, suggests a kind of universalism, embedding, and correlative thought.

Anastasia Kalyuta stresses one of the most important features of the Aztec metaphysical system, one we can also find in other Mesoamerican systems – the multiplicity of appearance, without reference to a single unifying substance. She writes that the Aztec view presents "simultaneous singularity and plurality of *teteo* and their respective capacity to manifest themselves in different forms at the same time..."[19] In addition to conforming to general views of embedded identity and metaphysics we find in other Mesoamerican traditions, we can make sense of much of the seemingly contradictory Aztec evidence in just this way.

This evidence can be found in a number of sources, including the *Florentine Codex* and the sixteenth century *Historia de los mexicanos pur sus pinturas* (History of the Mexicans According to their Paintings), which appears to be based on earlier precolonial glyphic texts. According to the latter text, the creator god is known as Ometeotl (Two Teotl), a combination of male and female forms, a dual principle of creation. This follows a common Mesoamerican theme we saw in Chapter 5. This duality of Ometeotl gave rise to other gods, the Texcatlipocas, associated with the cardinal directions, and thus the organization of the cosmos. Leon-Portilla interpreted Ometeotl as a formative cosmic energy on which all things are dependent. The omnipresence of Omoeteotl, he argues, is suggested by the following passage in the *Florentine Codex*:

---

[19] Kalyuta, "What Is Teotl?"

Mother of the gods, father of the gods, the old god, spread out on the navel of the earth, within the circle of turquoise. He who dwells in the waters the color of the bluebird, he who dwells in the clouds. The old god, he who inhabits the shadows of the land of the dead, the Lord of fire and time.[20]

Ometeotl is clearly the ancestor of all things, as the formative ancestor of the gods as well, and is in this sense present in all things. Since all beings are descendent from Ometeotl, Ometeotl is manifest in all beings, and any being can *substitute* Ometeotl. We can think of Ometeotl as the ultimate ancestor, the ancestor all things share. This pervasiveness of Ometeotl does not in itself show that *teotl* is a basic single stuff of the world, however. The existence of Ometeotl as *two* is one hint as to what is going on here. Origins in Mesoamerican literature almost always begin with the dual principle, as we have seen in Chapter 5. The Framer and Shaper, the "Two Teotl," the hero twins, and so on. There is a fundamental duality underlying all creation, destruction, and change. Two distinct dualist metaphysical interpretations are given of this, by Lopez Austin and Leon-Portilla respectively, while Maffie offers a monistic interpretation and a response to the dualistic arguments. All three of these scholars are right about aspects of the Aztec view, but each of them overlooks another possible solution that fits better with what we find through much of Mesoamerican philosophy. We can call this the *universalist* view – one that links unity and duality, denying that one of these or the other has to be primary. If we think of Aztec (and other Mesoamerican) views in terms of *correlative* rather than *reductive* metaphysics, we can make perfect sense of this.

Lopez Austin's interpretation of Aztec metaphysics attributes to it a dualism, understanding everything in the cosmos as ultimately constructed of "two types of substance." He bases this on the clear continual use of dualistic oppositions connected to creation and the constitution of things in Aztec texts (as we find in other Mesoamerican sources as well). Multiple kinds, but always at least *two* kinds of key features are found in all things, including the gods (as seen above). The dualism of this view is a kind of inherent substance dualism[21] – the cosmos is constructed of

---

[20] Leon-Portilla, trans., *Florentine Codex* Book 7, in *Aztec Thought and Culture*, 32.

[21] Isabel Laack calls it a "constitutional dualism of light and heavy matter that is reminiscent of the well-known dualism of the spiritual and the material." (Laack, *Aztec Religion and the Art of Writing*, 129).

two substances interacting within everything. While this sounds something like a Cartesian substance dualism, Lopez Austin suggests that the
dual substance may be different with each particular kind of thing in the
world. He distinguishes these into "heavy" and "light" substances, holding
that the two substances manifest themselves differently by object. The
view does sound very close to Cartesian substance dualism when the light
substance is associated with spirit and the heavy substance with body.[22]
There are also clearly correlative aspects here, as a Lopez Austin mentions
a number of dualities he thinks are related to and reducible to this fundamental duality.

We find a different kind of dualism in Leon-Portilla's interpretation of
Ometeotl as ontologically distinct from the rest of the cosmos. Rather than
a claim that dual substances interact within the cosmos, Leon-Portilla's
dualistic view resembles much more closely the kind of Platonic dualism
of realms that is at the basis of many Christian understandings of the
nature of God and the world. Ometeotl is "behind" the work of the other
gods and all creation, in terms of transcendence. Leon-Portilla writes:

> The *tlamatinime* [philosophers] went beyond mere polytheism. In their
> quest for a sumbol, through "flower and song," which might lead them
> to comprehend the origin of all things and the mysterious nature of
> an invisible and intangible creator, the *tlamatinime* conceived the most
> profound of all their "*difrasimos*," Ometecuhtli-Omecihualtl, Lord and Lady
> of duality. Beyond all time, beyond the heavens, in *Omeyocan*, Ometeotl
> Moyocoyani existed by self-invention, and continued to exist by virtue of
> his perpetual creative activity.[23]

Leon-Portilla's argument, while compelling in some places, ultimately
attempts to read the Aztec tradition as sufficiently close to the Christian
and Platonist traditions of the West to deserve respect. While existence
requires perpetual activity in exactly the way he claims here in most
Mesoamerican traditions, there is no evidence in Mesoamerican texts that
origin ideas like Ometeotl or other gods were associated with a transcendent, mysterious, "invisible and intangible" creator standing outside the
world. This is very much the importation of a Greco-Christian conception

---

[22] López-Austin, *The Myths of the Opossum*, 38–55; Maffie, *Aztec Philosophy*, 50.
[23] Leon-Portilla, *Aztec Thought and Culture*, 97.

of divine transcendence pasted onto a context where we do not seem to find it. In the places the Aztec tradition does claim that the old gods and the origins of things are unknowable, as in Book One of the *Florentine Codex*, it does so not because these things are transcendent or metaphysically distinct, but because none of us were there at the time and so cannot really know. We can only pass down what we have heard, and they could only have gotten it from investigation of the way things might have been. The opening passage of Book 3 of the *Florentine Codex*, on the origin of the gods, reads:

> How the gods had their beginning. Where they had their beginning, cannot be known.[24]

This is not because they are transcendent entities, but rather this is an epistemological claim – human knowledge only extends as far as human experience, and the beginnings of the gods falls far outside of human experience. To claim knowledge about such a thing, then, would be presumptuous and necessarily false.

Maffie's argument against Leon-Portilla's interpretation takes a different direction. He argues that Leon-Portilla makes an unwarranted move from the fact that the fundamental reality, Ometeotl, is imperceptible or unknowable, to the view that it must be ontologically distinct or transcendent. Maffie is certainly right to point out that this does not follow. There could be many reasons for epistemic opacity, so this cannot necessitate ontological distinctness. The simple reason I gave above, for example, which seems to explain the claim of the *Florentine Codex*, can explain such opacity. The beginning is unknowable because no one was there, it's not happening now (other than through its continual creation), so we could never access it.

There is another difficulty here, however. The beginning *should be* knowable if creation is continually unfolding in the same way at every moment. By then witnessing continual creation *now*, we should thereby be able to know how creation happened at every moment into the (potentially infinite) past. Thus, if this claim from the *Florentine Codex* is not based on European influence, it suggests that this is about the

---

[24] *Florentine Codex* Book 3, Anderson and Dibble trans., 1.

nature of the continually unfolding cosmos itself – while we can know how its creation happens (thus the story told about the origin of the gods), we cannot know how, why, or when this continually unfolding process came to be.

There are a number of possible explanations for the fact that Aztec, Maya, and other Mesoamerican texts and traditions speak of things both in terms of duality and also in terms of underlying unity. The best explanation here, consistent with much of what we have seen so far in Mesoamerican thought, is that metaphysics in Mesoamerica is for the most part *correlative* rather than reductive. There is no basic one or two to which all things reduce. Rather, all things exist as such, and the way we understand these things is via their relationships with one another, the identities that can be drawn between them, and the ways in which they can transform into one another.

Reductionism? Conceptualization? How Do We Get "Things" from the Basic Stuff

Given the generalized "basic stuff," or being, inherent in the Mesoamerican traditions, there is a question of how this stuff, *itz*, *teotl*, *ch'ul*, *tonalli*, etc. manifests as individual objects. In particular, when we have a view that seems very much processual in nature, how do we make sense of distinct individual things, particularly ones that might share their essence with other things? An essence can belong to two or more things at the same time, or *represent* two or more things at the same time. The cosmos itself and the things within it are manifestations of this basic stuff or essence, which is always moving and thus things are always transforming. Individual objects can only be understood in such a system as *features* of the over-arching process, or as somehow conceptualized, and mind-dependent. Mesoamerican traditions generally accept both of these positions. The basic stuff of the cosmos, being in itself, is conceptualized or constructed in particular ways by human convention, just as the days are created and kept. Different individual things can come into being and transform on the basis of this human construction – this is why communal recognition, for example, is a necessary feature of personal identity. And given that the same essence, the same *teotl* or *itz*, can be manifest as distinct things, even at the same time, these distinct individual things can be understood as features of being itself, the underlying stuff of reality.

Is this then a kind of reductionism? It seems on the face to amount to the claim that all things can be reduced to the underlying stuff of reality, *teotl* or *itz.* – that any given object can be understood more fundamentally as simply a construction of this underlying stuff of reality. Mesoamerican traditions would resist the idea of understanding the relationship between things in the cosmos and the underlying stuff of reality as one that admits of reduction, for a couple of reasons.

First, if we look at the point of reductionist explanation, the idea is that a theory can be translated into the terms of another kind of theoretical explanation, where one of these is real or fundamental and the other is not, or is less so. Reductionism generally boils down to a view that some particular level of theoretical description is "no more than" some other, that one is the ultimately correct or legitimate theory and others to which this can be translated are somehow either shorthand, conventional, or less real. This is the case at least with respect to reductionism about ontology. If Mesoamerican traditions accepted such a reductionist picture about *teotl* or *itz*, the claim would be that only *teotl* or *itz* exists, and that everything else we posit is nothing more than *teotl* or *itz.* The reason the Mesoamerican views *do not* amount to such a reductionism is that while *teotl* or *itz* is fundamentally the nature of all things, the facts about how *teotl* or *itz* manifests, how it moves and changes, and the things that are of the nature of *teotl* or *itz* are not constituted by or explicable solely in terms of this fundamental stuff of reality. Even though we can say that individuals are of the nature of *teotl*, it is not quite right to say that they are *nothing more than teotl*. Despite their seeming opposition, it turns out that there are only subtle differences between the views that 1) all things are ultimately only one: *teotl, itz*, etc. (the monist view) and 2) all things are at the same time the one *and* themselves and *teotl* or *itz*, and there are infinite possible (and thus actually existent) things (the universalist view). I argue here that given the views we find concerning the mind-dependence of the cosmos, substitution, transformation, embedded identity, the nature of being and transshipment of essence, it is much more plausible to take a universalist system as central to Mesoamerican philosophical traditions than a monist system, although the two have a great deal of overlap. This is one of the key implications of the various types of soul discussed in both Maya and Aztec traditions. The *tonalli* of the Aztec tradition and *ch'ul* of the Maya tradition constitute only *one* aspect of the human soul. These aspects are closest to representation of the related concepts *teotl* and *itz*, respectively (as pointed out above). The Addition of further soul concepts alongside these, coexisting in the same individual, suggests just the kind of "embedding" that we see in the case of personal identity. This framework of ontological embedding appears consistent across the variety of metaphysical topics discussed in Mesoamerican traditions. Given the discussions surrounding embedding in other contexts, as well as the way concepts such as *teotl* or *itz* are dealt with, it seems likely that here too, in consideration of being and the cosmos, we find a view of embedding. A thing can be *at the same time* itself and *teotl* or *itz*, and this entails that there are things other than *teotl* or *itz*, even if at the same time these things are *identical* to *teotl* or *itz*. Just as the same activity can embed or manifest distinct persons, the same stuff can be both *teotl* and its individual manifestation. A tree is *both* a tree *and* a manifestation of *teotl*, not only a manifestation of *teotl* that can be understood solely through reference to *teotl*. Thus, reductionism would not work either ontologically or epistemologically. Describing the world in terms only of *teotl* would leave out everything else that exists, and would make it impossible to know all facts about the world.

Take the Ometeotl of the Aztec tradition as an example. If the point was to stress the fundamental duality of all things and the constitution of the world by two metaphysically distinct substances, the two aspects of Ometeotl would have been separated from one another, made distinct, not combined in a single entity. If the focus is duality, why would this duality be unified? On the other hand, however, if the focus was the unity of all things and monism, why would the dual nature of Ometeotl be stressed? Ometeotl could have been presented as simply *teotl itself*, much as the unity of God is stressed in the texts of the Abrahamic tradition, or the unity of Brahman is stressed in Advaita Vedanta. The fact that here with Ometeotl, and throughout the Mesoamerican traditions, we find *duality within unity*, is metaphysically relevant. This is just what we find when we look to issues such as personal identity, time, and other metaphysical issues. In the *Popol Vuh*, for example, the beginning account of the construction of the cosmos refers to a number of pairs of gods, who are together unified in a pair referred to as Midwife and Patricarch, Xpiyacoc and Xmucane. The passage reads:

> Here we shall gather the manifestation, the declaration, the account of the sowing and dawning by the Framer and the Shaper, She Who Has Borne Children and He Who Has Begotten Sons, as they are called; along with Hunahpu Possum and Hunahpu Coyote, Great White Peccary and Coati, Sovereign and Quetzal Serpent, Heart of Lake and Heart of Sea, Creator of the Green Earth and Creatior of the Blue Sky, as they are called. These collectively are evoked and given expression as the Midwife and the Patriarch, whose names are Xpiyacoc and Xmucane, the Protector and the Shelterer, Twice Midwife and Twice Patriarch, as they are called in Quiché [K'iche'] traditions. They gave voice to all things and accomplished their purpose in purity of being and in truth.[25]

Here, we see a statement of both unity and duality. All of the various pairs of gods are unified in a basic pair going under different names, and this pair can also be understood as unified. The unity of the pairs here should not be seen as a denial of their fundamental parthood, any more than a claim of duality should be seen as a denial of their fundamental unity. Within Mesoamerican traditions we generally find acceptance a fundamental coexistence of unity and plurality, without the need to reduce one to the other. Their metaphysics tends not to be *reductive* metaphysics. We can understand the connection between these various aspects of the cosmos in terms of a correlative metaphysics and in terms of embeddedness.

This is also demonstrated by the existence of gods who are at the same time humans, or humans who are at the same time spirit entities such as a *nahual* or *way*. There is no reduction entailed here – it is not that Queztalcoatl's *true* nature is as a god, and his nature as a human reduces to this, or vice versa – rather it is that he is both, one and the same (which ought to be a familiar view for those with understanding of Christian doctrine, in which Jesus is both fully human and fully God). Likewise, *teotl* is both many and one. The cosmos is both multiple and unified. The metaphysics of reduction, whether reduction to a single fundamental

---

[25] *Popol Vuh*, Christenson trans.

metaphysical substance or multiple substances, is largely foreign to Mesoamerica.[26] Things correlate with one another, can be identical to one another despite change, transform into one another – but they do not *reduce* to any particular thing or things.

We find this lesson reinforced when considering activity and roles. Barbara Tedlock discusses the idea of accrual of roles in K'iche' Maya thought. One fundamental role does not undermine or preclude another, just as one identity does not preclude another – a thing can have multiple essences. Discussing her initiation as a daykeeper (*ajq'ij*), Tedlock writes: "[F]rom my teacher's point of view, there was never any question of having to make a final choice between being an anthropologist and becoming a calendrical diviner. Among the [K'iche'], new roles are properly added to old ones, not substituted for them."[27]

Realms and Interconnectivity

Given this relational metaphysics and views of interconnectivity, we should expect to find similar connectivity and transformative potential between different realms, such as Xibalba and the upper world. These realms are connected in the same way different beings are connected to one another, with each having the possibility of being or becoming the other. Even though these realms are discussed in numerous sources in some way "separate" from one another, just as we take distinct objects, persons, and other things to be separate or distinct, they are at the same time identifiable with and always transformable to one another. Mesoamerican traditions stress the simultaneous separation and connectivity of these worlds.

The underworld is understood as not generally or easily accessible to humans, absent death, a long journey, or ritual extension of vision. There are certain ritually important areas in the visible world associated with entrances to the underworld or otherwise supernatural realms.

---

[26] I do not want to make the stronger claim here that reduction is completely *absent* from Mesoamerican traditions, as such strong claims require a demonstration that it cannot be found *anywhere*. Such claims, given the diversity of human viewpoints and the prevalence of disagreement, tend to be wrong.

[27] Tedlock, *Time and the Highland Maya*, 10.

Throughout Mesoamerica, caves were associated with such entrances[28], and were understood in a host of different ways. In addition to being seen as openings to the underworld, they were also sometimes associated with fertility and birth – the opening in the earth reminiscent of the vaginal opening, from which a newly constructed human emerges. Some scholars have argued that caves are associated with creation and emergence more generally, with the cave as the birthing place of the cosmos. Duncan Earle writes that "the cave was the epitome of the emergence location, as exemplified by the pan-Mesoamerican notion of the sun, moon, sky, and planets (all gods) coming out of caves, and as the origin and emergence place for winds and rain."[29]

In Maya imagery, entering or emerging from the earth, in caves or through other openings, seems to often be connected to movement between aspects of the world. We see in the sarcophagus lid of the ruler Janaab Pakal at Palenque the ruler descending to the underworld through an opening in the world tree – a portal or route through which he can travel to this realm. Alan Sandstrom discusses contemporary Nahua shamans who consider caves to be entrances to Mictlan, the underworld and realm of the dead.[30] Rituals concerning the dead and ancestors will commonly take place at such sites. There is discussion in a number of Mesoamerican contexts of emerging from the earth. A nineteenth century text on Mixtec grammar by the priest Antonio de los Reyes discusses those who consider themselves true Mixtecs, referred to as *tai nuhu* ("men of the earth"), based on the view that they originated in and emerged from the center of the earth.[31] In the Yucatan, *cenotes*, large sinkholes filled with wells of water, play a similar symbolic role to the cave in other areas.

Interconnectivity between these realms or aspects of the world involves transformation – birth from one into the other, ritual communication, or the symbolic journey as in the descent of the hero twins to Xibalba in the *Popol Vuh*. The interconnectivity between these realms is most closely

---

[28] Chládek, *Exploring Maya Ritual Caves*, 9–17.

[29] Earle, "Maya Caves across Time and Space", 81.

[30] Sandstrom, "The Cave-Pyramid Complex among the Contemporary Nahua."

[31] Smith, "The Relationship between Mixtec Manuscript Painting and the Mixtec Language," 68.

associated with creation, generation. As we have seen in previous chapters, creation requires duality. This is marked in terms of worlds by dual aspects of the world, operating both antagonistically and sympathetically with one another to bring about new things through transformation. Each operates on the other. The realm of the dead destroys that of the living, and the living reconstitutes that of the dead. Thus, we can make sense of the dual associations of these openings in the earth: Entrance to the underworld and point of emergence of created beings. The intersection between two aspects of the world plays both roles. The stress on realms and separation, then, is not so much a claim that there are separate or separable worlds or domains (how then could they interact and be essential for one another), but rather a claim of the necessary duality of creation and maintenance of the cosmos. Creation requires life and death, sacrifice and rebirth, god and human.

Further Reading

For more on a number of the issues discussed in this chapter, see Friedel, Schele, and Parker, *Maya Cosmos*; Stuart, *The Order of Days*, Maffie, *Aztec Philosophy*; McLeod, *Philosophy of the Ancient Maya*. Full publication details for all of these works can be found in the bibliography.

7   Knowledge, Seeing

Seeing

We have briefly discussed in previous chapters the image of "seeing" and vision as associated with knowledge in numerous Mesoamerican traditions. The theme of seeing is central in Mesoamerican conceptions of knowledge. Indeed, the concept of knowledge in Mesoamerica would be better described in English as the concept of "seeing." The sense of sight is associated both with our ability to process images of the world, and with our ability to access truths, to understand how things are. We find this association in a number of cultural contexts. In modern English, the word "see" can be used for "understand" or "know," as in "I see what you're saying." This connotation is found in numerous other linguistic and cultural contexts as well – in Chinese, terms for light and visual clarity can express knowledge or understanding, such as *ming* 明 (bright, clear, understand).

The senses in general might be understood as intimately connected to a concept of knowledge, as knowledge generally has to do with cognitive access of facts about *how things are* in some broad sense, and our most direct and intimate familiarity with how things are we take to be through the senses. Insofar as we can gain knowledge through more indirect means such as reasoning, we generally take this knowledge to be *about* the world accessible through the senses. Some even understand reasoning to be a kind of sense, akin to vision, through which we access certain kinds of truth about the world. The separation of reason from sensation largely depends on a certain kind of soul/body dualism. While Mesoamerican traditions do seem to draw a distinction between the soul(s) and body, it is not a substantive metaphysical distinction.

Just as scent and touch are different, and access different features of the world inaccessible through vision alone, reasoning can access yet other features of the world. This in itself does not show that reasoning has any distinct metaphysical status from the senses. One distinction that is sometimes drawn is that the senses are *passive*, which distinguishes them from abilities such as reasoning. The precolonial Mesoamerican traditions had a different view on this, however. According to them, the senses *are not* passive, but rather play an active role in accessing and manifesting things in the world. When we see, hear, or touch, it is not that we are simply receptacles for the world imposing itself on us and thus leaving its impression, but our minds play active roles in constructing what we access. In this way, the Mesoamerican traditions actually had greater insight into the nature of sense than Indo-European traditions. We know today that sense cannot be understood in terms of passive impression, and that structures and activities of the brain are responsible for sensation. In addition, we understand that despite our attempts to access the "mind-independent" world by canceling out the effects of sensation, there appear to be certain things that are ineliminably associated with mental construction.

Knowledge, then, necessarily is not just going to be a matter of accessing stable and completely mind-independent truths about the world (separate from us), but is also going to involve an aspect of creativity and construction. The association of this with *seeing* specifically, and the other senses more peripherally, in Mesoamerican traditions, also tells us something important about sensation. There is always a creative and participative aspect of sensation, according to Mesoamerican traditions. We *contribute* to sensation as active partners with the world. Recall the focus on activity and its association with being, discussed in previous chapters. To be is to act – so also to perceive, to sense, to know is to act, and to create. Houston, Stuart, and Taube note this active aspect of sensation in the Maya tradition:

> By means of graphic devices such as speech, scent, and sight scrolls, the Classic Maya communicated the presence, nature, and semantic content of sight, smell, hearing, touch, and taste to an extent unparalleled in most other parts of the ancient world. The visual conveyance of sense suggests that it was understood to be projective, meaning that the body did not

passively but actively reached out to see, smell, taste, touch, and hear, as though through tendrils extending from the body.[1]

While the senses in general were associated roughly with knowing and understanding, in most Mesoamerican traditions vision in particular was centrally associated with these concepts. Vision or seeing was sometimes understood as summative, with other sense concepts falling under its purview (just as in English, to access facts about something through taste or hearing could be expressed via the language of "seeing"). Houston, Stuart, and Taube mention a Tzotzil Maya summative notion of vision as including "total physical apprehension."[2] It was in other cases understood as at the top of a hierarchy of senses. Senses are associated with understanding in numerous texts. In the *Primeros memoriales* compiled by Sahagun, we see association of age with declining sensation and understanding ("the very elderly man: now is work is nothing, now he does not understand, he can no longer hear, etc."[3]). Likewise, we see that the grandfather is associated with broadening the senses of others, a reference to instruction: "[T]he good grandfather is an admonisher, an instructor... He opens people's eyes, he opens people's ears."[4] Book 10 of the *Florentine Codex*, in a passage on the human eye, reads:

> [I]t illuminates one, it enlightens one, it leads one, it guides one, it sustains one ... our mirror, instrument for seeing, that by which all live, precious, the esteemed, guardian of honor, it illuminates, it illuminates one, it enlightens one, it leads...[5]

Houston, Stuart, and Taube discuss the *creative* aspect of sight in the Maya tradition, where it is associated with knowing and also with a "procreative" constructive capacity. They mention ethnographies of Yucatec Maya associating vision with agentive and willful activity[6] and creativity. This association is enhanced in noticing the connection between the eye

---

[1] Houston, Stuart, and Taube, *The Memory of Bones*, 134.

[2] Houston, Stuart, and Taube, 138.

[3] *Memoriales*, Lopez Austin trans., 693.

[4] Lopez Austin trans., 274/703.

[5] *Florentine Codex* Book 10, Anderson and Dibble trans., 103.

[6] Houston, Stuart, and Taube, 167; Hanks, *Referential Practice: Language and Lived Space among the Maya*, 89.

and the Sun, given the clearly central role of the Sun in both creation and in knowledge. We also see this in associations between terms in a number of Maya languages. As Allen Christenson points out,[7] the K'iche' term for giving birth is "to dawn" or "to give light" (*-ya' saq*). Solar and eye imagery are combined and associated in both Maya and Aztec sources, such as the *Dresden Codex*. The association of vision with the god Itzamnaaj/Itzamna is doubly symbolic – in numerous images, including sun god imagery at Palenque, the god's eyes are rendered in a cross-eyed manner in which the eyes themselves are duplicates of the glyph for "mirror" (and darkness – based on obsidian as discussed above).

Seeing is something that happens not only on an individual level, but also communally. The community can come to "see" through rituals devised to allow shared access to certain aspects of the world. To know is often to *share* knowledge. Sometimes, what makes a piece of information knowledge is its foundation in a shared belief system, constructed by experts of various kinds. Today, we say that we *know* that Tom Hanks is an actor or that Ottawa is the capital of Canada. This knowledge is rooted in shared communal features – Tom Hanks and Ottawa have these features on the basis of communally visible roles, and the knowledge of these roles is based on access to the community. To know that Ottawa is the capital of Canada is a very different kind of knowledge from knowing that my car keys are in my pocket. It is a kind of knowledge that also shares similarity to knowledge as *familiarity* – in the sense that we know a friend. To say that we know a friend in this sense is to say that we are familiar with them, close to them, associated with them. We can be familiar with or associated with communally held information in a similar way.

Knowledge as seeing in this communal sense requires communally accessible and co-creative activity. Knowledge cannot be generated by the sole scholar operating independently, but requires the force of the ritual of the community. This is part of the reason for the centrality of practices such as daykeeping – playing the human role in the continual creation of the cosmos is not the work of an individual, but of a society, and it requires communication between ritual experts, leaders, and spectators in the community. The vision of the community, in witnessing the continual

---

[7] Christenson, *Popol Vuh*, 49.

creation of the cosmos through performances such as that of the *Popol Vuh* and other rituals, is itself a key part of the creative act. This is why the *Popol Vuh* text claims that the *Popol Vuh* can "no longer be seen." It is not because the text is not written, or even that no one can perform it – surely there could have been small secret performances. It could no longer be seen in the way that we might say an unreleased film cannot be seen. It cannot be partaken in by the community in the requisite way, and thus while it exists in some sense – the copy may exist for example – it is not a complete or functional entity given its intended role. Houston, Stuart, and Taube discuss the power of this communal vision:

> …[W]hen the Classic Maya regarded individual perception, at least in their glyphic texts, it was not simply as a vista or a bracing view of architecture, but as a reciprocal, heavily social context involving other people or beings. In truth, this was a "communion-oriented" vision, an "ecological event" of a very special sort. With the gods in particular, the *-ichnal* [visual field, space of perception] would have been extended, presumably, by the field of view of multiple participants.[8]

Seeing in Mesoamerican traditions is connected to ritual and generation of knowledge as well. The community requires certain people and rituals to serve as link to unseen aspects of the world. Just as in the modern world, we rely on experts and specialists to generate what we think of as a kind of shared communal knowledge of our world (which is why we say things such as "we know that the sun is a product of nuclear fusion"). Our ability to access certain features of the world is dependent on the abilities of particular groups and individuals who can demonstrate or more directly access relevant facts. I know that the Sun is a product of nuclear fusion not because I scientifically demonstrate that this is so, or even know how that would be done, but because I rely on trustworthy sources who *did* demonstrate this. Their epistemic work makes my true belief into knowledge. Likewise, the communal work of ritual performance and the individual work of activities like daykeeping on behalf of the community contributes to communal *seeing* – and this seeing, as we have already discussed above, has a creative element. The epistemic creative ability of the community, then, is a central aspect of knowing.

---

[8] Houston, Stuart, and Taube, *The Memory of Bones*, 174.

In order to understand what it is humans can come to know through this ritual work and through the particular kinds of special access certain members of the community have to unseen aspects of the world, we have to understand what those rituals are, how they work, and what aspects or activities of the individuals involve have this effect, and how this works. *Ritual* and *special perceptual ability*, then, are key aspects of a theory of knowledge in precolonial Mesoamerican traditions.

Rituals for Seeing

Much of the written material of the Mesoamerican traditions, both precolonial and postcolonial material, deals with ritual and religion. We see from both these sources that communal rituals were fundamental in the lives of early Mesoamerican cultures, connected to organization of the world (thus the heavy focus on calendrics and location – fixing time and place), and the location of communal and individual life in the context of a broader time and place, linking generations. The rituals, as numerous scholars have pointed out,[9] provide the community with a sense of time and community. This is a function ritual generally has throughout the world, in all traditions. Even in the modern West, in which ritual has been personalized to a large extent as response to cultural pluralism (the wrong response, I think, as it disallows shared communal rituals in order to preserve earlier individual ones), there are some shared rituals that allow us to have a conception of ourselves in a particular community, in a time and place, etc. Thus, the "winter holidays," are generally shared by everyone even if one does not belong to a particular religious tradition. Rituals have many functions, and one of its most important is to create a cohesive community and organize the life of this community in terms of time and place.

In Mesoamerican traditions, an additional purpose of ritual is generation of knowledge. At the beginning of the *Chilam Balam of Chumayel*, we find a detailed account of a ritual fixing the space of the cosmos. Roys translates this as the "ritual of the four world-quarters." This establishes a number of correlative associations between a number of aspects of and things in the cosmos and the different directions. For example, we find:

---

[9] See Van't Hooft, *The Ways of the Water*, 53.

The white flint stone is their stone in the north. The white ceiba tree of abundance is the arbor of the white Mucencab. White-breasted are their turkeys. White Lima-beans are their Lima-beans. White corn is their corn. [...] The white wild bees are in the north, The white pachea is their flower. A large white blossom is their cup.[10]

This opening ritual comes just before the focus of the rest of the text, a mytho-historical account of the people of the Yucatan, creation, and accounts of calendrics and other important information for the community. The placement of these rituals seems to fix the human construction of time, place, and the cosmos as the beginning of the project of creating and recounting the kind of knowledge contained in texts such as the *Chilam Balam* texts. We find very much the same kind of picture in the *Popol Vuh*, in the attempts of the gods to create humanity and their early failures, first because the physical constitution of the created beings failed (the people made of mud), then because they did not have the proper minds, abilities, and understanding (the people of wood). When the gods finally created humanity from maize, one of its central defining characteristics was *knowledge*, the ability to see, perfect vision. This vision/knowledge was so vast that it alarmed the gods themselves. The *Popol Vuh* describes the ability:

Perfect was their sight, and perfect was their knowledge of everything beneath the sky. If they gazed about them, looking intently, they beheld that which was in the sky and that which was upon the earth. Instantly they were able to behold everything. They did not have to walk to see all that existed beneath the sky. They merely saw it from wherever they were. Thus their knowledge became full. Their vision passed beyond the trees and the rocks, beyond the lakes and the seas, beyond the mountains and the valleys.[11]

Their knowledge of everything that they saw was complete – the four corners and the four sides, that which is within the sky and that which is within the earth.[12]

The vision here associated with knowledge is perceptual, and the key is its ability to span great distance, to cover all aspects of the world. Imagery throughout Mesoamerica linking vision to knowledge presents

[10] *Chilam Balam of Chumayel*, Roys trans., 22.
[11] *Popol Vuh*, Christenson trans., 183–4.
[12] *Popol Vuh*, Christenson trans., 185.

one with preternatural understanding as having many eyes, or as having eyes extending far outside of the body. These distant or otherwise inaccessible aspects of the world accessed through ritual become accessible through the enhanced perception and more generally enhanced powers of apprehension of features of the world of one engaged in certain kinds of ritual. Just as we may hold that our powers of apprehension are enhanced through reading a book or performing an internet search, according to Mesoamerican traditions certain rituals have the power to extend human vision in the general sense of knowing.

The Seeing Individual: *Ajq'ij, itz'aat, tlamatini*

When we discuss philosophy and the specialized roles concerned with generation and transmission of knowledge, a few different types of people can be considered. The "daykeeper" in Maya tradition, scribes, the priest, such as the mythical (or more likely semi-mythical) "Chilam Balam" said to be responsible for the texts associated with his name from the Yucatan, and most famously (and perhaps controversially), the Aztec *tlamatini* ("knowledgeable person"), which Leon-Portilla, following Sahagún, translates and understands as *filósofo* (philosopher). While I discuss in this section all of these categories of knower, it is on the Maya daykeeper (*aj q'ij, ah kin* in Yucatec Maya) and the Aztec *tlamatini* that I will spend most time, as these two figures represent the two major methods of generating knowledge discussed by Mesoamerican traditions – the ritual and discursive.

An important figure in the Maya tradition in terms of the construction and maintenance of communal knowledge is the *aj q'ij*. The knowledge and practices of the *ajq'ij* is described even by practitioners in contemporary contexts as philosophical and nature, as opposed to religious (taking Christianity as the key example of religion). One of the *aj'qijab* in Quetzaltenango interviewed by Daniel Fitjar discusses this:

> I don't practice Christianity, in other words, I have no religion. The Maya is not religion. [...] It's philosophy. The "Maya religion" is not a religion, it is philosophy. In Guatemala, as *ajq'ijes*, we are spiritual guides.[13]

---

[13] Fitjar, *Balancing the World*, 34.

Interestingly here, when Fitjar asks the *ajq'ij* about the distinction between spirituality and philosophy, he answers that they accept both, and not just a single determination of what Maya thought amounts to. "We are dualists," he says. "We're not monists like in the Christian religion."[14] This reinforces the idea discussed earlier that Maya thought (and Mesoamerican thought more generally) should not be understood as reductionist, with things and their differences fundamentally grounded in *one* kind of thing.[15] It is possible to recognize the distinctions between things, without collapsing or reducing them to something else, while at the same time recognizing the ways in which these things do also represent the same structures of the world and can transform to one another, and can be reconceptualized. Contemporary *ajq'ijab* will often refer to themselves as philosophers or as "spiritual guides." These two roles are not separate in Mesoamerican traditions. In this way, we can see the Mesoamerican conception of the philosopher (surely influenced by precolonial Mesoamerican ideas) as closer to that of the Socratic conception of the philosopher than that of the contemporary academic conception. Just as Socrates saw himself as a "midwife" helping others to birth knowledge and thus liberate the soul, the essential role of the *ajq'ij* is guidance, for the community and individual, which requires the ability to *see*, to know.

A literal translation of *ajq'ij* would be "keeper of days" or "maker of days," a human activity that we see in the *Popol Vuh* plays a critical role in the maintenance of the cosmos and community. We see that in the association of *aj* with "making," there is a stress on the creative aspect of human activity here. One who keeps the days does not merely passively record what is independently happening in the world, but plays an active role (with the community) in constructing the cosmos as we experience it. Generation of knowledge, then, is not a matter of simply accessing the mind-independent world, but creativity and shaping of the world by the mind is part of the process of generating knowledge.

---

[14] Fitjar, *Balancing the World*, 34.

[15] It's also interesting here that the *aj q'ij* quoted here sees Christianity as holding a monist view of the world, in distinction from the Maya view. He could have in mind here the idea of a single god at the center of the religion, whereas we find a fundamental duality behind creation in Maya and other Mesoamerican traditions.

A particularly powerful image used by one of the contemporary *ajq'ijab* to whom Fitjar spoke is that of the *ajqi'j* as "balancing the world, balancing the universe." (Fitjar, 41). The *ajq'ij* plays this role, and their guidance role, in part through their ability to see, to access normally unseen parts of the world. Fitjar explains:

> In Maya communities, the *ajq'ij* is a person whom people can approach to solve all kinds of problems. The *ajq'ijab* possess the ability to communicate with beings and things normally not reached easily by others, and this gives them the possibility to find a spiritual solution to personal and social problems: to cure sickness; to give thanks or pray for harvests and many other tasks.[16]

The *ajq'ij* in the contemporary context seems to correspond to some extent then with the shaman/priest in precolonial contexts, such figures as the *chilam* of Postclassic Yucatan, or the priests/rulers of the Classic Period. The intermediating ability of the *ajq'ij*, which can manifest as medical, moral, ritual, or any other form, is based on the knowledge of the *ajq'ij* in terms of their ability to access unseen aspects of the world. It is not the power of the *ajq'ij* that makes possible this advising, healing, etc., but rather the sacred vital power inherent in the world, associated above with *ch'ul* or *itz*. The shamanic ability of the *aj'qij* is to serve as a bridge between the community and the unseen aspects of the world from which humanity can derive power, meaning, ability, etc. The bearer of knowledge, in this view, is primarily a *guide*. Because of this, the *aj'qij* also must have understanding of and ability to maintain the key practices of Maya culture – most importantly the practice described in their name, "keeping the days." Part of this process is understanding of the ritual calendar and its day associations, but other knowledge we associate with "scholarship" must also be part of the store of the *ajq'ij*. Medicine, history, myth, and more. One contemporary *aj'qij* of Guatemala describes the role as "a repository – of history, legend, origins – the collective memory if you like of a community, sometimes a family."[17]

---

[16] Fitjar, *Balancing the World*, 41.
[17] Fitjar, *Balancing the World*, 76.

The role of the bearer of knowledge in Maya traditions is closely linked to political organization. As we have seen, knowledge and guidance of the community go hand in hand. Organization of the community thus will involve knowledgeable people in roles of leadership, who are able to be intermediaries for the entire community between the unseen aspects of the world and the seen. In the contemporary Maya region, there is a hierarchy of such knowledgeable persons, with the top occupied by a position likely closest to the precolonial role of shaman-priest – in K'iche' called the *chuchkajawib* ("mother-father"). This shamanic figure is the key individual responsible for communal rituals, serving in the hierarchy under the *ajaw*, a term still used in contemporary Maya languages, but in this context referring to *elders* at the head of the community, rather than the ruler figures of the Classic Period. The Classic Period *ajaw* in some ways combined aspects of all of the roles discussed here. The contemporary *chuchkajawib* can be understood as a higher rung of the hierarchy to which *ajq'ij* also belong as individual knowers. This hierarchy, like the hierarchies of academia, religious institutions, and similar groups, is meant to connect to the scope of roles and responsibilities – with those higher up the hierarchy having broader responsibility for the community and for the training and oversight of those below.

A related category in Maya traditions is the *itz'aat* (sage), found in the Maya lowlands. We see right away a connection to the key concept of being or vital energy, *itz*, with the *itz'aat* understood as "one who manipulates *itz*." The person of knowledge here is the person of *ability* – one who is able to use *itz* for practical purposes. Knowing a thing, in Mesoamerican traditions, is not to have a definition of it, but is to be able to control it, to shape it, to work with it. As we have seen above, knowledge and creativity are closely linked. As with being, knowledge is active and constructive, vital, constantly in motion.

The use of *tlamatini* in Aztec texts does not determine a specific class or role. A number of different people are described as *tlamatinime* (knowledgeable or wise persons), including the *nahualli* (*naoalli*, shaman or seer, connected to the concept of the *nahual*, animal spirit). The general term marked someone who had some official role connected to knowledge or teaching, a priest, scribe, physician, writer, or keeper of writings. A good parallel would be the ancient Greek conception of the "philosopher" (*philosophos*) or the contemporary conception of the professional scholar. It does not make sense in the precolonial Mesoamerican context, similar to other ancient societies, to distinguish between different types of scholars such as the philosopher, physician, or empirical scientist. In Mesoamerica, as in ancient Europe, China, India, and elsewhere in the world, there was considerable overlap in these areas, and we did not see the kind of specialization of scholarship that we find today. A scholar, a wise person, was one who dealt with many different subjects, though not necessarily all of them. Each learned person was different. There were some, of course, who had to have particular kinds of knowledge and ability, such as the ability to perform certain rituals, follow calendric systems, and other socially necessary knowledge. These tasks formed the main reason for the existence of scholars as such, as a distinct class in society, rather than leaving the task of learning and generating knowledge to nonspecialists in the community.

A passage in the *Primeros memoriales* of Sahagún describes the *tlamatini*, again linking knowledge to vision:

> The wise man: a light, a torch, a stout torch that does not smoke. A perforated mirror, a mirror pierced on both sides. His are the black and red ink, his are the illustrated manuscripts, he studies the illustrated manuscripts. He himself is writing and wisdom. He is the path, the true way for others. He directs people and things; he is a guide in human affairs. The wise man is careful (like a physician) and preserves tradition. His is the handed-down wisdom; he teaches it; he follows the path of truth. Teacher of the truth, he never ceases to admonish. He makes wise the countenances of others; to them he gives a face (a personality); he leads them to develop it. He opens their ears; he enlightens them. He is the teacher of guides; he shows them their path. One depends upon him. He puts a mirror before others; he makes them prudent, cautious; he causes a face (a personality) to appear in them. He attends to things; he regulates their path, he arranges and commands. He applies his light to the world. He knows what is above us and in the region of the dead. He is a serious man. Everyone is comforted by him, corrected, taught. Thanks to him people humanize their will and receive a strict education. He comforts the heart, he comforts the people, he helps, gives remedies, heals everyone.[18]

---

[18] *Primeros memoriales*, Leon-Portilla trans., in *Aztec Thought and Culture*, 27.

We can see from this that the *tlamatini* not only sees (knows), but causes others to see, brings his access of these unseen aspects of the world to the rest of the community. The specialized knowledge and ability of the *tlamatini* is ultimately for the use and benefit of the community, in extending its vision and thus serving as a guide, in matters moral and medical. Interestingly here, we see that the *tlatanimi* is associated with rectifying the lives of others, in terms of eliminating confusion and struggling, whether that be a matter of intellectual struggle, moral struggle, or physical struggle. The vision of the *tlamatini* into the realm of the dead, *mictlan*, is central here – and resonates with the crucial ability in the Maya tradition to see into the realm of the dead, *Xibalba*. The ability of the *tlamatini* to be a "guide in human affairs" requires his ability to see greater distances than most people can, to access generally unseen aspects of the world such as *mictlan*. The associations made in the above passage shows the connection between knowledge and seeing, light, and guidance – the wise person helps others along their *way* – the image of light and vision of course essentially connected to navigation and travel. Human life, like all things in the cosmos, is marked by continual movement and change, which leads many traditions to use a path metaphor to describe human life and activity (for example, the *dao* of the Chinese tradition). The far-reaching vision of the *tlamatini* allows him to direct others with lesser vision on their way, and in this way he serves as *substitute* for the vision of the community.

One interesting feature of the discussion of the *tlamatini* in the *Primeros memoriales* that also shows the essential connection to the community is mention of the false *tlamatini*. Such a person, according to this account, is concerned not about the community or even about the truth, but instead about his own ego, about having a name for being greater or more important than others. The entire thing is about satisfying vanity for the false *tlamatini*, and as a result of this, people are misguided on their paths, and ultimately "he causes the people to perish; he mysteriously puts an end to everything."[19]

We see here the concern with the distinction between truth and falsity and the association of the *tlamatini* with concern for truth, a close parallel to the Socratic conception of the philosopher. The accounts of

---

[19] Leon-Portilla trans., in *Aztec Thought and Culture*, 32.

the *tlamatinime* we find in Sahagún's collections may seem even *suspiciously* close to Socratic or early Greek conceptions of the concerns and activities of philosophers, and further from other parts of the Mesoamerican traditions than what we find in other sources.

The *tlamatini* played a similar role in the Aztec tradition to that of the *ajq'ij* in the Maya. Like the *aj'qij*, *tlamatinime* had a number of overlapping roles, including keeping the ritual calendar and divining on its basis, guiding, healing, and serving as intermediary between the community and the unseen aspects of the world. The *tlamatinime* were responsible for the performance of rituals that brought various benefits to the community, for keeping important cultural and communal knowledge, including in the sacred books, and they took leadership roles in the community. The connection between knowledge, guidance, and political leadership is seen throughout Mesoamerican thought. A passage from the *Coloquios y Doctrina Cristiana* has an Aztec response to a Christian priest, referring to the *tlamatinime* as:

> [T]hose who guide us ... who receive the title of Quetzalcoatl ... They busy themselves day and night with the placing of incense, with their offerings, with the thorns to draw their blood. Those who see ... Those who arrange how a year falls.... To them falls to speak of the gods.[20]

We can see here the connection to the concept of substitution, as the *tlatmatine* is associated with the god Quetzalcoatl. (This may also give some hint as to the appearance of Queztalcoatl in Aztec history as both god and human). We also see connection here to the shamanic autosacrificial bloodletting ritual performed throughout Mesoamerica, demonstrating sacrifice as well as allowing a conduit for communication between different aspects of the world – the gods and ancestors on one side, and the living human community on the other.

Interestingly, a number of contemporary sources refer to figures like the *aj'qijab* and the *tlamatinime* as "philosophers." This choice of terminology suggests that some want to distinguish the knowledgeable person in the Mesoamerican context from that of the intermediary and sage in the context of religion, specifically Christianity. The key example of the sage or ritual intermediary in the most familiar Christian traditions in Mesoamerica (until

[20] Graña-Behrens, "Itz'aat and Tlamatini," 25.

the modern day) is the Catholic priest. There are certainly many similarities between this role and that of the *aj'qij*, *itz'aat* or *tlamatini*, yet a number of scholars and practitioners reject this association, preferring to refer to these roles as those of "philosophers." Bernardino de Sahagún himself translated the term *tlamatini* as "philosopher". Miguel Leon-Portilla followed this, and explained that the focus on wisdom, maintenance of knowledge, and ethical ability matched the concept of the philosopher as we find it in Western traditions. A number of *aj'qijab* interviewed by Daniel Fitjar also understood themselves as philosophers rather than religious experts or clerics, mainly because they associated the latter categories with Christian priests, and religion with Christianity specifically (perhaps a result of the hundreds of years of colonial Spanish insistence that Christianity is the only true religion).

One of the difficulties here, of course, is to distinguish the practice, knowledge, and role of the philosopher from that of similar figures such as the priest, political advisor, scholar, or spiritual guide. This is notoriously difficult to do. Professional philosophers have been unable to come up with an adequate definition of philosophy or the philosopher that captures the practice of all of those we refer to with that name. This is certainly because the category is far too broad and variably understood to admit of a clear and precise definition, just like the other roles mentioned above. The term one uses for particular kinds of people will often be one of personal choice and inclination – those in Mesoamerica resistant to Christianity, for example, are more likely to call someone like an *ajq'ij* a philosopher, whereas someone less so may call them a priest or spiritual guide. It is very much the same as those antagonistic or ambivalent toward religious groups in the West who refer to themselves as "spiritual but not religious." Religion is there associated with particular organizations, most often the organizations most prominent in their communities or culture (mainline Protestant churches and the Catholic church in the USA, for example), and the person is, in rejecting the title of "religious" to themselves, rejecting affiliation with those groups. The person's own practices or communities might perfectly well be considered religious under any reasonable scope of the term, but such a person uses "religion" in a narrower sense than would most scholars of religion. The "philosopher," we see for at least some in Mesoamerica, is understood as a non-Christian alternative to the knowledgeable authority figure and intermediary between the divine and human found in the church.

Knowledge and Reduction

The knowledge of the daykeeper, the *tlamatini*, or other sage in Mesoamerican traditions is tied to life and practice, just as is the case for knowledge in most other philosophical traditions. While on occasion in contemporary philosophy we have lost sight of the reasons behind our concern with knowledge (in part because of our sometimes myopic move toward specialization in philosophy), in most traditions, the discovery of knowledge was tied to particular kinds of practical concerns. Why do we want to know about the world? What is it we can know about the world? Our experience, according to Mesoamerican traditions, teaches us what there is. One of the key features of some parts of the wider Indo-European philosophical tradition is the idea of knowledge as something extra-experiential, something to which our experience or our perception might blind us or trick us somehow. We find this, for example, in the views of Plato and of the Advaitins (among many others). Gaining knowledge is a matter of accessing something beyond the ultimately illusory appearances, the changing and non-eternal world of our experience. One does not have knowledge of a thing, according to Plato, until one has a *definition* of it, unchanging and eternal. And our experience does not provide us with definitions – indeed it could never do so, as our experience only familiarizes us with things in the continually changing physical world, not the eternal realm of the forms on which definitions are based.

Conceptions of knowledge in precolonial Mesoamerica are different than this, in that they take knowledge to be closely connected to experience, to perception. Mesoamerican traditions do not discount the realm of human experience as contributing to knowledge – indeed, such experience is *all there is* to knowledge. Lacking knowledge is not, according to these traditions, a matter of being unable to access the unifying definitions behind the illusions of our experience, but rather a matter of lacking certain kinds of experience. I lack knowledge of a thing when I have not experienced it, when I have not *seen* it. A common feature of Mesoamerican traditions is to accept the world the way we find it as the world, rather than taking it as illusory, constructed of some more fundamental aspect or substance, or less than fully real. When we ask of our experience "but what is it *really*?", we are simply looking for a way around having to accept the reality of what we experience. This is why rather than the reductive approach, we find much more commonly in Mesoamerican thought the *syncretic* approach.

This also largely explains the kind of syncretism and response to religious development and change that we find in Mesoamerica still today. The typical mode of Mesoamerican thought is syncretism, and we find it in metaphysics as well as religious expression. Contemporary *ajq'ijab* who are also Christians find no difficulty in adopting these two worldviews we often see as very different. To hold and follow one is not to dismiss and disbelieve the other. Any new worldview or way of thought does not *displace* others, but exists *alongside* others. The world is how we find it, with its multitude of ways. This is quite a different stance to that we find in Abrahamic religions, which have for the most part insisted on the reduction of religious experience to a single true way.[21] A vivid expression of a single unchanging and eternal truth lying behind the natural world (and in this case likely influenced by Platonism as well) can be found in the 6th *sura* (chapter) of the Qur'an, discussing Abraham's discovery of the one God, beginning with changing things:

> When the night grew dark upon him, he saw a star and said "this is my Lord!" But when it set, he said "I do not love things that set." Then when he saw the moon rising, he said "this one is my Lord!" But when it disappeared, he said "if my Lord does not guide me, I will certainly be one of the misguided people." Then when he saw the sun shining, he said "this must be my Lord – it is the greatest!" But again when it set, he declared, "O my people! O totally reject whatever you associate with God in worship."[22]

The desire to reduce is closely linked to the desire to *get rid of* some aspect of our experience, to explain it away, reject it, render it something we can ignore or devalue. Mesoamerican traditions tend to oppose this idea, and thus we do not see appeal to reduction as explanation. Generation of knowledge then is not the abstraction of some general or unified thing behind the less real changing things and experiences of the world, but a greater vision, an ability to see *more* of those numerous things of the world. Generation of knowledge is associated with experience rather than

---

[21] This is, of course, not without exceptions – there are universalist or syncretic traditions within Abrahamic religions as well, even if these are less common or prominent.
[22] Qur'an 6:76–78.

abstraction, with inflation rather than reduction. One who knows is not one who sees *one* thing in many, but one who sees many things where others see only one. This is why the person of knowledge is able to serve as a guide and intermediary, just like a person with a familiarity with terrain we've never traveled can serve as a guide through a region.

Barbara Tedlock refers to the Maya syncretic or universalist view as "complementary dualism" as opposed to the "analytical or oppositional dualism" of the imported European tradition.[23] What she means by this is the idea that the multiple kinds of things in the world are not reduced or explained in terms of some other thing, not collapsed into some ultimately real category and thus deprived of their own individual reality. Rather, in the Maya tradition things are accepted as themselves, as fully real alongside one another. The tradition, as others in Mesoamerica, is not uncomfortable with *multiplicity*. There is no single explanation for a given thing, rather there are *explanations*. While Tedlock's contrast between Maya and Western thought overlooks the diversity within each tradition, there certainly is an important strain of explanatory reductionism within Western tradition more generally, in particular within the form of Christianity imported to Mesoamerica by the Spanish in the sixteenth century. This tradition insisted on its own hegemony – that it could only be true if everything else was false. Maya thought generally did not take this position. This is why one could see then, and can still find today, those who take both Christianity and Maya religious thought as explanations of the world, as two ways of understanding how things are. The truth of one does not necessarily undercut the truth of the other, in just the same way that experiencing a scene as a serene and calming event does not make impossible another experiencing that same scene as chaotic and violent (or even the same person experiencing it as such). Given that the world, according to Mesoamerican traditions, is constantly in motion, transforming, correlatively interrelated, it does not make sense to talk about any one formulation, worldview, or understanding as *the* correct one, to the exclusion of the others. To account for the others by reducing them to something else to explain why they are mistaken is to fail to understand the ways these experiences and worldviews capture how things are in certain places and perspectives. To have knowledge, then, is not to have

[23] Tedlock, *Time and the Highland Maya*, 44.

an understanding of how all of those other perspectives are wrong and how they reduce, but to have an understanding of how they capture the world as one finds it, and how those with these perspectives find the world that way. One with this kind of knowledge, like a good therapist, will serve as the best kind of guide. An excellent guide is not one who can tell you why you're wrong based on a reductionist conception of the world, but rather one who can understand the way you see the world, where you are going, how you are moving, and thus can help you navigate this world.

A good example of knowledge here is to consider motivation and explanation. When we know how an individual acts, we can give an explanation for what they do. Often we look for a *single* overarching explanation, denying that there can be overdetermination. Perhaps one engages in an act that is politically expedient, personally enjoyable, and morally right. What is one's reason for performing this action? One may appeal to all three of these reasons, but we generally take one or the other as the true motivational reason. Which would have led the person to act in this way, even in the absence of the others? Would the person have done the act if it was morally right but neither politically expedient nor enjoyable? Or some other combination? One might act for all of these reasons, and there is no need to reduce the reasons to one foundational one (although there certainly may be cases in which there is one central reason but an individual uses other justifications as cover for what they take to be a less noble reason, and such things). Likewise, knowing is seeing multiple different aspects of things – understanding the ways they manifest as well as their potential – their distinct essence as well as the way this essence is interconnected with that of other things in the world.

Further Reading

For more on knowledge and particular practices connected to the roles discussed here, see Tedlock, *Time and the Highland Maya*; Megged and Wood, eds., *Mesoamerican Memory*; Fitjar, *Balancing the World: Contemporary Maya Ajq'ijab in Quetzaltenango, Guatemala*; Molesky-Poz, *Contemporary Maya Sprituality*. Full publication details for all of these works can be found in the bibliography.

8 Ethics

Throughout most of this book thus far, we have looked at primarily precolonial Mesoamerican thought, and the ways in which these traditions understood themselves before the arrival of the Spanish (even though we've used some colonial period texts to do so). In the previous chapter, we got some glimpses into the ways that these ideas are still understood today in Mesoamerica. In this final chapter, the two merge, the ancient and the contemporary, the historical and the forward-looking. And what more natural topic with which to make this transition than ethics and social philosophy, which looks at the questions surrounding how we live, how we make our way through this world in which we find ourselves. Precolonial Mesoamerican traditions certainly had much to say about this, some of which we find in their colonial period writings. These ideas have inspired new and related ones, however, which are vital to guiding people in Mesoamerica today, and, like the metaphysical and epistemological issues we have seen in earlier chapters, have much to contribute to thought and practice in today's world outside of Mesoamerica as well.

In this chapter, we look at Mesoamerican views on human activity and life. How did precolonial Mesoamerican philosophers think about proper or right action, in the case of the individual and the wider community? This includes issues such as the role of the state, the ruler, and the individual's duties toward each.

Perhaps the fullest early textual accounts we have of ethical and political discussions are found in Book 6 of Sahagún's *Florentine Codex*, the *Cantares Mexicanos,* and the K'iche' *Popol Vuh*. In precolonial glyphic sources, we find a good deal on politics and rulership, but relatively little on ethics. This is for a number of reasons – most of the glyphic texts that have survived have been the memorial texts on stelae and architecture, which was generally intended to commemorate accessions of rulers or important political events in the life of a ruler or the state, or the state itself – these two being closely tied together. The few paper books from precolonial Mesoamerica to which we still have access generally include ritual, astronomical, and calendric, and divinatory information. The reason why most of these texts survive today is that they were taken as souvenirs or curiosities by Spanish and brought to Europe, where they were kept in sufficiently dry conditions to remain intact. While the greatest degree of attention has turned to figures like the Franciscan priest Diego de Landa for destroying native books, most of the destruction happened because these books simply were not kept in secure and preserving locations after Spanish colonization, as they fell into disuse, likely in part because of Spanish colonial power. After Spanish colonization, there was no institution or group able and committed to preserve these texts, so the ones that existed inevitably fell victim to the rapid decay of the rainforest. As in many other parts of the world, texts are often unearthed in tombs and excavations (some of the most famous have given us the texts of the Dead Sea Scrolls and the Mawangdui Silk Texts, for example). In Mesoamerica, remains of bark paper books are still discovered on occasion, but these discoveries most often end in frustration, because the warm and humid climate of most of the wider region is particularly ill-suited to the preservation of ancient texts. While bark paper texts have been found, they are manifestly decayed and unreadable, unlike unearthed text carved in stone or painted on ceramics, which is more often salvageable.

The early colonial period texts tell us an enormous amount about Mesoamerican ethics and politics, even though those accounts have to be taken with a grain of salt to some extent. In the *Florentine Codex*, for example, we see an account of proper human activity that mirrors very closely certain ideas of Christianity, and ideas that are hard to locate in any precolonial sources, or seem to conflict with ideas we find in those earlier sources. While these accounts almost certainly give us some sense of the shape of Mesoamerican ethical thought during the colonial period, the extent to which that thought is influenced by Christianity at that point, and in these particular cases, is hard to know. For texts such as the *Florentine Codex*, which in Book 6 gives an account of Aztec ethical and political thought, it is quite possible that a number of Spanish or more broadly Christian ideas made their way into the text. The fact that there is a good deal of overlap with Christian thinking about virtue in itself does not demonstrate such influence, as we often find similarities between cultures concerning ethical norms. But the sheer amount of similarity, combined with the fact that Sahagún and his Aztec informants were adherents of the Christian faith, suggests that this account could contain more of Christian morality than what we might find in a non-Christian Aztec account of morality.

In texts such as the *Popol Vuh*, also recorded by a Spanish Christian, but in this case likely copied more directly from precolonial sources and from contemporary Maya sources not directly connected to Christianity, we find seemingly less Christian influence. Though such influence is still certainly there (Christianity is even explicitly mentioned in a couple of places in the text), the *Popol Vuh* appears as a very different kind of text from those Christians or Europeans in general would be familiar with. In it, we see a very different world with very different assumptions, mores, ways of being. The divergences between what we find in the *Popol Vuh* and the account of morality we see in the *Florentine Codex* seem much more distant than the differences we find in most aspects of Maya and Aztec thought. All of this just contributes to the questions surrounding the "authenticity" of the *Florentine* account.

The question of authenticity here is even more difficult than it seems at first. What makes for an "authentic" Mesoamerican view? Much of Mesoamerican thought since the arrival of the Spanish has been influenced to some extent by European thought, but there was never any time prior to the Spanish arrival that Mesoamerican thought had not been influenced by some "outside" source. We see that the thought of Postclassic Yucatan Maya was influenced by central Mexican thought in a way that earlier Classic Period thought of the highland and southern lowland was not. But that earlier thought was itself influenced by ideas from Teotihuacan and other areas outside the Maya region. Should we take one of those periods as more authentically Maya than any other? The thought of one period, with its influences, adaptations, and syntheses, is as authentic as that of any other. Instead of trying to make a distinction between what is authentically Mesoamerican and what is not – Christianity is as much authentically Mesoamerican today as anything else, for example – we should focus on the distinction between what precolonial Mesoamerican thought looked like (in general, as there were certainly many adaptations and other changes that took place before the arrival of the Spanish as well) and the ways this thought looked in and after the colonial period. Since the focus here is on presenting the distinctive features of Mesoamerican thought before Christian influence, so as to introduce the foundational aspects of Mesoamerican traditions, this should be taken more as a useful heuristic than as a framework for determining what is legitimate or authentic Mesoamerican thought.

Thus, here we consider the moral thought presented in texts such as the *Florentine Codex* and other colonial period sources, along with what we can glean from earlier texts and from the practices and views of contemporary Mesoamerican people, to get as close as we can to the aspects of Mesoamerican ethics prior to the arrival of the Spanish. While colonial and later Mesoamerican thought should also be seen as legitimately Mesoamerican and as important, to understand the foundational thought of Mesoamerica prior to its engagement and synthesis with Western thought, we will try to keep as close to precolonial forms of thought as we can. It is not always an easy task.

Proper Human Activity

In Chapter 7, we discussed the role of particular classes of people charged with the task of bearing knowledge, facilitating ritual, guiding the community, and serving as intermediaries between the community and the unseen aspects of the world, including the gods and ancestors. Here, we look further at ideas about proper human activity for other kinds of people, outside of the category of specialists bearing knowledge. How should we act as ordinary humans?

As in a number of other traditions, there is no simple or blanket answer to this. We do not find in the Mesoamerican traditions the views of morality that become popular in the Enlightenment period in Europe, in which certain kinds of activity are understood as normative or morally binding for everyone as a result of one's humanity alone. Rather, we find here something much more akin to what we find in early Chinese or Indian thought, in which what is right or proper for one to do is linked to one's role or position in society. Consideration of proper individual action can never be abstracted away from consideration of the individual as member of a larger community, and thus position and role are always considerations in determining proper action.

Humility

In the *Popol Vuh*, we see that humans are first constructed primarily to keep the days and to recognize the gods, to "provide and sustain," to see/create, and have knowledge. We find examples early in the text of the kind of virtues associated with proper action, and the vices generally cutting against it, in a host of stories involving various aspects of creation. We see the first example of vice in the character of Seven Macaw, who is represented as prideful, lacking in humility, delusional, overestimative of his abilities, and desirous to place himself above others. Seven Macaw declares himself to be the Sun and the Moon, through a slick trick of reasoning and inflation of his own characteristics. Seven Macaw says:

> I am great. I dwell above the heads of the people who have been framed and shaped. I am their sun. I am also their light. And I am also their moon. Then be it so. Great is my brightness. By the brilliance of my silver and gold I light the walkways and pathways of the people. My eyes sparkle with glittering blue/green jewels. My teeth as well are jade stones, as brilliant as the face of the sky. This, my beak, shines brightly far into the distance like the moon. My throne is gold and silver. When I go forth from my throne, I brighten the face of the earth. Thus I am the sun. I am the moon as well for those who are born in the light, those who are begotten in the light.[1]

Seven Macaw skillfully talks himself into believing that he is the Sun and the Moon, through an overestimation of his qualities and his importance. He also claims a far reaching vision – which as we have seen in the last chapter is a symbol of knowledge. The famous (and often confusing) hero twins of the *Popol Vuh*, Hunahpu and Xbalanque, conspire to defeat Seven Macau, as his self-aggrandizement made it the case that "people will never be able to live here on the face of the earth." The arrogance and self-inflation of Seven Macau would make community impossible.

We find this view in a number of other Mesoamerican sources as well. Book 6 of the *Florentine Codex* records a ruler continually speaking of himself as lowly and unworthy. In a discussion of evil activity, he cites a number of vices, including the arrogance of lack of humility. He enjoins his people not to drink liquor because, among other negative effects, it makes

---

[1] *Popol Vuh*, Christenson trans., 77–78.

one arrogant: "[B]ecause of the pulque [liquor] he brags falsely of his noble lineage, he thinks himself superior, he vaunts himself, he esteems himself, he is grandiose, he regards no one with much consideration, he values no one, praises no one, he is disrespectful."[2]

This ruler stresses humility in his instruction to his sons in the same text, and there is reference to humility throughout. This was clearly an important trait in Aztec thought and life. In another passage from the *Florentine Codex*, this ruler connects humility to self-sacrifice, to acceptance of grief and pain on behalf of the community and in maintenance of ritual. This is a theme we commonly see in Mesoamerican text and imagery. He says:

> Heed in what manner there is life on earth, in what manner compassion is secured of the lord of the near, the nigh. It is only the weeper, the sorrower, who is required; he who sighs, he who is anguished. And the devout one who shows preference for, who welcomes, who gives himself wholeheartedly, and who holds vigil for the sweeping, the cleaning, the ordering of things, is the pleasure of our lord; and he takes care of, he takes charge of the incense ladle, the offering of incense.[3]

Book 6 of the *Florentine Codex* stresses, through numerous references, the importance of this virtue. Parents enjoin their children to be humble, to avoid bragging and elevating themselves. In one passage of Book 6 (echoed in other parts of the text), the ruler warns his daughter not to be presumptuous and arrogant about the impending birth of her child – the message here seems to be that tempting fate inevitably brings disaster (a theme we see in other Mesoamerican texts as well). If a person boasts, takes what they have for granted, or lords over others, they will inevitably bring disaster upon themselves. This happens for a number of reasons. First, the inevitability of losing everything one has through transformation and ultimately death means that the arrogant person will suffer a greater misfortune than the humble person. The vicissitudes of life can never be predicted, and a haughty attitude could lead to a greater disaster. A midwife tells a newly delivered mother in *Florentine Codex* Book 6:

---

[2] *Florentine Codex* Book 6, Anderson and Dibble trans., 68–69.
[3] *Florentine Codex* Book 6, Anderson and Dibble trans., 88.

Perhaps our lord will bless you each one [mother and child] separately; in separate times and places; perhaps you will lose the baby which has arrived. Or perhaps he who created the baby will just summon it, small as it is, will call it for himself. Perhaps he will come to take you. Do not go constantly bragging of it. Go appealing in sorrow to our lord...⁴

Second, the person arrogant and lacking in humility will make easily avoidable mistakes and be easily manipulated, based on their skewed and inaccurate view of the world, and their willingness to accept even unbelievable things that fit their chosen narrative. We see this same theme in the Hero Twins' defeat of Seven Macaw. They ultimately overcome the arrogant Seven Macaw by tricking him, destroying the features that he took to distinguish himself and put himself above others. Once this was gone, Seven Macaw perished.

The defeat and destruction of Seven Macaw and later his sons Zipacna and Cabracan can be understood on numerous levels. There is clearly an ethical dimension here, concerning lack of humility and its ultimate fruits, but there is also a symbolic discussion of the taming of nature by humanity. In destroying Seven Macaw, the Hero Twins render impotent the powers of other aspects of the world that threaten humanity. In defeating Zipacna, the twins tame the Earth – as the character is associated with mountains, and appears as a caiman. In defeating Cabracan, the twins overcome natural disasters, as he represents earthquakes, toppling mountains. The defeat of these arrogant characters was necessary to make the Earth a habitable place for humanity. The powers of nature here are linked with a kind of lack of humility and arrogance, and are ultimately brought low by the community, just as the person who lacks humility will ultimately be brought down by the community. This bringing low happens through communal intervention, as well as through the intervention of nonhuman aspects of the world.

This all suggests that humility is such an important concept for Mesoamerican traditions because it is closely tied to communal cohesion and well-being. The social purpose of humility is to bind together the community, to create bonds between the individuals comprising it, which are severed by lack of humility. Henry Selby discusses this aspect of humility for the Zapotec, in his ethnographic study in the 1970s:

---

⁴ *Florentine Codex* Book 6, Anderson and Dibble trans., 179.

> To [the Zapotec], humility is attendance on the desires of others; it is a pervasive sense of equalitarianism. Humility is the absence of selfishness, and it implies a rampant altruism and disregard for one's own immediate welfare, a subversion of self-interest. Humility is obedience to constituted authority. Humility is the granting of the rights of other people to free expression of their opinions and prerogatives. Humility is the ready granting of a favor to others. Humility is the admission that everyone is equal and that everyone is equally poor. Humility is the recognition in one's attitudes and daily conduct of the absence of distinctions between men.[5]

Humility is a community-building and maintaining feature of human character. This one reason is crucial for figures such as the Hero Twins to root it out, so that the human community can thrive, and for a ruler, such as we see in the *Florentine Codex*, to enjoin it to his people, so as to ensure the cohesiveness and thriving of the community. As we see in the discussion of the Zapotec above, humility is linked to selflessness. The person without humility overly focuses on their own accomplishments, talents, value. Humility takes our eyes off of these things, and evens us with other members of the community. For a person to be humble is for them to dwell not on those qualities that set one *apart* from others in the community, but on those qualities that make one the same as other members of the community. It is difficult, if not impossible, to undermine, scorn, reject, or work against the community insofar as one sees oneself as the same as other members of the community. As we know from history and psychology, setting oneself apart is the first part of the process of distancing and dehumanization that allows us to mistreat and harm others. If this happens within a community, there is no way a community can remain coherent. It will necessarily fall apart.

Humility seems to have special significance for rulers. In general, those who have power over the community will face a more difficult situation in generating humility. The ruler is at the head of society, occupies the most visible and powerful position. This role seems to lend itself to self-aggrandizement and arrogance. When one occupies the chief position in society, it is difficult to avoid the belief that one is somehow special, better than others, possessive of uniquely valuable abilities and features,

---

[5] Selby, *Zapotec Deviance*...

and overall superior to those around one. This is much of the reason that we often see the traits of self-absorption or arrogance in rulers and leaders. Sometimes it is the case that those who are vain, self-important, or arrogant are at an advantage in the competition to *become* leaders, but often it is the reverse – it is the role that makes the person. Psychological situationists would tell us just this. Look at the case of hereditary rulership or wealth – the beneficiaries of such systems are often far less humble in character than the average person. Surely this is not genetic – it is a feature of their privileged situation. The human mind is such that those who enjoy a situation of power and privilege tend to think of themselves as uniquely worthy of such power and privilege, rather than as beneficiaries of a system that has nothing to do with their own talents, features, or individual worth.

Features of a culture and ethical tradition, such as a focus on humility, can form a key restraint on our tendency to view ourselves as uniquely worthy or valuable. Psychological studies have shown that people have a tendency (far more pronounced in "individualist" cultures in the West) to view themselves positively. While there is debate as to whether this is a feature of human psychology universally or rather culturally driven, there is plenty of evidence from less "individualistic" cultures that absent the system of restraints offered by cultural norms, humans have a tendency to become self-absorbed and inflate our self-value. This is the reason the early Confucian philosopher Xunzi, for example, argued for the necessity of ritual. He saw ritual as a tool constraining the human natural tendencies to both continually widen the scope of our desires and demands, and to be continually focused on the self. We find this view to some extent in earlier Confucians as well, but Xunzi develops the most complete account of this. The existence of such a universal natural tendency toward self-concern and self-aggrandizement also seems to make the most sense of the continual focus on virtues like humility in a number of traditions, including Mesoamerican traditions. While, like Chinese traditions, we find far less self-concern in Mesoamerica than in the contemporary West, much of the reason for this is the cultural apparatus of Mesoamerica in which humility is taken as a necessary virtue. Humility was taught, continually reinforced, discussed, and the subject of constant reminders. We find stories like that of Seven Macaw and his sons that explain the need for humility, and why the lack of it leads to destruction. Indeed, even heroic characters such as the original Hero Twins One and Seven Hunahpu, in the *Popol Vuh*, brought death onto themselves, and presumably onto humanity in general, for arrogant and haughty action in the face of the lords of the underworld, Xibalba. If humans had a natural tendency toward humility, surely such a continual focus on it would be unnecessary. Moral norms are only necessary insofar as humans have a tendency not to follow them. We do not need to be taught or reminded of something we have a natural inclination to do, such as eat, breathe, or procreate.

Sacrifice

One feature of proper human activity closely connected to humility, and a major focus of Mesoamerican thought, is sacrifice. Mesoamerican traditions see sacrifice as essential for maintenance of community and for change and creation. The ability and willingness to sacrifice is a virtue according to Mesoamerican traditions. This virtue is important to cover here for a number of reasons: 1) it is central to Mesoamerican conceptions of proper human activity; 2) the focus on sacrifice is a very unique aspect of Mesoamerican ethics (which these traditions share to some extent with indigenous traditions elsewhere in the Americas, but which receive far less attention or at least central focus in Indo-European and Asian traditions); 3) it is one of the most misunderstood features of Mesoamerican thought and cultures, outside of (and even within!) Mesoamerica.

In the West (outside of Mesoamericanist circles at least), talk of sacrifice in Mesoamerica often invokes the image of ritual execution of humans (generally war captives) as an act of propitiation of the gods. This infamous practice received massive amounts of attention from Westerners, particularly in the early periods of European contact, and became a kind of symbol for Mesoamerican cultures in the eyes of Westerners, down to this day. This is unfortunate, and happened for a number of reasons.

First – from the earliest days of Spanish contact, Spanish and other Western observers misunderstood and purposely misrepresented the nature and the frequency of such ritual executions. Spanish accounts present Mesoamerican people, including the Maya and Aztecs, as engaged in mass slaughter, nabbing unsuspecting victims in their villages and massacring them en masse in their temples, as offerings to the sun (or other gods). This should be the first tip that something was wrong with those accounts. While human sacrifice was certainly an aspect of numerous Mesoamerican societies, particularly in central Mexico, no society could operate in a state of mass slaughter of its citizens at random.

Second – the image of Mesoamerican cultures as blood-soaked sites of mass slaughter served the purposes of Spanish colonizers, who presented the native people of Mesoamerica as hopelessly backward and in need of salvation (and of course of dispossession of the land and resources they used for such evil). In Spanish accounts of Mesoamerican people, we find constant stress on these so-called evil and barbaric aspects of their cultures. This was all part of the attempt to dehumanize and vilify Mesoamerican peoples, in order to facilitate their oppression and justify Spanish dispossession of their land and resources. We know from psychological studies and historical investigation that such dehumanization techniques make it psychologically easier to harm the targets of this dehumanization. Given that the Spanish interests in the Americas were financial and political, and required dispossession of native people, forced labor, cultural reprogramming, and genocide, they needed to advance the kinds of stories of Mesoamerican people as depraved, vicious, and dangerous that we find in their breathless accounts of ritual sacrifice.

Third – in focusing on the kinds of ritual execution found in certain ceremonies in Mesoamerica, Western observers overlooked or completely missed the most important forms of sacrifice in Mesoamerican traditions. The ethical meaning of these important rituals of sacrifice was completely lost on early commentators, and to this day continues to be overlooked by scholars as a result of this early neglect. Sacrifice is both a much broader concept than it is rendered by early European accounts, connected to a much wider array of practices, most of which occupied a more central role in Mesoamerican societies than ritual execution ever did, and one ultimately aimed at communal *welfare*. While the ritual executions that the Spanish denounced were certainly part of the overall picture of sacrifice, they were nowhere near the whole of it or even a large part of it, and this practice itself was notoriously misrepresented by the Spanish. The broader concept of sacrifice was (and still is) understood as both a necessary creative activity and a virtue of character in Mesoamerica.

There is an enormous amount of material in Mesoamerican traditions, textual and non-textual, precolonial and post, on the issue of sacrifice. Some of the most important rituals in Mesoamerican societies involved sacrifice, as well as the most well-known creation and origin stories. The most common sacrificial ritual in precolonial Mesoamerica was the auto-sacrificial bloodletting ceremony, recounted in all of the Mesoamerican cultures discussed in this book. The details of the ritual were fairly similar across cultural contexts. The bloodletting ceremony most often involved rulers and nobles, and in some contexts warriors, substituting particular gods. Participants would draw blood from some area of their bodies, usually the genitals, tongue, or ears (interestingly, the areas of the body most commonly pierced for decorative and other purposes in numerous cultures). The blood would often be offered to the gods, sometimes along with other sacred substances such as sap or nectar, through burning. There are a number of different interpretations of the significance of these ceremonies. Schele, Friedel, and Parker interpret the Maya bloodletting ritual as a shamanic ritual, in which the person who draws their own blood is granted through this act vision into the unseen aspects of the world, and thereby can channel the gods or ancestors. A number of famous images of Lady Xoc, a Queen at Yaxchilan, particularly Lintels 24 and 25, depict such a ceremony. In Lintel 24, Lady Xoc pierces her tongue, with the bowl that will collect her blood in front of her. Just in front of her stands a figure representing her husband, the ruler Itzamnaaj B'alam II (Shield Jaguar II, 681–742 CE), holding a torch to light the scene. In Lintel 25, a figure in the form of a serpent with a human head arises from an offering bowl containing Lady Xoc's drawn blood. The head of this serpent figure wears earrings in the style of Teotihuacan, which as some have suggested connect Lady Xoc (and by extension her husband) to the cultural and political authority of that formative city. There is some debate as to the identity of this serpent figure – whether it represents an ancestral founder, a god, or (most likely) some combination of these. What seems more clear is that the vision represents access to unseen aspects of the world through the power of the offering of blood. The serpent arises from the blood of Lady Xoc – it is a power associated with that blood that allows for the vision. Whether this is representative of ancestral connection – that is, the blood-line of Lady Xoc containing that of the illustrious ancestors, or through a shamanic power connected to the blood, it is clear that this sacrificial ritual has implications for vision and knowledge.

There are some additional hints here to the connection of the blood-letting ceremony with shamanic vision, including the role of obsidian, which as we have seen in previous chapters, is associated with vision/ knowledge, particularly of the normally unseen. But just *what is it* that the active participant in such a ceremony sees? Those aspects of the world closed off to most of us become available to those with particular kinds of special vision and ability. Sacrifice, in the variety of contexts in which is appears in Mesoamerican thought, is often connected to enhanced vision and ability.

Another key feature of sacrifice is its role in generation.Metaphysical systems in Mesoamerica generally took creation to be necessarily linked to destruction, as new things do not come into existence *ex nihilo*. All created things are recycled from other things, thus in order for there to be change and generation, there must be decay. We find images of this throughout Mesoamerican art and culture. Gods emerge from decayed objects, such as the maize god emerging from the earth or a turtle shell, which we find in many images on Maya artifacts, commonly paintings on containers and plates (which have obvious connection to maize). The growth of maize here is offered as a resurrection in recognition of the process of grow-ing maize, in which seeds from old plants are put into the earth and the decayed remnants of those old plants are used to fertilize the ground for the new. The death and decay of the previous plants are thus part of the process of the birthing of the new plants. And in this birthing of the new, there is also resurrection of the old. There is continuity of the essence of the maize throughout.

The *Popol Vuh* discusses sacrifice and rebirth throughout the text, with the image and the stories of the Hero Twins most clearly representing this theme. The first pair of Hero Twins, One Hunahpu and Seven Hunahpu, generate the Hero Twins Hunahpu and Xbalanque, from two separate acts of sacrifice. First, One and Seven Hunahpu are sacrificed by the lords of Xibalba, and the head of One Hunahpu removed and put into a calabash tree. The head of One Hunahpu (which the text says was also that of Seven Hunahpu, as they shared the same thoughts), generated and became the same as the fruit of the calabash tree. A daughter of one of the lords of

Xibalba visited the tree, and the head of One (and Seven) Hunahpu spit into her hands, which impregnates the woman with the Hero Twins of the rest of the story, Hunahpu and Xbalanque. The origin of the Hero Twins in this sacrifice also expresses the continuity of essence through sacrifice and rebirth. The Hero Twins themselves willingly go to sacrifice in Xibalba later in the story, and are resurrected in a number of forms.

Munson, Amati, Collard, and Macri discuss a common sociological view of what they call "costly ritual behaviors," in which painful, intense, and/or other difficult to perform rituals have the role in a community of demonstrating the ritual performer's commitment to the community and willingness to undergo severe pain on behalf of the community.[6] This ties rituals like the Maya bloodletting ceremony to other painful rituals such as the "sun dance" of people of the North American plains (Lakota, Cheyenne, etc.). This was likely part of the significance of self-sacrifice for the ancient Maya, but there were clearly more elements to the general conception of sacrifice. We know this in part because not all acts of sacrifice were of such intensity or pain, such as fasting (ch'ahb), which occupied a major role among the Classic Maya, and was likely also connected to creation and renewal, as with the bloodletting ritual. As I discuss below, creation is a central aim of sacrifice in its various forms throughout Maya history.

But how is the sacrifice good for the individual who sacrifices, as well as for the community that enjoys both the conditions for renewal and the transformative and revelatory benefits of this sacrifice? One possibility, suggested by the Yaxchilan Lintels, and put forward as a hypothesis by Linda Schele and Mary Miller, is that bloodletting facilitated visions and hallucinations that the Maya understood as shamanic encounters with other aspects of the world, giving the sacrificer him or herself a kind of mystical vision leading to a broadening of their own understanding or generation of additional powers of insight (although this interpretation has been challenged by some scholars, such as Sven Gronemeyer).[7] Some particular features of the bloodletting ritual in the Classic Period suggest

---

[6] Munson, Amati, Collard and Macri, "Classic Maya Bloodletting and the Cultural Evolution of Religious Rituals: Quantifying Patterns of Variation in Hieroglyphic Texts."

[7] Schele and Miller, *The Blood of Kings*, 1986. Gronemeyer, "Bloodletting and Vision Quest Among the Classic Maya: A Medical and Iconographic Reevaluation."

another element of the sacrifice, connecting it to creation. While women, such as Lady Xoc, pierced their tongues in the ceremony, the piercing point for males was the penis. Many scholars note the possible symbolism of creative potency captured by this. David Joralemon wrote, of a Classic Period image of the city of Palenque:

> In the Foliated Cross Tablet the great king Pacal is shown presenting the deified instrument of sexual self-sacrifice to the cruciform maize tree in the center of the composition. By metaphoric extension Pacal is also offering his own precious sacrificial blood to fertilize the sacred tree at the center of the world. Whatever other symbolic meaning blood-letting and sexual mutilation might have had in ancient Maya thought, there was a strong association of sexual self-sacrifice with rituals of agricultural fertility during the Classic Period.[8]

Joralemon also claims that drawing blood from sexual organs must have been seen by the ancient Maya as particularly potent. This connection between sacrifice and creation can be seen throughout Classic Period imagery, but becomes more explicit in later texts such as the *Popol Vuh*.

In the main story of the Hero Twins Hunahpu and Xbalanque, the twins are brought to Xibalba, like One and Seven Hunahpu before them. They are brought to Xibalba on the basis of their skilled and noisy playing of the ubiquitous Mesoamerican ballgame (pitz in Classic Mayan), which possibly represents the regular work of human life. In the midst of this life, the Hero Twins are challenged by the lords of the realm of death, who wish to silence them and overcome them. The imagery is not so straightforward as good vs. evil or life vs. death, however. As Barrois and Tokovivine point out:

> The underworld and the heavenly world in Classic Maya culture do not have the same connotations that hell and paradise do for Christianity. The underworld covers a whole set of different, positive and negative notions, just like the upper world does. In fact, if the Maya underworld is the place of darkness and death, it is as well the place of water, fertility, and life.[9]

The depiction of the lords of Xibalba elsewhere in the Popol Vuh also attests to this. In Part 4 of the text, the Xibalba lords intervene on behalf

---

[8] Joralemon, "Ritual Blood-Sacrifice," 67.
[9] Barrois and Tokovivine, "The Underworld and the Celestial World in the Maya Ball Game."

of humanity with the god Tohil to procure the knowledge of generating fire for humans, which becomes essential to their future. The struggle between the Hero Twins and the Xibalbans then clearly represents transformation and its means. Subjecting the Hero Twins to a number of seemingly impossible tests in order to defeat them, the Twins overcome one after another. Finally, the Hero Twins recognize that they must be sacrificed in Xibalba, and allow themselves to be sacrificed – a representation of self-sacrifice reminiscent of the bloodletting ritual of the Classic Period.

The Hero Twins, through this sacrifice, gain the ability to sacrifice themselves (in the sense of complete destruction) and return to life. The process begins by the Twins' leaping into a pit of fire created by the Xibalbans. They later reappear in different forms, and are able ultimately to overcome the Xibalbans through this ability to sacrifice and be reborn (which the Xibalbans lack). This is highly suggestive of the theme of renewal and creation through sacrifice. Events of Part 4 of the Popol Vuh strengthen this suggestion. There, humans (with the help of the Xibalbans) acquire fire in exchange for sacrifice, a deal made with the god Tohil. The image of the maize god being sacrificed and reborn underground is important in this connection, as fire was used for agriculture by the ancient Maya, in clearing fields. This sacrifice and rebirth of maize is a key symbol of the entire life cycle for the ancient Maya.

The symbol of procreation as rebirth is stressed in the story of the origin of the Hero Twins from the head of One (and Seven) Hunahpu as well. As we saw in Chapter 4, the essence of an individual can be continued in progeny, and various kinds of sacrifice are necessary for the generation and the development of those progeny.

Aztec origin stories likewise take the theme of sacrifice as central. In the *Florentine Codex* version of the story of the origin of the fifth sun, the visible cosmos was created through the act of self-sacrifice of the humble Nanahuatzin and the proud Tecuciztecatl, entering willingly into a fire, to be sacrificed and become the Sun and Moon. The idea of sacrifice, which was connected to the ritual executions discussed at the beginning of this section as well as other forms of sacrifice, was that sacrifice was necessary for the continued maintenance of the cosmos in such a way as to allow for human life and society. Why would this be? If we consider some of the key features of metaphysics in Mesoamerican traditions as we have seen them thus far, the reasoning behind this becomes clearer. The existence of the cosmos is the existence of a *process* rather than a static thing like a substance. A process can only continue in existence as long as it is active. If we think of an object such as a wave or a storm – as soon as there is no longer motion, these things perish. A fire needs fuel to be kept burning – we have to be careful to add more wood and to keep the conditions right, or the fire will go out. This process of continual activity can only happen through change, through transformation. Because, as we have seen, no new things come into existence from nothing, any change requires a destruction and a creation. The generation and renewal required for change and motion can only happen if there is destruction and decay, just as we can only build something new from a set of parts if we take apart the things previously constructed by those parts. If each thing in the cosmos holds onto itself, remains without death and decay, then the process necessarily will end. The fire goes out, the storm subsides, the water calms and the wave ceases to be. Thus, those things in existence at any given time must sacrifice themselves to facilitate the continual development of things, the continual unfolding of the process that is the cosmos.

The image of the soil, the earth itself, as fertile and fruitful in generating the crops we need to survive, involves decay and sacrifice. Images of the Aztec god Tlaltecuhtli, representative of the Earth, include numerous features referring to sacrifice, including a tongue resembling the flint knife used in certain forms of sacrifice, and a human skull on his back. Manuel Aguilar-Moreno writes, of one image of the god: "[T]his monument represents the devouring power of the Earth, which needs the sacrifice of humans in order to maintain its life and to continue to provide fertility." (*Handbook to Life in the Aztec World*, 189). This surely is connected to the idea of the fertilization of the soil, and extended to the idea of the giving of life. Tlaltecuhtli is often depicted as consuming and thus generating.

Sacrifice in terms of relinquishing, losing, and in the ultimate sense death and decay, is a matter of character because in order for this process to happen efficiently, one must engage in sacrifice as a giving of oneself, a willful relinquishment of what is one's own. Whether this is in terms of the giving up of one's wealth, one's time, or other things that one might enjoy but let go for the benefit of others, or one's life itself, having the ability to make sacrifice of oneself is a critical virtue, according to Mesoamerican traditions.

Qualified Goodness

One thing we do not find in Mesoamerican texts and traditions, for the most part, is a conception of good and evil in connection to character, as we find it in some other traditions. The gods, humans, and all aspects of the cosmos are complex in their character, and could not be called either good or evil, right or wrong. Likewise, the moral value of things is differential – sometimes good, sometimes not, depending on context. The same act can be both a good and evil act with respect to different observers. There are no universally prescribed actions, nor could there be, given the nature of continual unfolding and change of the cosmos. The most important human activities and characteristics are sometimes corrosive, and the most damaging and devalued can sometimes be essential. We see this throughout Mesoamerican literature and traditions as antagonists become protagonists, and vice-versa, or a trait heroic in one context becomes villainous in another.

In the *Popol Vuh*, we find such swings of character. The lords of Xibalba, who appear as antagonistic in the story of the Hero Twins, at the same time intervene on behalf of humanity to secure the secret of fire from the god Tohil. A bat-like figure from Xibalba assisted the early people of many nations on their way out of the origin place of Tulan, and advised them to entreat Tohil for the gift of fire. They made an exchange with Tohil for fire, that would require their sacrifice, in terms of first death, which then became the bloodletting sacrifice, through a kind of realization and knowledge that came from this sacrifice. The text recounts after the exchange with Tohil:

> Thus the nations gave their breasts beneath their shoulders and beneath their armpits. This, then, was the breast-giving spoken of by Tohil – all the nations were to be sacrificed before him. Their hearts were to be carved out from beneath their shoulders and armpits. This thing had not heretofore been attempted. [...] Now when they came from Tulan Zuyva, they did not eat. They fasted continuously. Yet they fixed their eyes on the dawn, looking steadfastly for the coming forth of the sun. [...] When they were there at the place called Tulan Zuyva, their gods came to them. But it was surely not then that they received their ultimate glory or their lordship. Rather, it was where the great nations and the small nations

were conquered and humiliated when they were sacrificed before the face of Tohil. They gave their blood, which flowed from the shoulders and the armpits of all the people. Straightaway at Tulan came the glory and the great knowledge that was theirs. It was in the darkness, in the night as well, that they accomplished it. Thus they came. They were pulled up like weeds as they came out from there, leaving the East behind. "This is not our home. Surely let us go to see where we shall begin," said Tohil. ... "You shall first give thanks. You shall carry out your responsibilities first by piercing your ears. You shall prick your elbows. This shall be your petition, your way of giving thanks before the face of god."[10]

The figure from Xibalba may seem to have ultimately tricked the humans into making this bargain with Tohil that appeared at first to have been to their detriment, but turned out to be a necessary step in the generation of knowledge and the human realization of the necessity of sacrifice. This also demonstrates that good is sometimes achieved *through* antagonism, through the attempt to harm, destroy, or devalue. Suffering or "evil" is not seen unnecessary or extraneous – rather, it is a necessary part of the continual unfolding of the cosmos, without which this cosmos could not continue to grow, move, and become, as is necessary for its existence. Just as the travails of the Hero Twins in Xibalba were necessary, the suffering of the people on their way from Tulan was necessary, and the normal and inevitable suffering humans endure in life is necessary and meaningful. As we see in some other traditions, this is one way of making human suffering more bearable and giving us a resilience and sense of purpose. If the suffering, the pain, the illness and death, the sadness, the indignities, the toil and grief of life is all just an unfortunate accident, signifying nothing and only marked in its failure to be what we want, then why endure it, unless the joys of life are worth that price? We endure this suffering, according to Mesoamerican traditions, because it ultimately benefits the world.

The lords of death, of Xibalba, also form a necessary aspect of generation and transformation. The Hero Twins recognize the necessity of their sacrifice in Xibalba in order to be resurrected – and the lords of Xibalba, the lords of death, are a necessary part of this continual unfolding of the

[10] *Popol Vuh*, Christenson, 202–204.

cosmos, of sacrifice and rebirth. They cannot then be seen as bad or to be avoided – they are necessary, and ultimately valuable, even if there is a continual struggle between life and death, between living things and the lords of Xibalba.

Further Reading

Martin, *Ancient Maya Politics: A Political Anthropology of the Classic Period 150–900 CE*; Rice, *Maya Political Science*; Read, *Time and Sacrifice in the Aztec Cosmos*. Full publication details for all of these works can be found in the bibliography.

Conclusion: Mesoamerican Philosophy and the Contemporary World

One of the most enduring falsehoods about Mesoamerican people and cultures, particularly those of the Maya and Aztec, is that they disappeared at some point in history, either before the arrival of the Spanish (Maya), or with the arrival of the Spanish (Aztec). One will often hear speculation (and in news and media sources that ought to know better, or at least consult experts) about "what killed the Mayans," or "how the Maya disappeared." These sources talk about Maya civilization being "destroyed" or "wiped out" before the Spanish arrived in the Americas. They talk about the Aztecs being destroyed by the Spanish, and themselves disappearing. The problem is, of course, that none of this is true, and even the briefest of surveys or a quick Google search would reveal that it's not true. I am occasionally asked, when I give public talks about the precolonial Maya, what happened to the Maya, or why they disappeared. At more frustrated times, my response will be something like "why don't you go down to Yucatán or Guatemala and ask them?" Of course, I can't blame the people who ask these questions for being misinformed about the history and people of Mesoamerica. Our society in general has done a shamefully poor job in promoting, understanding, and paying attention to Mesoamerica (and the Indigenous Americas in general). It is easy to find outright bald falsehoods and lies about people like the Maya and Nahua repeated in even respected sources in the West, even given the incredible resources we have at our fingertips for gaining information. Perhaps 20 or 30 years ago such misinformation about the people and cultures of Mesoamerica would have been more understandable, but today it's simply a sign of laziness and carelessness at best.

But how did we get to such a point? We didn't just all of a sudden wake up and decide to tell lies about Mesoamerica. There is a deep history of about 500 years that led to all of this, beginning with the arrival of the Spanish in Mesoamerica in the sixteenth century. The Spanish were the first Europeans to arrive in the Americas, and the contact with the native people of the Caribbean and Mesoamerica was the first between Europeans and indigenous people of the Americas. The early Spanish "conquistadors" along with their clerical and lay associates created a host of narratives about the indigenous people of the Americas, meant to facilitate their own goals of acquisition and exploitation of the land and its people. Among these narratives were ones that are still well known today, and unfortunately still popularly associated with Mesoamerican peoples. The elevation of and misunderstanding of forms of human sacrifice became a central theme in Spanish storytelling about Mesoamerica. Groups such as the Aztecs worshipped various "devils," and engaged in Satanic practices such as the ritual execution of random members of society to satiate the bloodlust of these devils. Much of the difficulty of gaining a proper understanding of Aztec life and culture around the time of Spanish contact is that many of the accounts we have of Aztec life during that time come from clearly biased Spanish writers. Bernardino de Sahagún's *Florentine Codex*, for example, is one of the most cited works for understanding Aztec life and culture in the early colonial and precolonial period, but we find in Book One a direct statement of Sahagún's bias that will give any modern reader looking for the truth pause about taking his account as trustworthy. Sahagún, as a priest and a subject of Spain, was interested primarily in spreading Christianity, in converting and "reforming" the native people of Mesoamerica–a project that of course also contributed to their exploitation by Spanish economic forces.A shared ideology made it easier for native people to adopt Spanish economic systems, and to take Spanish people as their benefactors, masters, and those to whom they owed service or deference. A key in any attempt to conquer or suppress a people is to undermine and displace their culture, traditions, intellectual systems, and sense of communal identity. Take away their individuality and the sense of their own importance, and instead make them adopt your worldview, which places *you* at its center. Such a people will be much more amenable to allowing and helping you to be the beneficiary of all benefits, the measure of goodness, success, beauty, intelligence, and everything valuable, and the entity in which value consists and thus at which all must aim. The Spanish deployed this tactic with great success, as did other colonial powers such as the English, Portuguese, French, and in earlier periods the Chinese, Arabs, and other people who constructed empires. The Maya and Aztecs themselves engaged in this in their interactions with other peoples, if on a smaller scale.

In Book One of the *Florentine Codex*, we see an explicit display of the bias of Sahagún and (perhaps) his informants, who were native students of his. He writes, in side-by-side Nahuatl and Spanish:

> You who were born here, in New Spain, you Mexicans, you Tlaxcalans, you Cholulans, you Michoaca; all you who are vassals dwelling in the land of the Indies—your ancestors—your fathers, grandfathers, and great-grandfathers—left you in great darkness, error, unbelief, and idolatry, as is evident in your ancient picture writings. [...] For error, in which you have lived in all past time, came to you. It has misled and deluded you. And with this light and splendor, you may attain true faith. And thus you may hear and accept the word of God, here written, which he, your lord, the King of Spain, has caused to be sent to you, as well as God's Vicar, the Holy Father, who dwells in Rome.[1]

The account continues like this for pages and pages. Just in this small passage we see a number of telling and important features of Spanish indoctrination of the natives and its goals. Native thought was denounced as deluded, evil, against God and nature. This thought originated with the ancestors of the native people. To get away from this, the natives of the day had to turn away from their fathers, grandfathers, etc., to cut them off, to erase their past. This destroys a sense of identity, tradition, rootedness. And what is put in its place? Spain. Rome. The light of the king of Spain, the head of the Church in Rome. These locations are specifically spelled out by Sahagún here. He does not just say the Holy Church or the light of Christ, or some such construct – he specifically references Spain and Rome. These are critical aspects of the allegiance he was trying to build, and the Spanish project in general. The point was not (or at least not *only*) to win souls over to Christ, but to win minds over to Spain. People such as Sahagún likely did not even see these projects as separate. Human motivation is often complicated and multifaceted. We build up

---

[1] *Florentine Codex* Book 1, Anderson and Dibble trans., 27.

layers of intertwined motivations, like vine branches curling around a tree, that even we are often not aware of. We construct stories to hide motivations we deem socially unacceptable or don't want others to know, but then these stories themselves create new motivations alongside the originals. There are so many different things that go into the structure of human motivation. Sahagún and others like him probably thought of themselves primarily as purveyors of the Gospel, on a mission to "save" the people of Mesoamerica, but they also likely linked this with Spanish domination. It would be a mistake to think that they saw their Christian evangelization as a ruse and a cover for the kind of cultural replacement that would create dependency on and slavish admiration of and valuation of the Spanish, even though that is in fact what it was (among other things). No doubt there were some (although we can't know how many) for whom the Christian proselytization was in their own minds just a cynical tool. Likely for many more it was not. Regardless of what they thought and convinced themselves, however, this is how it actually worked. Another thing humans excel at is creating and getting ourselves to actually believe motivational stories that track and are intended primarily to selfishly benefit us. Thus, the rapacious businessman crafts an image of himself not as a corporate raider, but as a "job creator." He begins to think of his actions in terms of job creation, convincing himself to some extent that this is what he is. While he thinks this way to retain his sense of his own goodness, from the outside it is clear that he is not primarily a job creator, since when the creation of jobs conflict with his personal gain, he will always go with his personal gain. Likewise, in the case of Christianity in the Americas. For most, when the message of the Gospel conflicted with the interests of Spain, or England (or whatever colonial power wielded this ideology), it was simply reinterpreted or discarded. At one point during the Atlantic slave trade, it was ruled that someone who was baptized as Christian could not be enslaved, but people who claimed to be interested in Christianization of the Americas got around this in numerous ways. One way was to refuse to allow baptism of slaves or potential slaves, and another (and more direct) way was to simply reinterpret the dictates of scripture – slaving interests led to the view that it was not incompatible with the Christian Gospel to enslave Christians. Economic and political interests clearly led the way.

Mesoamerican thought has long been under a kind of shroud of mystery, myth, and outright lies due to the overwhelming success of the colonial Spanish in perpetuating their narrative of Mesoamerican cultures. The people of Mesoamerica were the first indigenous Americans with whom the Europeans became familiar, and their depiction by the Spanish largely set the terms for all future relations between Europeans and indigenous American people. Although this topic could take up a book (or many volumes!) of its own, the stories the Spanish first told Europe about people such as the Aztecs and the Maya played a major role in forming the image of the "Indian" in the colonial European mind. This image was in line with Spanish interests in the Americas, rendering the native people of Mesoamerica in a way so as to make them appear in desperate need of Spanish intervention, guidance, and control. This image turned out to be extremely profitable for the Spanish, which would demonstrate its usefulness to the other colonial powers. It would be a well to which colonial powers returned again and again.

The view that Mesoamerican people and cultures have somehow disappeared is, and has always been, patently absurd. The Maya, Nahua, Mixtec, Zapotec, and other people of Mesoamerica never went anywhere. They are still there, and their cultures still thrive. There are over 6 million native speakers of Maya languages today, throughout the traditional Maya region. There are almost 2 million native Nahuatl speakers, and over 1 million who speak Mixtec or Zapotec. Mesoamerican cultures certainly changed radically during the colonial period, but so did European cultures. Spanish culture did not remain the same after the colonial experience as it had been prior to it, even though we often treat the cultures of Europe as if they are insulated from influence by those with whom they had contact. While Christianity became a dominant ideology in Mesoamerica beginning in the colonial period, it never displaced native modes of thought. Not only were there non-Christian groups, including those who resisted Spanish culture and encroachment for many years (indeed, the famous "Caste War" of the Yucatan from 1847 to 1915 involved resistance to Spanish power and ideas), but even where Christianity was adopted, it was often combined with or held alongside of native modes of thought. We see this still today, in examples such as the Maya *ajq'ijob* ("daykeepers") who engage in traditional ritual practices based on traditional religious and philosophical beliefs, sometimes alongside of Christianity, and sometimes not.

The "disappearance of the natives" view was deployed by numerous colonial powers in the Americas to justify the coopting of land and other resources and the dispossession of the people living in these places.[2] This went alongside of other equally false views, such as the view that native people had not developed the land and were not using it. Early claims that native people were not making use of the land were based on the disingenuous idea that "making use" of the land was to cultivate it using European-style agricultural techniques, rather than native ones. Some have claimed that Europeans simply did not recognize native agricultural techniques as such, but this is to attribute to them a naivete almost as unbelievable as that which would claim that Europeans actually thought the natives had disappeared and that there was no one on the land they were claiming for themselves. Policies of enslavement and removal throughout the Americas belie this. Colonials certainly recognized that native people existed on the land and engaged in all types of agricultural activity (indeed, how could they have survived on the land without doing so?), but constructed flimsy justifications for their activity of dispossessing native people of their land and resources. Many of these justifications have outlived the colonial project in the minds of its descendants.

Despite the focus of this book on Mesoamerican philosophy prior to contact with Europe, Mesoamerican thought continued to develop and change through the colonial period and beyond, down to today. The cultures of the Maya, Nahua, and other Mesoamerican people continue to thrive, though certainly in different forms today than in precolonial times. This, of course, is the case for every culture. The cultures of Spain, the USA, China, and everywhere else look very different in the modern world from the way they did hundreds or thousands of years ago. While the thought

---

[2] The extent to which there was a "disappearance" was due to the massive population decline created by diseases such as smallpox that were introduced to the Americas through European contact. While there is disagreement on exactly the extent of the population decline in the Americas (including Mesoamerica), it was significant, killing anywhere from a quarter to a half of the population of the valley of Mexico in the early sixteenth century, and surely played a significant role in the fall of the Aztec Empire to the Spanish. While vast numbers died of disease, however, nowhere near enough people died to eliminate native cultures or peoples, who clearly continued on to become colonial subjects, resisting in various ways through the rest of colonial history.

of Mesoamerican people today has been heavily influenced by first Spanish Christian thought, and then the subsequent broader global systems with which the region came into contact in the modern period of globalization, there are still many elements of precolonial Mesoamerican thought present. Many traditions and practices continue, and others that have declined are reemerging, as indigenous people in Mesoamerica look to reclaim aspects of precolonial culture that were suppressed or fell into neglect in the colonial period. Some understand this as presenting an alternative and resistance to the political structure of the region, the dominance of European-based elites, and the subordination of indigenous peoples.

The continuation of Mesoamerican traditions in the contemporary world is an expression of the uniqueness and value of the indigenous people of this region, which they hold in the face of centuries of denigration of their traditions and active attempts to undermine them and to "convert" them to different forms of thought and practice. Thus early Mesoamerican thought is clearly of value to contemporary indigenous people of the region. It is of wider value to the rest of us as well. First, as with any intellectual tradition, these philosophical traditions help us understand how humans have grappled with the fundamental philosophical issues in various times and places in the world. Philosophy is largely a discipline engaged in "from the armchair" – it relies on intuition, background knowledge, and understanding of the basic structures of human thinking. We cannot possibly have reliable or well-formed intuitions and the like without having a broad understanding of different kinds of human responses to the fundamental philosophical questions we face. Without this, our intuitions and background knowledge are merely provincial, and the answers we thus come up with to philosophical questions are bound to be likewise provincial. Second, if what we seek in philosophy is the truth, then we should be open to the philosophical resources and thinking of people in the various times and places in the world outside our own. To think that all the possibilities have been covered by the figures and traditions of one or a limited number of traditions is presumptuous, and will certainly lead to intellectual stagnation, just as surely as the thought that we can understand the nature of human language by looking only at a single language, or understand animals by studying only cows. Third, and perhaps most importantly for the purposes of the philosopher, we find in Mesoamerican traditions many highly plausible views in metaphysics, epistemology, and ethics that can help us develop adequate theories in these areas. Common Mesoamerican views of the nature of personhood, for example, give us perhaps the best account of the person and the relationship between individual and community we find in all of global philosophy. We find striking insights in Mesoamerican philosophy that we do not commonly find in other traditions – insights that can transform and improve our own understanding. Mesoamerican philosophy, is not only a relic of the past, but is also a strong and often highly plausible account of the nature of humanity, the cosmos, and the relationship between them. It is my hope that readers of this book will both look more deeply into Mesoamerican philosophical traditions and integrate many of the important insights and positions from these traditions into their own thinking about the philosophical issues of interest to us all.

Bibliography

Adams, Richard. 2005. *Prehistoric Mesoamerica*, 3rd ed. Norman: University of Oklahoma Press.

Adams, Richard and Murdo Macleod. 2000. *Cambridge History of the Native People of the Americas, Volume II: Mesoamerica, Part I.* Cambridge: Cambridge University Press.

Aguilar-Moreno, Manuel. 2007. *Handbook to Life in the Aztec World.* Oxford: Oxford University Press.

Anderson, Arthur and Charles Dibble, trans. 1953. *Florentine Codex, Book 7.* Salt Lake City: University of Utah Press.

Anderson, Arthur and Charles Dibble, eds. 2012. *Florentine Codex (Books 1–12),* 2nd ed. Salt Lake City: University of Utah Press.

Aveni, Anthony. 1992. *Conversing with the Planets: How Science and Myth Invented the Cosmos.* New York: Crown.

Aveni, Anthony, ed. 2008. *Foundations of New World Cultural Astronomy: A Reader with Commentary.* Boulder: University Press of Colorado.

Aveni, Anthony, ed. 2015. *The Measure and Meaning of Time in Mesoamerica and the Andes.* Cambridge, MA: Harvard University Press.

Barrera-Vasquez, Alfredo and Silvia Rendón, trans. 1963. *El libro de los libros de Chilam Balam.* Mexico City: Fondo de Cultura Económica.

Barrois, Ramzy and Alexandre Tokovivine. 2004. "The Underworld and the Celestial World in the Maya Ballgame." *Presented at XVII Simposio de investigaciones arqueológicas en Guatemala.*

Bassett, Molly. 2015. *The Fate of Earthly Things: Aztec Gods and God-Bodies.* Austin: University of Texas Press.

Bassie-Sweet, Karen and Nicholas Hopkins. 2015. "The Family of Ancient Creator Deities." In K. Bassie-Sweet, ed. *The Ch'ol Maya of Chiapas.* Norman: University of Oklahoma Press.

Bassie-Sweet, Karen and Nicholas Hopkins. 2019. *Maya Narrative Arts.* Boulder: University Press of Colorado.Berdan, Frances. 2014. *Aztec Archaeology and Ethnohistory.* Cambridge: Cambridge University Press.

Bierhorst, John. 1985. *Cantares Mexicanos: Songs of the Aztecs.* Palo Alto: Stanford University Press.

Bierhorst, John, trans. 2009. *Ballads of the Lords of New Spain: The Codex Romances de los Señores de la Nueva España*. Austin: University of Texas Press.

Bierhorst, John, trans. 2011. *Codex Chimalpopoca: The Text in Nahuatl with a Glossary and Grammatical Notes*. Tucson: University of Arizona Press.

Boone, Elizabeth. 2000. *Stories in Red and Black: Pictorial Histories of the Aztecs and Mixtecs*. Austin: University of Texas Press.

Boone, Elizabeth and Walter Mignolo, eds. 1994. *Writing without Words: Alternative Literacies in Mesoamerica and the Andes*. Durham: Duke University Press.

Brown, Joshua and Alexus McLeod. 2020. *Transcendence and Non-Naturalism in Early Chinese Thought*. London: Bloomsbury.

Burke, Janet and Ted Humphrey, eds. 2012. *Bernal Díaz del Castillo's the True History of the Conquest of New Spain*. Indianapolis: Hackett.

Cabezas, Horacio. 2005. "Unidad Geográfica-Cultural." In H. Cabezas, ed. *Mesoamérica*. Guatemala: Universidad Mesoamericana.

Carlsen, Robert. 2011. *The War for the Heart and Soul of a Highland Maya Town*, Revised ed. Austin: University of Texas Press.

Carrasco, David. 2000. *City of Sacrifice: The Aztec Empire and the Role of Violence in Civilization*. Boston: Beacon Press.

Carrasco, David. 2011. *The Aztecs: A Very Short Introduction*. Oxford: Oxford University Press.

Carrasco, David. 2013. *Religions of Mesoamerica*, 2nd ed. Long Grove: Waveland Press.Chinchilla Mazariegos, Oswaldo. 2017. *Art and Myth of the Ancient Maya*. New Haven: Yale University Press.

Chládek, Stanislav. 2011. *Exploring Maya Ritual Caves: Dark Secrets from the Maya Underworld*. Lanham, MD: AltaMira Press.

Christenson, Allen. 2003. *Popol Vuh: The Sacred Book of the Maya*. Norman: University of Oklahoma Press.

Christenson, Allen. 2007. *Popol Vuh, Vol. 2: Literal Poetic Version, Translation, and Transcription*. Norman: University of Oklahoma Press.

Coe, Michael and Stephen Houston. 2015. *The Maya*, 9th ed. London: Thames and Hudson.

Coe, Michael and Rex Koontz. 2013. *Mexico: From the Olmecs to the Aztecs*. London: Thames and Hudson.

Coe, Michael and Mark Van Stone. 2005. *Reading the Maya Glyphs*, 2nd ed. London: Thames and Hudson.

Cummins, Thomas. 2011. "Tocapu: What Is It, What Does It Do, and Why Is It Not a Knot?" In E. Boone and G. Urton, eds. *Their Way of Writing: Scripts, Signs, and Pictographies in Pre-Columbian America*. Washington, DC: Dumbarton Oaks Research Library and Collection.

Earle, Duncan. 2008. "Maya Caves Across Time and Space: Reading-Related Landscapes in K'iche' Maya Text, Ritual, and History." In John Staller, ed. *Pre-Columbian Landscapes of Creation and Origin*. Dordrecht: Springer.

Earle, Duncan and Dean Snow. 1985. "The Origin of the 260-Day Calendar: The Gestation Hypothesis Reconsidered in Light of Its Use among the Quiche-Maya." In M. Robertson and V. Fields, eds. *Fifth Palenque Round Table, 1983*. San Francisco: Pre-Columbian Art Research Institute.

Eberl, Markus. 2013. "Nourishing Gods: Birth and Personhood in Highland Mexican Codices." *Cambridge Archaeological Journal* 23(3), 453–475.

Edmonson, Munro. 1982. *The Ancient Future of the Itza: The Book of Chilam Balam of Tizimin*. Austin: University of Texas Press.

Eliade, Mircea. 1959. *The Sacred and the Profane*. New York: Harcourt.

Fitjar, Daniel. 2014. *Balancing the World: Contemporary Maya 'Ajq'ijab' in Quetzaltenango, Guatemala*. Frankfurt: Peter Lang.

Foster, Lynn. 2005. *Handbook to Life in the Ancient Maya World*. Oxford: Oxford University Press.

Friedel, David, Linda Schele, and Joy Parker. 1995. *Maya Cosmos: Three Thousand Years on the Shaman's Path*. New York: William Morrow and Co.

Furst, Jill. 1997. *The Natural History of the Soul in Ancient Mexico*. New Haven: Yale University Press.

Gingerich, Willard. 1987. "Heidegger and the Aztecs: The Poetics of Knowing in Pre-Hispanic Nahuatl Poetry." In B. Swann and A. Krupat, eds. *Recovering the Word: Essays on Native American Literature*. Berkeley: University of California Press.

Graham, Angus. 1990. *Studies in Chinese Philosophy and Philosophical Literature*. Albany: SUNY Press.

Graña-Behrens, Daniel. 2012. "*Itz'aat* and *Tlamatini*: The 'Wise Man' as Keeper of Maya and Nahua Collective Memory." In A. Megged and S. Wood, eds. *Mesoamerican Memory: Enduring Systems of Remembrance*. Norman: University of Oklahoma Press.

Gronemeyer, Sven. 2003. "Bloodletting and Vision Quest among the Ancient Maya: A Medical and Iconographic Reevaluation." *Human Mosaic* 34(1–2), 5–14.

Hajovsky, Patrick. 2015. *On the Lips of Others: Moteuczoma's Fame in Aztec Monuments and Rituals*. Austin: University of Texas Press.

Haly, Richard. 1992. "Bare Bones: Rethinking Mesoamerican Divinity." *History of Religions* 31(3), 269–304.

Hanks, William. 1990. *Referential Practice: Language and Lived Space among the Maya*. Chicago: University of Chicago Press.

Hinojosa, Servando. 2015. *In This Body: Kaqchikel Maya and the Grounding of Spirit*. Albuquerque: University of New Mexico Press.

Houston, Stephen. 2014. *The Life Within: Classic Maya and the Matter of Permanence.* New Haven: Yale University Press.

Houston, Stephen, Oswaldo Chinchilla Mazariegos, and David Stuart, eds. 2001. *The Decipherment of Ancient Maya Writing.* Norman: University of Oklahoma Press.

Houston, Stephen and David Stuart. 1989. "The *Way* Glyph: Evidence for 'Co-Essences' among the Classic Maya." *Research Reports on Ancient Maya Writing,* 30.

Houston, Stephen, David Stuart, and Karl Taube. 2006. *The Memory of Bones: Body, Being, and Experience among the Classic Maya.* Austin: University of Texas Press.

Hvidtfeldt, Arild. 1958. *Teotl and Ixiptlatli: Some Central Conceptions in Ancient Mexican Religion.* Copenhagen: Munksgaard.

Jansen, Maarten and Gabina Pérez Jiménez. 2010. *The Mixtec Pictorial Manuscripts: Time, Agency and Memory in Ancient Mexico.* Leiden: Brill.

Jansen, Maarten and Gabina Pérez Jiménez. 2017. *Time and the Ancestors: Aztex and Mixtec Ritual Art.* Leiden: Brill.

Joralemon, David. 1974. "Ritual Blood-Sacrifice among the Ancient Maya: Part I." In M. Robertson, ed. *Primera Mesa Redonda de Palenque, Part 2.* Pebble Beach, CA: Robert Louis Stevenson School of Pre-Columbian Art Research.

Joyce, Arthur. 2009. *Mixtecs, Zapotecs, and Chatinos: Ancient Peoples of Southern Mexico.* Hoboken: Wiley-Blackwell.

Justeson, John and Peter Mathews. 1983. "The Seating of the Tun: Further Evidence Concerning a Late Preclassic Lowland Maya Stela Cult." *American Antiquity* 48(3), 586–593.

Калюта, Анастасия В. 2018. "What Is Teōtl? Some Observations the Meaning of One Word in Classical Nahuatl." www.academia.edu/41231839/What_is_teōtl_Some_Observations_the_Meaning_of_One_Word_in_Classical_Nahuatl

Karttunen, Frances. 1983. *An Analytical Dictionary of Nahuatl.* Norman: University of Oklahoma Press.

Katan-Schmid, Einav. 2016. *Embodied Philosophy in Dance: Gaga and Ohad Naharin's Movement Research.* London: Palgrave Macmillan.

Knowlton, Timothy. 2012. *Maya Creation Myths: Words and Worlds of the Chilam Balam.* Boulder: University Press of Colorado.

Kólar, Petr. 1999. "Truth, Correspondence, Satisfaction." In J. Peregrin, ed. *Truth and Its Nature (If Any).* Dordrecht: Springer.

Kowalski, Jeff, and Cynthia Kristan-Graham, eds. 2011. *Twin Tollans: Chichen Itza, Tula, and the Epiclassic to Early Postclassic Mesoamerican World,* Revised edition. Washington, DC: Dumbarton Oaks Research Library and Collection.

Laack, Isabel. 2019. *Aztec Religion and the Art of Writing*. Leiden: Brill.

Leon-Portilla, Miguel. 1979. *La filosofía Nahuatl*. Mexico City: Universidad Nacional Autónoma de Mexico.

Leon-Portilla, Miguel. 1990. *Time and Reality in the Thought of the Maya* (trans. of *Tiempo y realidad en el pensamiento Maya*). Norman: University of Oklahoma Press.

Leon-Portilla, Miguel. 2012. *Aztec Thought and Culture* (trans. of *La filosofia náhuatl*, 1956). Norman: University of Oklahoma Press.

Lind, Michael. 2015. *Ancient Zapotec Religion: An Ethnohistorical and Archaeological Perspective*. Boulder: University Press of Colorado.

Looper, Matthew. 2009. *To Be Like Gods: Dance in Ancient Maya Civilization*. Austin: University of Texas Press.

López Austin, Alfredo. 1988. *The Human Body and Ideology: Concepts of the Ancient Nahuas* (trans. of *Cuerpo humano e ideologia*). Salt Lake City: University of Utah Press.

López Austin, Alfredo. 2011 (trans. of 1990). *The Myths of the Opossum: Pathways of Mesoamerican Mythology*. Albuquerque: University of New Mexico Press.

Lounsbury, Floyd. 1976. "A Rationale for the Initial Date of the Temple Cross at Palenque." In M. Robertson, ed. *The Art, Iconography, and Dynastic History of Palenque*. San Francisco: Pre-Columbian Art Research Institute.

Macri, Martha and Matthew Looper. 2003. "Nahua in Ancient Mesoamerica: Evidence from Maya Inscriptions." *Ancient Mesoamerica* 14(2): 285–297.

Macri, Martha and Matthew Looper. 2013. *The New Catalog of Maya Hieroglyphs, Volume One: The Classic Period Inscriptions*. Norman: University of Oklahoma Press.

Maffie, James. 2013. *Aztec Philosophy*. Boulder: University Press of Colorado.

Martin, Simon. 2020. *Ancient Maya Politics: A Political Anthropology of the Classic Period, 150–900 CE*. Cambridge: Cambridge University Press.

McKillop, Heather. 2004. *The Ancient Maya: New Perspectives*. Santa Barbara: ABC-CLIO.

McLeod, Alexus. 2015. *Theories of Truth in Chinese Philosophy: A Comparative Approach*. London: Rowman and Littlefield International.

McLeod, Alexus. 2017. *Philosophy of the Ancient Maya: Lords of Time*. Lanham, MD: Lexington Books.

McLeod, Alexus. 2018. "*Itz* and the Descent of Kukulkan: Central Mexican Influence on Postclassic Maya Thought." *Parergon* 35(2), 147–173.

McLeod, Alexus. 2019. "Sacrifice: A Maya Conception of a Misunderstood and Underappreciated Component of Well-Being." *Science, Religion, and Culture* 6(1), 34–41.

Megged, Amos and Stephanie Wood, eds. 2012. *Mesoamerican Memory: Enduring Systems of Remembrance*. Norman: University of Oklahoma Press.

Mignolo, Walter. 2003. *The Darker Side of the Renaissance*. Ann Arbor: University of Michigan Press.

Mikulska, Katarzyna. 2011. "'Secret Language' in Oral and Graphic Form: Religious-Magic Discourse in Aztec Speeches and Manuscripts." *Oral Tradition* 25(5), 325–363.

Milbrath, Susan. 2000. *Star Gods of the Maya: Astronomy in Art, Folklore, and Calendars*. Austin: University of Texas Press.

Molesky-Poz, Jean. 2006. *Contemporary Maya Spirituality: The Ancient Ways Are Not Lost*. Austin: University of Texas Press.

Monaghan, John and Peter Just. 2000. *Social and Cultural Anthropology: A Very Short Introduction*, 9th ed. Oxford: Oxford University Press.

Moore, Christopher. 2019. *Calling Philosophers Names: On the Origin of a Discipline*. Princeton: Princeton University Press.

Munson, Jessica, Viviana Amati, Mark Collard, and Martha Macri. 2014. "Classic Maya Bloodletting and the Cultural Evolution of Religious Rituals: Qualifying Patterns of Variation in Hieroglyphic Texts." *PLOS One* 9(9), 1–13.

Nail, Thomas. 2018. *Being and Motion*. Oxford: Oxford University Press.

Nichols, Deborah and Enrique Rodríguez-Alegría. 2020. *The Oxford Handbook of the Aztecs*. Oxford: Oxford University Press.

Osborne, Grant. 2006. *The Hermeneutical Spiral: A Comprehensive Introduction to Biblical Interpretation*. Downers Grove, IL: IVP Academic.

Outlaw, Lucius. 1990. "African Philosophy; Deconstructive and Reconstructive Challenges." In Henry Odera Oruka, ed. *Sage Philosophy*. The Netherlands: E. J. Brill, 230.

Palmer, Colin and Colin Clifford. 2020. "Face Pareidolia Recruits Mechanisms for Detecting Human Social Attention." *Psychological Science* 31(8), 1001–1012.

Park, Peter. 2013. *Africa, Asia, and the History of Philosophy: Racism in the Formation of the Philosophical Canon, 1780–1830*. Albany: SUNY Press.

Pharo, Lars. 2013. *The Ritual Practice of Time: Philosophy and Sociopolitics of Mesoamerican Calendars*. Leiden: Brill.

Phillips, Henry, trans. 1883. "History of the Mexicans as Told by Their Paintings." *Proceedings of the American Philosophical Society* XXI.

Pratt, Scott. 2002. *Native Pragmatism: Rethinking the Roots of American Philosophy*. Bloomington: Indiana University Press.

Read, Kay. 1998. *Time and Sacrifice in the Aztec Cosmos*. Bloomington: Indiana University Press.

Rice, Prudence. 2004. *Maya Political Science: Time, Astronomy, and the Cosmos.* Austin: University of Texas Press.

Rice, Prudence. 2007. *Maya Calendar Origins: Monuments, Mythistory, and the Materialization of Time.* Austin: University of Texas Press.

Rosenswig, Robert. 2009. *The Beginnings of Mesoamerican Civilization: Inter-Regional Interaction and the Olmec.* Cambridge: Cambridge University Press.

Roys, Ralph. 1933. *The Book of Chilam Balam of Chumayel.* Washington, DC: Carnegie Institution of Washington.

Sanders, William and Susan Evans. 2006. "Rulership and Palaces at Teotihuacan." In J. Christie and P. Sarro, eds. *Palaces and Power in the Americas.* Austin: University of Texas Press.

Sandstrom, Alan. 2005. "The Cave-Pyramid Complex among the Contemporary Nahua of Northern Veracruz." In J. Brady and K. Prufer, eds. *In the Maw of the Earth Monster: Studies of Mesoamerican Ritual Cave Use.* Austin: University of Texas Press.

Schele, Linda and Mary Miller. 1992. *The Blood of Kings: Dynasty and Ritual in Maya Art.* New York: George Braziller Inc.

Scherer, Andrew. 2015. *Mortuary Landscapes of the Classic Maya.* Austin: University of Texas Press.

Selby, Henry. 2011. *Zapotec Deviance: The Convergence of Folk and Modern Sociology.* Austin: University of Texas Press.

Sharer, Robert. 2005. *The Ancient Maya*, 6th ed. Palo Alto: Stanford University Press.

Sharer, Robert. 2009. *Daily Life in Maya Civilization*, 2nd ed. Santa Barbara: Greenwood.

Smith, Mary. 1973. "The Relationship between Mixtec Manuscript Painting and the Mixtec Language: A Study of Some Personal Names in Codices Muro and Sanchez Solis." In E. Benson, ed., *Mesoamerican Writing Systems.* Washington, DC: Dumbarton Oaks Research Library and Collection.

Soud, David. 2016. *Divine Cartographies: God, History, and Poesis in W. B. Yeats, David Jones, and T. S. Eliot.* Oxford: Oxford University Press.

Soustelle, Jacques. 1984. *The Olmecs: The Oldest Civilization in Mexico.* New York: Doubleday.

Stuart, David. 1996. "Kings of Stone: A Consideration of Stelae in Ancient Maya Ritual and Representation." *RES: Anthropology and Aesthetics* 29(30), 148–171.

Stuart, David. 2012. *The Order of Days: Unlocking the Secrets of the Ancient Maya.* New York: Crown.

Taube, Karl. 1992. *The Major Gods of Ancient Yucatan.* Washington, DC: Dumbarton Oaks Research Library and Collection.

Tedlock, Barbara. 1992. *Time and the Highland Maya*, Revised edition. Albuquerque: University of New Mexico Press.

Tedlock, Dennis. 1996. *Popol Vuh: The Definitive Edition of the Mayan Book of the Dawn of Life and the Glories of Gods and Kings*. New York: Touchstone.

Tedlock, Dennis. 1998. "Toward a Poetics of Polyphony and Translatability." In Charles Bernstein, ed., *Close Listening: Poetry and the Performed Word*. Oxford: Oxford University Press.

Tedlock, Dennis. 2005. *Rabinal Achi: A Mayan Drama of War and Sacrifice*. Oxford: Oxford University Press.

Terraciano, Kevin. 2002. *The Mixtecs of Colonial Oaxaca: Nudzahui History, Sixteenth Through Eighteenth Centuries*. Palo Alto: Stanford University Press.

Townsend, Camilla. 2019. *Fifth Sun: A New History of the Aztecs*. Oxford: Oxford University Press.

Urcid, Javier. 2005. *Zapotec Writing: Knowledge, Power, and Memory in Ancient Oaxaca*. Waltham: Department of Anthropology, Brandeis University.

Vail, Gabrielle and Christine Hernández. 2013. *Recreating Primordial Time: Foundation Rituals and Mythology in the Postclassic Maya Codices*. Boulder: University Press of Colorado.

Van Norden, Bryan. 2012. *Virtue Ethics and Consequentialism in Early Chinese Philosophy*. Cambridge: Cambridge University Press.

Van Norden, Bryan. 2017. *Taking Back Philosophy: A Multicultural Manifesto*. New York: Columbia University Press.

Van't Hooft, Anuschka. 2006. *The Ways of the Water: A Reconstruction of Huastecan Nahua Society through Its Oral Tradition*. Amsterdam: Amsterdam University Press.

Weeks, John, Frauke Sachse and Christian Prager. 2009. *Maya Daykeeping: Three Calendars from Highland Guatemala*. Boulder: University Press of Colorado.

Welch, Shay. 2019. *The Phenomenology of a Performative Knowledge System: Dancing with Native American Epistemology*. London: Palgrave Macmillan.

Welch, Shay. 2022. *Choreography as Embodied Critical Inquiry: Embodied Cognition and Creative Movement*. London: Palgrave Macmillan.

Whittaker, Gordon. 2021. *Deciphering Aztec Hieroglyphs: A Guide to Nahuatl Writing*. Berkeley: University of California Press.

Wittgenstein, Ludwig. (Peter Winch, trans) 1984. *Culture and Value*. Chicago: University of Chicago Press.

Worley, Paul and Rita Palacios. 2019. *Unwriting Maya Literature: Ts'iib as Recorded Knowledge*. Tuczon: University of Arizona Press.

Index

For EU product safety concerns, contact us at Calle de José Abascal, 56–1°,
28003 Madrid, Spain or eugpsr@cambridge.org.